THE
ROYAL AIR FORCE

A CENTENARY OF OPERATIONS

OSPREY
PUBLISHING

THE
ROYAL AIR FORCE

A CENTENARY OF OPERATIONS

MICHAEL NAPIER

CONTENTS

OSPREY PUBLISHING
Bloomsbury Publishing Plc

PO Box 883, Oxford, OX1 9PL, UK
1385 Broadway, 5th Floor, New York, NY 10018, USA
Email: info@ospreypublishing.com

OSPREY is a trademark of Osprey Publishing, a division of
Bloomsbury Publishing Plc

First published in Great Britain in 2018

A CIP catalogue record for this book is available from the
British Library.

Hardback: 978 1 4728 2540 7
ePub: 978 1 4728 2539 1
ePDF: 978 1 4728 2538 4
XML: 978 1 4728 2541 4

Conceived and edited by Jasper Spencer-Smith.
Artwork by Nigel Pell.
Index by Shaun Barrington.
Produced by Editworks Limited, Bournemouth, UK
Originated by PDQ Digital Media Solutions, Bungay, UK
Printed in China at C & C Offset Printing Co., Ltd.

19 20 21 22 23   12 11 10 9 8 7 6 5 4 3

Image acknowledgements
All images are from the author's own collection, unless
otherwise stated.

Front cover: An RAF Typhoon appears like a shark from the depths.
This photograph was taken from the back of a transport aircraft
over a lake in the Baltic region where the Typhoons were deployed
in the NATO Baltic Air Policing Role. (MoD/Crown Copyright 2014)

Back cover: A Spitfire Mark VB, R6923 of No 92 Squadron RAF
based at Biggin Hill, Kent, banking towards the photographing
aircraft. (Photo by G Woodbine/IWM/ Getty Images)

Title page: A Victor K2 from 55 Squadron RAF Marham on one
of its last flights before the end of the aircraft type's operational era.
(Crown Copyright 2006)

Contents page: Two Harrier GR7s in formation.
(Crown Copyright 2002)

Foreword: Air Chief Marshal Sir Stuart Peach (Crown Copyright)

The Woodland Trust
Osprey Publishing supports the Woodland Trust, the UK's leading
woodland conservation charity.

www.ospreypublishing.com
To find out more about our authors and books visit our website.
Here you will find extracts, author interviews, details of
forthcoming events and the option to sign up for our newsletter.

FOREWORD

Air Chief Marshal Sir Stuart Peach
GBE, KCB, ADC, DL, Chief of Defence Staff

As the Royal Air Force prepares to celebrate 100 years of independence, this book offers an important record of the significant contribution of the Royal Air Force over the last century. From the strategic to the tactical, the structure and reputation of the Service has grown through the application of technology by incredible people.

The author, himself a former Royal Air Force Tornado pilot, describes the journey in a chronological format. This works well to describe the transformation of the aeroplane from an object of wonder in 1914 to a formidable part of the national defences in 1918. Following the Great War, little wars went on. In the expanded mandate of the British Empire, air elements were despatched to Iraq and Afghanistan. One hundred years later the British Government still despatches the Royal Air Force to support sovereign governments, to counter terrorism and to support our vital national interests. That much has not changed.

What has changed is the range and breadth of capabilities of the Royal Air Force. The types of mission remain constant: deterrence, presence, precision strike, reconnaissance, mobility, refuelling, and force protection. The way we conduct those missions has evolved to include space and cyber warfare. The chronology demonstrates through world wars, small wars and the Cold War that the people remain committed, determined and brave.

As the Royal Air Force turns one hundred, this book adds to our knowledge. In the spirit of *per ardua ad astra*, I commend it.

CHAPTER 1

AN INDEPENDENT SERVICE

1918-1922

In late 1917, air power throughout the British Empire was exercised by the Royal Naval Air Service (RNAS) and the Army Royal Flying Corps (RFC). Each arm had its own command structure and was serviced by its own procurement and supply chain. As might be expected, the RNAS was mainly a maritime force, operating both land and seaplanes, as well as flying boats, balloons and airships from coastal bases around the UK, but with units also based on the north coast of France and in the Mediterranean and Aegean Seas. Additionally, naval seaplane carriers gave the RNAS the mobility to operate further afield (such as East Africa and the Far East) if needed. RNAS aircraft were mainly employed for anti-submarine operations and coastal reconnaissance, but there was also a small number of fighter and bomber aircraft based in both France and the Aegean. The main bulk of the RFC was deployed on the Western Front in France and Belgium, but RFC squadrons also supported the army in Italy, Greece, Palestine, Mesopotamia and India. A handful of fighter squadrons were retained in the UK for home defence against German heavy bombers and Zeppelins (airships); another small number of bomber squadrons in France were positioned for independent operations over Germany; all other front-line RFC flying squadrons were allocated to the army at division level in each theatre of operations. These units were divided into 'Army' and 'Corps' squadrons. The Army squadrons comprised fighter units, tasked with achieving air superiority over the enemy air services, and bomber units tasked with

A Fairey IIID of 267 Squadron is hoisted aboard the seaplane carrier HMS *Ark Royal* in the early 1920s. The fledgling RAF inherited all of the commitments of the Royal Naval Air Service (RNAS), including the provision of aircraft and flying personnel to support naval operations. HMS *Ark Royal* was closely involved with the deployment of RAF aircraft to Russia, Turkey and Somaliland in the immediate post-war years. (Jarrett)

attacking military targets such as headquarters units and similar facilities behind the enemy frontlines. The Corps squadrons were chiefly used for artillery observation and photographic reconnaissance, which were, perhaps, the two least glamorous yet most important and successful of the roles fulfilled by aircraft during the entire war. During army offensives, Corps aircraft would also be used for 'contact patrols' in which they would fly low over the battlefield to establish the positions of the forward army units and report them back to headquarters.

However, the failure of both air arms to stop the German air service from bombing the British mainland in 1917 led to serious questions about how the UK should be defended by its own air forces. These led to the larger question as to how British air power should be organized, and the man tasked by the government to answer all of those questions was J.C. Smuts, a South African lawyer who had distinguished himself fighting the British army during the second Boer War.

GENERAL SMUTS

Jan Christiaan Smuts was, by almost any measure, a genius: Albert Einstein is reputed to have numbered Smuts amongst the handful of people who actually understood his general theory of relativity and he was also named, along with Milton and Darwin, as one of the three outstanding graduates over five centuries at Christ's College, Cambridge. In 1917, Smuts, who was at the time both a Lieutenant General in the British army and a leading member of the South African government, was invited to join the Imperial War Cabinet. On 11 July 1917, Smuts was tasked to examine, firstly, the arrangements for the defence of the British Isles against air raids and, secondly, 'the air organization generally and the direction of aerial operations'. In a report published later that month, Smuts addressed the first subject, but wrote that 'the second subject of our enquiry is the more important and will consequently require more extensive and deliberate examination.' His second report followed a month later.

While Smuts acknowledged, in his second report, that the separate RNAS and RFC had grown from the perception that air power would be subordinate to the needs of the navy and the army, he wrote that 'unlike artillery, an air fleet can conduct extensive operations far from and independently of, both army and navy... and the day may not be far off when aerial operations with their devastation of enemy lands and destruction of industrial and populous centres on a vast scale may become the principal operations of war, to which the older forms of naval and military operations may become secondary and subordinate.' He concluded that an Air Ministry should be established without delay and that the RNAS and RFC should be amalgamated into a single independent air service. The recommendations made by Smuts were accepted and the Royal Air Force (RAF) was formed from the RNAS and the RFC on 1 April 1918. Thus, Jan Smuts became the progenitor of the world's first independent air force.

Unfortunately, the first appointee to the post of Chief of the Air Staff (CAS), Major General Sir H.M. Trenchard KCB, DSO, suffered a personality clash with Lord Rothermere, the Air Minister, and he resigned; his place was taken on 12 April by Major General F. H. Sykes CMG, who steered the new service through its first year of existence.

A GLOBAL REACH

From its inception, the RAF was involved in operational flying on a front that stretched from Ireland across to India. In fact, in April 1918 the last campaign of the war in India (in Baluchistan) was coming to a close and the resident units in India, 31 and 114 Squadrons, (which were both equipped with BE2e aircraft) saw no further action during the year. However, further west of them, the RAF units in Mesopotamia were very active in the late spring of 1918 as British forces in the region advanced northwards along the River Tigris, driving the Turkish forces back towards Kirkuk. The RAF contingent comprised two Corps squadrons,

Wearing the uniform of a Field Marshal, the South African statesman, scholar and soldier Jan Christiaan Smuts (1870 –1950), whose report *Air Organisation and the Direction of Aerial Operations*, published in August 1917, was the catalyst for the establishment of an independent Royal Air Force the following year. (Official Photographer/ IWM/Getty)

An Airco de Havilland DH4 day bomber of 475 Flight (later 220 Squadron) at Imbros. The unit carried out anti-submarine patrols over the Aegean Sea, as well as bombing raids over the Dardenelles and Salonika. (Jarrett)

30 and 63 Squadrons, operating the RE8 and a single Army squadron, 72 Squadron, which was equipped with the Bristol M1C Monoplane Scout, Martynside G.100 and SE5a fighters and also de Havilland (DH) 4 bombers. Although it was primarily intended for air-to-air work, the Bristol Monoplanes proved particularly effective at this time for ground strafing the retreating Turkish forces.

The Turkish armies were also fighting a defensive battle in Palestine, having retreated from Gaza during the winter of 1917. In April 1918, the frontlines had stabilized, temporarily, just to the north of Jerusalem while the British forces re-grouped. After struggling with barely adequate aircraft in the previous year, the RAF units in-theatre had been recently re-equipped with more modern types: the Corps units, 14 and 113 Squadrons, now flew the RE8 while 142 Squadron operated the Armstrong-Whitworth (AW) FK8; additionally two fighter squadrons, 111 Squadron and 1 Squadron Australian Flying Corps (AFC), were equipped with the SE5a and Bristol F2b respectively. Another two squadrons, 144 Squadron (DH9) and 145 Squadron (SE5a) would join the frontline during the summer. All of these units were supplemented by 'X' Flight, a small independent flight which operated

directly in support of Arab forces led by Col T.E. Lawrence. Unlike Mesopotamia where there was little air opposition, the RAF aircraft had often been engaged by Turkish or German fighters over Palestine; however, the advent of the SE5a and Bristol F2b in early 1918 meant that the balance of air superiority had tipped decisively towards the RAF. Apart from directing a sustained campaign of artillery counter-battery work, one of the major tasks of the Corps squadrons in Palestine was to photograph the terrain: there were virtually no maps of the Levant so the army depended on aerial surveys in order to produce suitable charts. The squadrons of the Palestine Wing were also active supporting army operations against the Turkish forces and transport infrastructure to the east of the River Jordan: the tasks carried out included contact patrols, tactical reconnaissance, bombing and aerial resupply of medical equipment.

RAF units were also busy in the eastern Mediterranean: seaplanes based in Malta, Santa Maria di Leuca (southern Italy), Crete, Port Said and Alexandria (Egypt) carried out routine anti-submarine patrols and convoy escort duties and there were two maritime wings, each comprising four squadrons of DH4s and Sopwith Camels based in southern Italy and the Aegean. Much like the work of the land-based Corps squadrons, the tasks carried out by the seaplane units were not particularly glamorous, but they were very effective in limiting the effectiveness of the Austro-Hungarian U-boat service. The DH4 and Camel units based in Italy at Otranto (224 and 225 Squadrons) and Taranto (226 and 227 Squadrons) were used for attacking naval and military targets on the Adriatic coast of Albania and Montenegro. From April to late August, they bombed the submarine bases at Cattaro and Durazzo frequently and the same squadrons were also used to support the Italian offensive in Albania in early July 1918. In the Aegean sector, the four land-based units were more widely dispersed across eastern Greece and the north Aegean islands: 220 Squadron was based at Imbros, 221 Squadron at Stavros, 222 Squadron at Thasos and 223 Squadron at Mudros. Apart from anti-submarine patrols of the Aegean and reconnaissance patrols over the Sea of Marmaris, these units bombed targets in the Dardanelles region as well as carrying out bombing and reconnaissance sorties over the Salonika (or Macedonia) front.

In April 1918, the Salonika front was formed as an approximately 50-mile arc around the city of Thessaloniki: here an Allied force was dug in, facing combined Turkish, Bulgarian and Austro-Hungarian armies. Following the pattern in Mesopotamia, the RAF contingent in Thessaloniki comprised two Corps squadrons, 17 and 47 Squadrons (both with FK8s and DH9s) and a single Army squadron, 150 Squadron (equipped with the SE5a, Bristol Monoplane M1 and Camel). Often working in co-operation with 221 and 222 Squadrons, and enjoying the air superiority won by the fighters, the aircraft of 17 and 47 Squadrons were used to bomb airfields and storage depots deep behind the enemy frontlines throughout May.

Further north, and on the opposite side of the Adriatic Sea, a British contingent fought alongside Italian troops on the Piave front in northeast Italy. They were supported by a somewhat substantial air arm based to the northwest of Padua, comprising 34 Squadron (RE8) at Villaverla, 66 Squadron (Camel) at San Pietro-in-Gu and two more Camel squadrons, 28 and 45 Squadrons, at Grossa; a further flight of Bristol F2b, which was later to become 139 Squadron, was attached to 34 Squadron to help with the task of routine reconnaissance. The Camel squadrons were tasked to escort the RE8 reconnaissance aircraft and also to carry out offensive patrols against Austro-Hungarian aircraft. In May, it became apparent that an offensive by the Austrians was imminent and on 30 May a force of 35 Camels carried out a pre-emptive low-level bombing attack on enemy hutments in the Val d'Assa area. When the offensive was launched in mid-June, the RAF

A Bristol M1C Monoplane fighter, on an airfield near Baghdad in 1920. Fast and manoeuvrable, this type was used very effectively during 1918 by 72 Squadron in Mesopotamia and by 47 and 150 Squadrons in Salonika. Although 125 of these aircraft were ordered, it seems likely that less than 20 saw active service, largely because of a general prejudice within the RFC and RAF against monoplanes. (Flintham)

Probably the most successful aeroplane produced by the Royal Aircraft Factory, the SE5a fighter aircraft along with the Sopwith Camel enabled the RAF to establish air supremacy over the Western Front. The type also served in the Mediterranean and Middle Eastern theatres. This particular aircraft was flown by Maj Fred Sowrey MC, while commanding 143 Squadron, a home defence unit. (Pitchfork)

sent large formations of Camels, again operating at low level, which were effective in helping to repel the attack.

THE HOME FRONT

In 1918, home defence of the UK against enemy aircraft was provided by an integrated system of anti-aircraft guns, searchlights and fighter aircraft, served by a rudimentary early warning system. The latter was provided by observer stations manned by the police of the Observation Corps, sometimes backed up by wireless-equipped aircraft which could relay the position and altitude of enemy aircraft. The RAF contribution to the Home Defence organization was divided into a Northern and a Southern Group, covering the areas to the north and south of the Wash. The northern group comprised five squadrons equipped with Bristol F2b and Avro 504K aircraft, while the southern group mainly focussed on the defence of London with 11 squadrons equipped with FE2b, SE5a, Bristol F2b, Camel and Avro 504K aircraft. After an absence of a month from the UK mainland, the *Deutsche Luftstreitkräfte* (German air service) carried out a raid on the Midlands with five Zeppelin airships on the night of 12/13 April. Taking advantage of poor weather which prevented many RAF fighters from taking off, the airships were untouched by the defences and were able to drop their bombs on targets including Wigan, Birmingham and Coventry. Only one interception was made, that of the Zeppelin L62 by Lt C.H. Noble-Campbell of 38 Squadron, but he was wounded and his aircraft damaged by the defensive fire from the Zeppelin, which escaped safely.

Another large raid by German aircraft took place on the night of 19/20 May. On this occasion, a force of 43 bombers, mainly Gotha and Giant aircraft, attacked Dover and London under the light of a full moon. This time the defences, which included 84 fighter aircraft, were much more effective and seven of the German bombers were brought down.

However, the greater part of the RAF's operational strength in the UK was involved in anti-submarine operations around the coast. One surprisingly cost-effective measure introduced in the summer of 1918 was to use surplus DH6 training aircraft to patrol coastal shipping lanes. The presence of an aeroplane was usually enough to deter a U-boat commander from making an attack and submariners were unaware of the limited offensive capabilities of the DH6.

Left: The distinctive silhouette of a Blackburn Kangaroo anti-submarine patrol aircraft of 246 Squadron, escorting a naval convoy. Despite its ungainly appearance, the type proved to be particularly effective in the anti-submarine role: despite being deployed only in small numbers in the last six months of the war they attacked eleven U-boats. Unfortunately, the value of long-range maritime patrol aircraft was forgotten after the war and had to be re-learnt during World War II. (Cross & Cockade)

Below: The Felixstowe F2A flying boat equipped seven squadrons during World War I and was used for patrols over the North Sea. The aircraft carried a crew of four and had an endurance of some 6 hours. Despite its large size (including a wing span of nearly 100ft), the Felixstowe F2A was a remarkably manoeuvrable aeroplane and was capable of combat against enemy fighters and flying boats as well as Zeppelins and submarines.

Above: Only some 14 Blackburn Kangaroos were built, of which ten served with 246 Squadron at Seaton Carew, near Hartlepool, during 1918. The aircraft was powered by two Rolls-Royce Falcon II engines and carried a crew of four, who enjoyed good visibility from the two open cockpits. (Jarrett)

Right: Most of the 8,000 Avro 504 aircraft built during World War I were used as training aircraft, but in 1918 some 200 of the type were converted as single-seat night fighters. These aircraft equipped six home defence squadrons. (Jarrett)

Furthermore, as the aircraft was very simple to fly, it gave the opportunity for pilots who were unsuited to front-line flying (for example those with disabilities incurred in previous operational flying) to continue to be useful to the service. Seaplanes were also used for anti-submarine work and coastal patrols, while larger flying boats carried out long-range reconnaissance sorties along the German and Dutch coasts. They were also used for long-range interception of enemy airships: the Zeppelin L62, which had evaded the home defences in April, was destroyed after being attacked off Heligoland on 10 May 1918 by an RAF flying boat.

The coastal waters off the Netherlands and Germany were the scene of almost continuous action between German seaplanes and RAF seaplanes and flying boats, as the *Luftstreitkräfte* sought to prevent RAF aircraft from interfering with mine clearance

operations. One of the largest actions was fought on 4 June 1918 between five RAF Felixstowe F2A flying boats (two from Felixstowe, Suffolk and three from 228 Squadron at Great Yarmouth, Norfolk) and approximately 15 German seaplanes based on the island of Borkum; although the two flying boats from Felixstowe were lost in the combat, six enemy seaplanes were shot down in this action.

On the continental side of the Strait of Dover were the two naval wings at Dunkirk, one of which comprised a fighter unit (213 Squadron), an anti-submarine unit (217 Squadron), and a reconnaissance unit (202 Squadron), the other of which consisted of a fighter unit (204 Squadron), a day bomber unit (211 Squadron) and three night bomber units (207, 214 and 215 Squadrons). The latter wing was intended for operations against the German U-boat, motor gunboat and seaplane bases at Ostend and Zeebrugge; they remained active in doing so throughout the rest of the war. They also supported the naval raids on Zeebrugge on 23 April and Ostend on 10 May. Another two naval fighter squadrons (201 and 210 Squadrons) had been transferred from Dunkirk to the Western Front at the end of March to reinforce the hard-pressed squadrons. Other former naval fighter squadrons had preceded them, including 209 Squadron, which was involved in the shooting down of Manfred von Richthofen ('The Red Baron') on 21 April.

THE WESTERN FRONT

The RAF was born into the aftermath of the German spring offensive on the Western Front, which had broken through Allied lines in the Somme area on 21 March 1918. As the army staged a fighting retreat, RAF aircraft were instrumental in slowing the German advance. On 1 April, all single-seat fighter units in V Brigade were involved in almost continuous low-level bombing and strafing attacks on enemy troops; meanwhile the Corps squadrons carried out contact patrols in order to establish the positions of friendly ground units. The main role of these units, though, was to co-ordinate artillery fire, but it proved to be a difficult task when many batteries either abandoned their wireless equipment,

Due to the powerful gyroscopic effect of its heavy rotary engine and a centre of gravity well forward in its short fuselage, the Sopwith 1F.1 Camel enjoyed what one test pilot described as 'very lively handling characteristics.' Extremely manoeuvrable and armed with two forward-firing Vickers machine guns the Camel was perhaps the most successful RAF fighter aircraft of World War I. By October 1918, the RAF had over 2,500 Camels on strength. (Flintham)

or did not re-erect their aerials when they moved to new positions. The day bomber units were also busy on that day, attacking targets in the enemy rear areas: 205 Squadron bombed enemy aerodromes, while 18, 57 and 206 Squadrons concentrated on the railway stations at Cambrai, Bapaume and Menin. Air activity continued into the night, with attacks by 58 and 83 Squadrons on the railway system and 101 and 102 Squadrons attacking road transport travelling under headlamps. A Handley Page O/100 bomber of 214 Squadron also dropped 14 bombs on Valenciennes that night. Similar operations continued through 2 April, and although Marshal Foch issued an order that 'the first duty of fighting aeroplanes is to assist the troops on the ground by incessant attacks,' the RAF policy remained that artillery direction was the prime role and that at least some fighter units should be used to protect the Corps and ground-attack aircraft from the attentions of enemy aircraft. Indeed, the following day, force of some 30 Pfalz and Albatros fighters bounced Camel and SE5a fighters at 1,500ft near Rosières. Five German aircraft were shot down during the engagement, at no cost to the RAF squadrons, and thereafter, as a result of this action, continuous patrols,

each of two-squadron strength, were mounted by the RAF specifically to seek out and destroy enemy aircraft.

The German advance in the Somme area was halted just to the east of Amiens two days later, but no sooner had that part of the line been secured, than a second offensive (Battle of the Lys) was launched in Flanders. On 9 April, after an initial bombardment of chemical shells, German forces advanced along a front from Armentières to Festubert. The advance was covered by thick fog which prevented RAF aircraft from taking off during the morning. After being warned that German forces were about to overrun the aerodrome at La Gorgue, the resident 208 Squadron burnt their Camels before abandoning the base. The fog lifted into low cloud in the early afternoon and a contact patrol by an RE8 from 4 Squadron revealed the positions of German troops, enabling low-level attacks against them by Camels of 4 AFC, 203, and 210 Squadrons and the SE5a aircraft of 40 Squadron. Poor weather continued the following day, which also saw a second German thrust developing opposite Messines. When the weather cleared sufficiently, the low-level attacks by RAF fighter squadrons resumed, as did the work of the Corps squadrons, but these operations were

An Airco de Havilland DH9 bomber in flight. Intended to replace the DH4 as a day bomber, the DH9 was handicapped by the mediocre performance of the 230hp Siddeley Puma engine. Nevertheless, some 3,200 of these aircraft were built and they saw action with RAF units in France, the Mediterranean and the Middle East. (RAFM)

complicated by the presence of low-flying German aircraft over the battlefield. Like their counterparts in the Somme area, the day bomber squadrons operated behind the German lines throughout the day attacking the rail infrastructure and reinforcements. As darkness fell most airfields became fog-bound, which limited the activities of the night bombing units; nevertheless, bombers were able to carry out night attacks on 10/11 April. The next day, with the ground situation critical, Field Marshal Sir Douglas Haig issued the order that 'every position must be held to the last man; there must be no retirement. With our backs to the wall and believing in the justice of our cause, each one of us must fight on to the end.' Indeed, 12 April proved to be the pivotal day of the battle, during which RAF fighter aircraft carried out many low-level attacks while Corps aircraft ensured effective gun direction and contact patrols. During the day six German observation balloons were destroyed and that night, the bomber squadrons were active again attacking rail and road transport as well as troop billets. After fierce fighting, the German advance lost momentum and slowed: the frontline in Flanders was eventually stabilized by 29 April.

Further German offensives followed in May, June and July in the largely French-held sectors in Champagne and the Chemin des Dames. In early June eight RAF units, comprising three DH9 day bomber squadrons and five fighter squadrons were dispatched to the area to help to contain the German advance. From 9 to 10 June these aircraft were used primarily for low-level gun and bomb attacks on advancing German troops, and from 11 June they also supported the successful French counterattack that followed at Noyon.

INDEPENDENT OPERATIONS

A wing of bomber aircraft had been established at Nancy-Ochey in late 1917 in order to attack targets in Germany: these operations were intended as a reprisal against German air raids on the British mainland. The wing initially comprised 55 Squadron with the DH4 for day operations, and 100 Squadron equipped with the FE2b also 16 (Naval) Squadron (which became 216 Squadron) equipped with the Handley Page O/100 and O/400 for night operations; it was

Handley Page O/400 heavy bombers, of which some 550 were built, saw service with seven squadrons in France, including 97, 115, 215 and 216 Squadrons of the Independent Force. The largest aeroplane operated by the RAF in World War I, it could carry a weapons payload of 2,000lb including the largest 1,650lb 'SN' bomb. (Flintham)

In the summer of 1918, various schemes were tried to improve the tactical range of aircraft operating over the North Sea. Attempts to tow or carry seaplanes proved too dependent on sea conditions, but trials using a Sopwith Camel 2F.1 flying off a lighter towed by a destroyer were successful. On 11 August 1918, Lt S.D. Culley launched from a lighter towed by HMS *Redoubt* and shot down Zeppelin L53. (Flintham)

enlarged in May 1918 by the addition of 99 and 104 Squadrons flying the DH9. From Nancy, the RAF aircraft could reach into Germany to cover an arc from Köln (Cologne) to Stuttgart: operating within that area whenever the weather was suitable, they attacked factories, military barracks and railways by both day and night. For night operations, steelworks made the best targets, as the blast furnaces showed up clearly in the dark. The wing officially became the Independent Force in June 1918, recognizing that the operations were strategic in nature and were independent of land operations; it was further expanded with the addition of 110 Squadron, equipped with the DH9 and 97, 115 and 215 Squadrons with Handley Page O/400 bombers. Although operations by the Independent Force caused relatively little physical damage in Germany, it was considered that they had been effective in undermining the morale of the civilian population. Night operations were also carried out against German airfields, but the results of these attacks were inconclusive.

However, German night operations against RAF aerodromes, and other military facilities, in France in early 1918 were successful and they resulted in the transfer of night-fighter squadrons to France. Of these, 151 Squadron, equipped with the Sopwith Camel, which arrived in June, proved to be particularly effective: in the five months after arriving in France it shot down some 26 German night bombers without any losses.

By August, the German night bombing campaign against Britain had ground to a halt, not least thanks to the effective anti-aircraft defence system. The last raid by the *Luftstreitkräfte* was on the evening of 5 August, when five Zeppelin airships approached the coast of East Anglia. They were intercepted by a DH4 from Yarmouth flown by Maj E. Cadbury with Capt R. Leckie, who destroyed Zeppelin L70; seeing this engagement, the remaining airships then turned and headed back to Germany; no bombs were dropped on the mainland.

Another Zeppelin, the L53, was destroyed six days later. The previous evening a small naval force comprising light cruisers and destroyers had sailed for the Dutch coast. Three of the destroyers each towed a lighter (small barge), carrying an aeroplane as a means of giving the machine a longer tactical range. Two of these aircraft were flying boats, but a lighter from HMS *Redoubt* carried the Sopwith Camel to be flown by Lt S.D. Culley. The following morning, near the island of Terschelling, a formation of Yarmouth-based flying boats reported the presence of a Zeppelin and Culley was launched to make an interception; this he successfully did and then shot down the airship. As it was not possible for him to land back on the lighter he ditched his Camel in the sea and was picked up by a naval ship.

RUSSIA

A modest task force, including an RAF contingent comprising eight DH4 bombers, five Fairey Campania seaplanes and two Sopwith Baby seaplanes, had been dispatched to northern Russia in May 1918. Its purpose was twofold: firstly, to secure the British military equipment which had been provided to the Russian army and prevent it from falling into Bolshevik hands, and secondly, to support White Russian forces. After arriving in Murmansk, the force split into two: 'Syren' Force set up the defence of Murmansk and the air arm started operations in support of White Russian forces along the railway line which ran southwards to Kandalaksha via Kem and Lake Onega. Meanwhile

'Elope' Force moved on by ship towards Arkhangelsk. After a brief action, which included bombing Bolshevik artillery on Modyuski Island by Fairey Campania floatplanes of the RAF, Arkhangelsk was taken on 7 August. Here the RAF contingent found enough new (still in their delivery crates) Sopwith 1½ Strutter aircraft to form two squadrons, which were manned by RAF and Allied personnel. Once again, DH4 bombers and seaplanes were used for operations along the railway line (which led to Moscow) and the River Dvina. The aircraft of both the Syren and Elope forces were used for long-range reconnaissance and artillery observation, but also carried out bombing attacks against Bolshevik ground forces.

Further south in the same month, two Martinsyde G100 aircraft of 72 Squadron were dispatched from Iraq to support 'Dunsterforce,' a British army detachment which was holding Baku against Turkish forces. The aircraft began operations on 20 August and were fortunate in having no enemy air opposition. They were initially used for reconnaissance, bombing and leaflet dropping, but also carried out intensive low-level strafing attacks against enemy troops during the Turkish offensive which started on 26 August. However, the Turkish force was overwhelming and despite a

The Martinsyde G100 Elephant entered service with the Royal Flying Corps in early 1916, but by 1918 only a handful of the type remained in service, with 72 Squadron in Mesopotamia. In May 1918, two of these aircraft were attached to 'Dunsterforce' a British Army detachment which attempted to hold the city of Baku against Turkish forces. (RAFM)

Above: The Armstrong Whitworth FK8, known as the 'Big Ack' was used by 8 Squadron in the first co-ordinated actions by tanks and enemy aircraft during the Allied offensive of August 1918. Although it was superior in many ways to the RE8, the FK8 was only produced in relatively small numbers and equipped just five squadrons in France, and a further three in Macedonia and Palestine. (Jarrett)

Right: The distinctive 'backward stagger' of the wings of the Sopwith 5F1 Dolphin is clearly visible in this view. The type saw service in France with 19, 23, 79, 87 and 90 Squadrons.

spirited rear-guard action covered by the aircraft of 72 Squadron, the inevitable evacuation took place on 14 September, after the aircraft had been burnt.

AUGUST OFFENSIVE

After the unsuccessful attempts by the German army to break through on the Western Front in the spring, it was the turn of the Allied forces to attack in late summer 1918. The British offensive opened near Amiens in the thick mist of the morning of 8 August. Just as it had in the German offensive five months earlier, the mist prevented aircraft from operating over the battlefield until late morning; however, as the weather cleared, single-seat pilots found that the ground was rich with targets. Meanwhile, the swift advance of British and Empire forces made artillery direction by the Corps aircraft challenging as friendly

troops began to advance beyond the range of the guns; in this fluid situation, contact patrols became even more important as the only means to keep track of the positions of ground units. The Corps aircraft were also tasked with some new roles: the RE8 aircraft of 3 AFC, 5, and 9 Squadrons dropped phosphorous bombs to provide smoke screens for the Australian and Canadian Corps as they attacked German strongpoints, while the FK8 aircraft of 8 Squadron experimented with close support of tanks. At this stage co-operation was limited to locating tanks, and dropping messages at the brigade headquarters notifying the staff of their progress; later tank contact patrols would also engage German anti-tank guns with bombs and machine-gun fire.

By late afternoon on the first day of the offensive, a large German force was trapped by the River Somme where it curves south at Péronne. The bridges over this stretch of river formed choke points and the RAF

An RE8 of 59 Squadron over the Western Front. Aircraft from this squadron were tasked with artillery spotting and direction during the offensive, but the crews frequently took direct action to support infantry troops. On 23 August 1918, the crew of an RE8 from the squadron strafed and neutralized an enemy machine gun position which had halted the advance of the New Zealand Division to the west of Bapaume. (RAFM)

bomber squadrons were tasked with the destruction of the 12 bridges between Péronne and Offoy. That evening and throughout the next day, RAF squadrons fought a sustained campaign against the Somme bridges: DH9 and DH4 bombers, supported by Camel and SE5a patrols, carried out numerous bombing attacks. On the first afternoon 205 bombing sorties were flown, but they were hotly contested by an increasingly aggressive *Luftstreitkräfte*, which resulted in the RAF losing 45 aircraft and a further 52 wrecked. At night, follow-up attacks were flown by FE2b night bomber squadrons and the Camels of 151 Squadron. On 9 August, the bombing missions started again at 05:00hrs and carried on throughout the day, culminating in a simultaneous attack by four DH9 squadrons against five bridges in the evening. This latter mission was directly supported by an offensive patrol comprising Sopwith Dolphin, Bristol F2b, SE5a and Camel squadrons; when darkness fell, night attacks continued, including bombing of the bridge at Voyenne by 207 Squadron equipped with the Handley Page O/400. However, it soon became apparent that despite significant air effort, little damage had been done to any of the bridges. The reasons for this were twofold; firstly, although some of the bombs were delivered from heights of around 2,000 or 3,000ft, most of the bombing had been carried out from 11,000 or 12,000ft, from which altitude bombing was not accurate enough to hit a target as small as a bridge. Secondly, even if hits were scored, the 25lb and 112lb bombs were too small to cause any significant damage to such a robust structure.

On 10 August, the bombing squadrons' attentions were switched to the more realistic objective of disrupting the railway traffic at Péronne and beyond. The first raid was carried out by 12 DH9s, escorted by a formation of 40 Camels and Bristol F2bs and seven SE5as. This sizeable formation was attacked over the target area by a force of 15 Fokker DVIIs and although one German fighter was shot down, five British aircraft were lost. The railway bombing continued into the night and on through the following day. By then the British advance had slowed, but the German army had already commenced a general withdrawal eastwards.

The next thrust came in the Bapaume area on 21 August. Once again, poor weather limited the effectiveness of air power on the first day. However, the weather cleared as darkness fell and RAF night bombers were able to operate, concentrating on the enemy airfields; the following morning, the day bomber squadrons began to attack the railway lines fanning out from Cambrai. On 23 August, the main offensive began along a wider front between Péronne and Bapaume. One innovation was the establishment of a Central Information Bureau (CIB) which acted as a reporting point for wireless-equipped Corps aircraft: the idea was that ground targets would be identified for low-level ground strafing and the CIB would then pass that information on to the relevant fighter aerodromes for action. Another innovation, which had been frustrated by the weather two days earlier at Bapaume, was the use of a fighter squadron (73 Squadron) to support tanks in combat by attacking German anti-tank guns. As in previous offensive actions, other fighter squadrons were tasked with supporting the infantry by making low-level attacks on the battlefield. Also the Corps aircraft often found that the quickest way to support the troops on the ground was by taking a direct role in engaging enemy machine-gun posts. Meanwhile, the railway system and road transport in the German rear area received the full attention of the day and night bomber squadrons. The weather was poor for much of the next few days and nights, but low-level attacks continued as well as the work of the Corps squadrons, often in driving rain under a 300ft cloud base; during this time RE8 aircraft were also regularly used to drop supplies of ammunition to troops in forward areas.

Further north, another assault was launched from Arras on 26 August, once again under low cloud and heavy rain. The weather prevented the day bomber squadrons from flying, but the Corps squadrons, 5 and 52 Squadrons, were active, flying at 200ft, while the Camel and the SE5a squadrons carried out close-support attacks. The following day the weather was little improved, but again the fighter squadrons were tasked with carrying out regular patrols at low level over the battlefield. Additionally, 73 Squadron

continued its work of neutralizing anti-tank guns in the path of the advancing tanks. By the end of August, the German army had been pushed back almost to the Hindenburg Line.

However, one major obstacle remained: the Drocourt–Quéant Line. This 15-mile stretch of defensive fortifications, which was centred approximately seven miles east of Arras, was the objective for two Canadian and one British division on 2 September. The infantry was supported by low-flying Camels of 54, 208 and 209 Squadrons and SE5a fighters of 64 Squadron, while the artillery was directed by the RE8 aircraft of 4, 6, and 52 Squadrons and the tanks were supported by FK8s from 8 Squadron and Camels from 73 Squadron. The result was an almost continuous presence of aircraft

operating at low level over the battlefield. By dusk the German line had been broken and that night the enemy troops fell back to the line of Canal du Nord.

MACEDONIA & PALESTINE

As the British armies in France were poised to attack the Hindenburg Line in mid-September 1918, those in Macedonia and Palestine were also about to commence major offensives. The first of these was in Macedonia, when British and Greek forces attacked the Bulgarian positions to the west of Lake Dojran on 18 September. The ground forces were supported by 17 and 47 Squadrons; both units operated a mixture of FK8 and DH9 aircraft and fulfilled the corps, reconnaissance

An RE8 over the Jerusalem to Bireh road. During the Battle of Megiddo in Palestine, which began on 19 September 1918, the aircraft of 14 Squadron and the FK8 aircraft of 142 Squadron carried out artillery direction and tactical reconnaissance; they also participated in the decimation of the Turkish 7th Army in the Wadi Fara – which remains a definitive example of the destructive capability of air power. (14 Squadron Association)

and bombing roles. They in turn were protected by Camels and SE5a fighters of 150 Squadron. Two days of heavy fighting followed, during which RAF aircraft carried out low-level bombing and strafing attacks, but their crews found it difficult to observe much detail because of the smoke and dust on the battlefield. Artillery direction against enemy batteries was more successful, as were attacks by the DH9 bombers against equipment dumps in the enemy's rear areas. The only appearance over the battlefield by Bulgarian aircraft was swiftly repelled by 150 Squadron and thereafter the skies were uncontested. On the ground Bulgarian forces fought back fiercely and by 20 September it seemed that the Allied forces had made no progress. However, the following day, a DH9 returned from a reconnaissance patrol and reported that the Bulgarian army was withdrawing northwards en-masse. Aircraft were immediately detailed to bomb enemy troops and their transport and over the coming days the retreating Bulgarians were continuously harassed by RAF aircraft. Long-range reconnaissance flights were also mounted in an attempt to discover what exactly was happening behind the Bulgarian frontlines. On 28 September, a sizeable column of troops was found in the Kryesna Pass where it was subjected to sustained bombing and strafing attacks, resulting in many enemy casualties. This was the last action by the RAF in Macedonia: an armistice was signed by the Bulgarian government on 30 September and hostilities ceased on that front.

The offensive in Palestine (the Battle of Megiddo) began on 19 September. The SE5a fighters of 111 and 145 Squadrons had already established air supremacy over the area, so the German crews of the reconnaissance aircraft were unable to see the preparations for the assault. From early September, the Turkish army had been deceived into believing that the assault would be delivered in the Judean Hills on the eastern flank, rather than on the coastal plain. On the morning of the attack, the Turkish command and control channels were seriously disrupted by air attacks on their corps and divisional headquarters and military telephone exchanges. Handley-Page O/400 bombers from 'X' Flight attacked the telephone

exchange at El Affule and this attack was followed up by another raid, this time by DH9 bombers of 144 Squadron. Earlier, this squadron had also attacked targets at Nablus, while 142 Squadron (FK8) and 14 Squadron (RE8) also carried out dawn raids. A standing patrol of two SE5a fighters over the Turkish aerodrome at Jenin throughout the day also ensured that enemy aircraft were unable to intervene. The British infantry attack quickly broke through the Turkish lines in the coastal sector. The main problem for the Corps squadrons was that the advance was so rapid that it quickly moved beyond the range of the artillery that they were directing. In the afternoon of 19 September, a large number of Turkish troops was discovered on the road from Tul Karm to Nablus and it was subjected to a prolonged attack by all of the RAF squadrons. Aircraft flew continuously along the column dropping bombs or grenades and machine-gunning any signs of movement. However, this massacre was only a rehearsal for an even greater slaughter two days later, when the Turkish 7th Army attempted to withdraw through the Wadi Fara, into the Jordan Valley. The entire army was caught in the Wadi on a narrow road which was bounded by a steep uphill slope on one side and a precipice on the other; with no means of escape, the Turkish troops were entirely at the mercy of RAF aircraft. Throughout the day, the troops were subjected to a relentless attack by all the aircraft that could be mustered. In the course of this attack, over 9 tons of bombs were dropped into the Wadi Fara. By the evening the Turkish 7th Army had been annihilated. The tactical emphasis now switched to the east of the River Jordan and the aircraft of 1 Squadron AFC and 144 Squadron bombed Turkish positions in support of the advance towards Amman; the city was captured on 25 September.

THE HINDENBURG LINE

The offensive against the Hindenburg line commenced on 27 September, with attacks by the 3rd Army on the northern flank and the 1st Army

The Royal Aircraft Factory RE8 was, arguably, the most important aircraft type in service with the RAF during the World War I. Known to its crews at the 'Harry Tate' after a music hall comedian of the day, the RE8 was the mainstay of the Corps squadrons, equipping a total of 19; the type saw active service in all theatres of operations. Over 4,000 were built to carry out the unglamorous but vitally important work of artillery direction and photographic reconnaissance. Although the type did not enjoy a particularly good reputation on the Western Front, it was regarded favourably in other theatres. (Pitchfork)

on the southern. Once again, the infantry assault was supported by low-level attacks by fighter aircraft, which in turn were protected from German aircraft by offensive patrols. German aircraft were also contained by bombing attacks on their aerodromes by the day bomber squadrons. The Corps squadrons of both armies were mainly involved with directing artillery counter-fire against German gun positions. An RE8 from 13 Squadron on a contact patrol found a formation of German infantry preparing for a counterattack and was able to call down artillery fire to neutralize the threat. That night, despite heavy cloud rolling in, the night bombers operated behind German lines attacking transport. The 4th Army, in the centre of the British line, opened its attack on the morning of 29 September. The ground forces included three tank brigades, which once again were supported by the FK8 aircraft of 8 Squadron and Camels of 73 Squadron. Flying conditions over the battlefield were difficult for the first days because of mist and cloud, mixed with smoke, but the weather improved on 1 October.

Further north, the Belgian army offensive (which included the British 2nd Army) had begun in Flanders on 28 September and once again low-level attacks by aircraft were integrated as part of the assault plan. Although there was no CIB on the Flanders front, Corps squadrons in this sector (7, 10 and 53 Squadrons) made good use of wireless (radio) equipment to pass on their reports. The aircraft were also used to drop rations to the forward troops at the end of the day. Through the rest of the month, the British, Empire and Allied forces continued to advance eastwards and the RAF units continued to support the army operations in the pattern that had been established so successfully.

OCTOBER OFFENSIVES

At the beginning of October 1918, the frontline in Mesopotamia ran approximately east–west close to the south of Kirkuk and British forces were positioned on both sides of the River Tigris. The offensive began on the night of 23/24 October and the following morning reconnaissance patrols by 72 Squadron located Turkish forces retreating northwards. The campaign in Mesopotamia was more fluid than that in other theatres and the contact patrols by the RE8 aircraft of 63 Squadron assumed vital importance in feeding the army commanders with up-to-date information about the dispositions of friendly and enemy forces. Over the next five days the battle moved swiftly along the Tigris back towards Mosul until, on 31 October, the Turkish army in Mesopotamia surrendered.

In Palestine, the Turkish army had been routed at Megiddo and British and Empire forces advanced swiftly to take Damascus on 1 October. In order to keep some semblance of aerial contact with advancing cavalry units, 14 and 113 Squadron used their RE8 aircraft to ferry petrol and oil to a forward operating base at El Affule so that they could be used by the FK8 aircraft of 142 Squadron for reconnaissance sorties and contact patrols. On 25 October Aleppo was captured and on 31 October, Turkish forces capitulated.

In northern Italy, the Battle of Vittorio Veneto opened with an Allied push across the River Piave on 27 October. Mapping for the offensive had been produced from the aerial photographs taken by the Bristol F2b aircraft of 139 Squadron in the preceding days. The initial RAF participation in the battle was through contact patrols by RE8 aircraft of 34 Squadron, but as the Austrian resistance crumbled, the other squadrons were deployed in low-level attacks against the retreating enemy forces. Hostilities came to an end in Italy with the signing of an armistice by the Austria on 4 November.

Meanwhile the Allied armies in France and Flanders continued their advance. The German retreat was made more difficult by a campaign of bombing attacks (both day and night) against the railway system in occupied territory and the German border. The *Luftstreitkräfte* vigorously opposed the bombers, sometimes flying in formations of 50 fighters. The hardest day's fighting in the air was on 30 October, when 67 German aircraft were destroyed, for the loss of 41 RAF aircraft. The RAF continued to bomb and strafe German troops over the next week until the war was ended by the armistice with Germany on 11 November 1918.

DEVELOPMENTS IN RUSSIA

Although the war against the Central Powers was now over, RAF units were still involved in combat operations in Russia. Over the autumn of 1918, the RAF in North Russia was bolstered by a flight of RE8s and six Camels. By October the various units from Murmansk were based on the northern tip of Lake Onega: DH4, RE8 and Camels were at Lumbushi (just north of the lake) while the seaplanes were at Medvegigora (on the northern tip of the lake); the Arkhangelsk units were split between 'A' Flight, covering the Moscow railway, at Obozerskaya on the railway 75 miles south of Arkhangelsk and 'B' Flight, covering the River Dvina, at Bereznik, along the river some 140 miles southeast of Arkhangelsk. Aircraft from all of these bases were operating in support of White Russian forces.

In early 1919, the scope of operations in Russia was increased with the dispatch of aircraft to support the British naval flotilla on the Caspian Sea in their efforts to contain the Bolshevik fleet based at Astrakhan. The first aircraft to arrive at Petrovsk (Makhachkala) on the western coast of the Caspian were DH9s and DH9As of 221 Squadron which commenced bombing missions against the railway systems at Kizlyar and Grozny early in February. In March, 221 Squadron was joined by 266 Squadron, equipped with various Short-built seaplanes, and both units began operations against Bolshevik shipping and military targets in the Volga delta. In May, 221 Squadron established a forward operating base at Chechen Island, which enabled the aircraft to reach as far as Astrakhan. On 20 and 22 May, 266 Squadron also attacked the Bolshevik naval base at Fort Alexandrovski on the eastern shore of the Caspian Sea.

Over the summer of 1919 both northern and southern RAF detachments in Russia were significantly reinforced and a third front was opened in the eastern Baltic. In southern Russia, 47 Squadron plus a flight from 17 Squadron were dispatched to Beketovka, on the outskirts of Tsaritsyn (later Stalingrad) for operations north of the Caucasus. The squadron, which was equipped with DH9A bombers, commenced flying operations on 22 June and over the next months, their targets ranged from Bolshevik ground troops and railway rolling stock to barge traffic on the River Volga. Unlike northern Russia where there was no viable

enemy air force, operations over the River Volga were challenged by Nieuport fighters flown by Bolshevik forces, which were based at Tcherni-Yar; in answer to this threat 47 Squadron received more Camels in September.

A naval force which included the aircraft carrier HMS *Vindictive* deployed to the eastern Baltic in July 1919. Operating from the Björkö Sound the force sought to contain Bolshevik naval forces in Petrograd. A number of raids were carried out by RN coastal motor boats, and also by the RAF air component embarked on HMS *Vindictive*, comprising Sopwith Camels and Short seaplanes. Most of the bombing attacks were against the naval installations at Kronstadt, which was attacked on an almost daily (and nightly) basis from

July through until October. On some occasions, the aerial bombing was designed to distract the defenders while the motor boats attacked. Naval and aerial attacks were also carried out against the fortress at Krasnaya Gorka.

The RAF's northern Russian detachments were reinforced by a number of volunteers in June 1919. Their arrival coincided with new aircraft being delivered which included the DH9, DH9A and the Sopwith Snipe as well as Fairey IIIC and Short 184 seaplanes. Daily sorties, lasting around 2 hours, were flown in support of White Russian ground forces by bombing enemy villages, railway junctions and strongpoints. Bolshevik naval craft operating on the lake were also attacked.

A Short Seaplane taking off from the River Dvina at Bereznik in late 1918 or early 1919, in support of White Russian forces fighting the Bolsheviks in northern Russia. From Bereznik, the aircraft could patrol over the river and rail approaches to Arkhangelsk from the southeast. Further to the west, seaplanes operating from Lake Onega and landplanes from Lumbushi covered the railway linking Moscow to Murmansk.

Above: An Airco DH9A in northern Russia during 1919. Operating from Lumbushi on the northern tip of Lake Onega, these aircraft were flown by volunteers in support of the White Russian army fighting Bolshevik forces. (Jarrett)

Right: A DH9 aircraft of 221 Squadron over Petrovsk during operations in early 1919 against Bolshevik forces in southern Russia. In the spring of 1919, working with the White Russian army, the aircraft bombed enemy forces and their transport infrastructure to the north of the Caucasus, reaching along the coast of the Caspian Sea as far as Astrakhan. (RAFM)

The Caspian Sea squadrons flew their last sorties in August and were then withdrawn. The RAF personnel in northern Russia were evacuated in October 1919 and HMS *Vindictive* and her air component also left the Baltic that month. That left only 47 Squadron, now renamed 'A' Detachment, in Russia: it continued to attack rivercraft and gunboats on the Volga between Astrakhan and Tsaritsyn, until it was also withdrawn in March 1920.

THE AFTERMATH OF WAR

Meanwhile the RAF, like the other services, had shrunk rapidly in the immediate aftermath of World War I. Of the 204 squadrons that existed in late 1918 only 29 remained by March 1920. A small number of flying units remained stretched across the Middle East and India, but the majority of flying squadrons had been reduced to cadre strength, or disbanded completely. Twenty squadrons had been deployed to Germany as part of the occupation force, mainly based at Bickendorf near Köln (Cologne); their role was largely restricted to flying mail runs and the last of the squadrons, 12 Squadron, was disbanded in 1922. As all three services reduced in size, both the Admiralty and the War Office fought to divide the RAF, and its budget, between them; it was only through adroit staff work and political patronage that the service survived these critical years. One unfortunate casualty of this political in-fighting was Major General Sykes, whose vision of an independent globally-positioned imperial air force proved to be too expensive for the post-war Treasury; he was replaced on 22 January 1919 Major General Trenchard, who had proposed a more affordable alternative. Ironically, during World War II, the RAF developed into an organization that closely resembled that of Sykes' original vision. After taking over as Chief of the Air Staff (CAS), Trenchard proposed a future RAF comprising 32 flying squadrons, of which 18 would be based overseas to police the Empire; furthermore

Sopwith Snipes of 70 Squadron. The unit was part of the occupation force based at Bickendorf in 1919. (Jarrett)

he wrote on 25 November 1919 that 'it is intended to preserve the numbers of some of the great squadrons who have made names for themselves during the war, in permanent service units with definite identity, which will be the homes of the officers belonging to them, and will have the traditions of the war to look back upon.' Thus was born the concept of squadron seniority which would underpin the traditions of the service over the next 100 years.

In April 1919, civil unrest erupted in India, which from the RAF's perspective had been relatively quiet over the previous 12 months. At first, the two resident RAF units, 31 and 114 Squadrons were called to assist the army in dealing with civil disturbances, but at the beginning of May intelligence sources indicated that an invasion by Afghan troops was imminent. The squadrons, still equipped with the BE2c, a type that had long been withdrawn from front-line service elsewhere, were put on standby for operations. A reconnaissance flight by 31 Squadron reported the disposition of the Afghan troops, supported by local

tribesmen, who crossed into India via the Khyber Pass on 6 May and occupied the settlement of Bagh. Three days later 16 aircraft carried out bombing attacks on the main Afghan encampment at Dakka while the Indian army carried out a counterattack at Bagh; although this action was unsuccessful, a second counterattack on 11 May drove the Afghans back across the border, hotly pursued by aircraft of 31 and 114 Squadrons and also the Indian army. The aircraft of 31 Squadron were also used to bomb Jalalabad. Meanwhile a Handley Page V/1500 bomber, which had been flown from the UK a few months earlier, was pressed into service. On 24 May, the aircraft was flown from Risalpur to bomb Kabul by Capt R. Halley DFC, AFC. Not only did his bombs cause damage to the palace of Amir Ammanulla, but they also had a significant personal and psychological effect on the Amir. Four days later, the Afghans counterattacked the British and Indian forces and laid siege to their camp at Thal. RAF aircraft played an important role in the relief of Thal on 1 June when they carried

Although it arrived too late for wartime service, the four-engined Handley Page V/1500 was the first truly strategic bomber to enter RAF service and was capable of reaching Berlin from the UK. This particular aircraft, 'Old Carthusian,' had been flown from England to India in January 1919 and was used to bomb Kabul during the Third Afghan War of 1919. (Jarrett)

out bombing attacks against Afghan positions and directed the artillery fire from the relief force. The Third Afghan War ended in an armistice on 2 June.

On the same day plans were approved in London for the RAF to assist in quelling another insurrection in Somaliland, led by the 'Mad Mullah,' Mohammed bin Abdullah Hassan. In the past, such uprisings had been put down, at great cost, by large columns of ground troops, but Trenchard saw the opportunity to demonstrate that the RAF could carry out such work more cost effectively. The RAF contingent, known as 'Z Unit,' comprised just 12 DH9 bombers, plus their supporting personnel. After embarking on HMS *Ark Royal*, Z Unit arrived in Berbera on 30 December 1919 and was ready for action three weeks later from an airstrip at Eil dur Eilan (some 100 miles southeast of Berbera). The plan was for the aircraft to operate independently for four days and then co-operate with the Somaliland Field Force (SFF) comprising troops from the Camel Corps, the King's African Rifles and local tribal levies; the Royal Navy would also provide support in coastal areas.

Intelligence sources reported that Hassan was at the village of Medichi (Midhisho) some 100 miles

northeast of Eil dur Eilan and between 21 and 24 January the aircraft carried out daily bombing raids against the village and the nearby fort at Jidali. However, during this time Hassan left the area to return to his main base at Taleh, so over the next five days, reconnaissance flights were made in an attempt to locate his party. The rebel forts at Jidali and Galibaribola were also bombed and both of these, as well as that at Badhan, were captured by the SFF. Meanwhile, a forward operating base was established at El Afweina, almost halfway between Medichi and Taleh: in this phase of the operation, a DH9 which had been converted to an ambulance proved particularly useful for transporting personnel and equipment to the new base. On the morning of 31 January, a reconnaissance flight located Hassan's caravan and made an attack; the next day another pair of aircraft also bombed and strafed the party. Thereafter Hassan and his supporters managed to remain invisible to reconnaissance aircraft. The last offensive action by aircraft of Z Unit was to bomb Hassan's palace and fortress complex at Taleh on 4 February. From that date, the aircraft were used exclusively for transport and communications, two roles which were essential

Operations in early 1920 to quell the insurrection in Somaliland led by the 'Mad Mullah' Mohammed bin Abdullah Hassan provided an opportunity for the RAF to demonstrate the concept of independent air control. One of the DH9 aircraft allocated to 'Z' Unit was modified to carry a stretcher, but during the campaign it proved to be more useful as a rudimentary transport aircraft. (Flintham)

in co-ordinating the widely-dispersed elements of the SFF. The Somaliland levies intercepted the main body of Hassan's supporters on 5 February and captured the Taleh complex on 10 February, but Hassan had already slipped away. By 12 February 1920 it was clear that he had escaped to Italian Somaliland and was no longer a threat. The revolt had been put down effectively – at a cost of just four aircraft written off in accidents without casualties.

In India, the RAF had been reinforced by the arrival of three squadrons, 20 Squadron (Bristol F2b), 97 Squadron (DH10) and 99 Squadron (DH9A), in the summer of 1919. All of these units saw action when violence flared up in Waziristan in November. Rebel gangs from two major tribal groups, the Tochi Wazir and the Mahsud, objected to foreign rule and sought to overthrow the colonial administration in the tribal areas. The government response was to issue an ultimatum for all weapons to be surrendered to the authorities and a fine paid. The first ultimatum was issued to the Tochi Wazir and when this did not elicit any response, their villages were bombed. The bombing commenced in the morning and by mid-afternoon, the weapons had been handed in and the fine paid. The aircraft of 20 Squadron then dropped leaflets in the Mahsud areas. Once again there was no response, so the town of Kaniguram was bombed by 20, 97 and 99 Squadrons, but this time the bombing did not have immediate results. In fact, the Mahsud

proved to be very reluctant to conform and a major army operation to restore order dragged on for the next three years. RAF aircraft played a significant part in these operations: the Bristol F2b aircraft of 20 and 31 Squadrons were used for co-operation with the ground troops, carrying out reconnaissance ahead of patrols. The squadrons also patrolled the areas around company-sized (picket) posts to advise if hostile parties approached, since the hilly terrain often provided excellent cover for any enemy advances. The bombers of 97 and 99 Squadrons attacked villages and also intercepted any potential reinforcements to Mahsud gangs. The bombing was carefully controlled so that it caused minimal damage: it was intended primarily as a show of force, but one that caused sufficient damage to keep the villagers too busy repairing their buildings and livestock shelters to support the insurrection.

However, despite the theoretical strength of six squadrons in theatre, the RAF in India was actually in a parlous state. Although the RAF was supposedly an independent service, the Indian government merely regarded it as part of the Indian army and it had no separate budget. Perhaps not surprisingly the senior officers of the Indian army were not sympathetic to the requirements of the RAF, which was emasculated in India by a chronic lack of funds. This situation was further exacerbated by a rather bizarre moratorium from the Indian government

The replacement of the Siddeley Puma engine in the DH9 by a 400hp Liberty engine produced the DH9A – the aeroplane which epitomized the RAF during the 1920s. Known in service as the 'Nine-Ack', the DH9A served with squadrons in the UK, Iraq, Palestine, Aden, Egypt and India. These aircraft are from 30 Squadron in Iraq during the late 1920s. (Pitchfork)

on the import of any aircraft spares. Reporting in August 1922, Air Vice Marshal (AVM) Sir John Salmond wrote 'it is with regret that I have to report that the Royal Air Force in India is to all intents and purposes non-existent as a fighting force.'

MESOPOTAMIA

In the summer of 1920, discontent at the British occupation of Iraq erupted into a violent rebellion by Arab nationalists in Baghdad. The British authorities lost control of a large swathe of the country, notably the regions around Karbala, Najaf and Samawah along the mid-reaches of the Euphrates. On 30 June, an army unit was besieged by a large force of Arabs in the centre of Rumaythah city; the Bristol F2b aircraft of 6 Squadron and

RE8 aircraft of 30 Squadron played a vital role in supporting the beleaguered troops during three weeks of siege, mounting bombing sorties each day and also dropping supplies of food and ammunition. Indeed, the two squadrons were active across the whole area carrying out reconnaissance and taking offensive action, often in direct support of the forces on the ground. At the end of July, the situation had deteriorated sufficiently for there to be a major reinforcement of the army. At this stage 84 Squadron was formed at Baghdad, using DH9A aircraft which had originally been intended to re-equip 30 Squadron; additionally, 55 Squadron (equipped with Bristol F2b) was transferred to Iraq from Turkey later in the summer. Slowly the balance of power was restored: Kufah was retaken on 6 October by a military column which was supported by 6 Squadron and Samawah was

An Airco de Havilland DH10 Amiens bomber of 60 Squadron (re-numbered from 97 Squadron) in India. The aircraft saw action on the Northwest Frontier in late 1920 and early 1922. (Jarrett)

A Bristol F2b on the approach to land at Ramleh, Palestine. During civil disorder in the region in 1921, F2b aircraft of 14 Squadron prevented Arab insurgents from sacking the Jewish settlements of Petah Tiqva and Hadera. These incidents are credited with planting the idea of building an Israeli Air Force into the minds of the Yishuv leadership. (14 Squadron Association)

relieved on 14 October, following an action which was heavily supported by air power. Najaf was subdued in early November, followed by Falujah and then Diwaniyah at the end of the month. In January the RAF mounted a show of force by flying a formation of 28 Bristol F2b aircraft over Baghdad. The revolt was formally considered to be over when Suq Al-Shuyukh capitulated on 3 February 1921.

PALESTINE

In Palestine, tensions between Palestinian Arabs and Jewish settlers had been building since the end of Ottoman rule. Inter-communal violence broke out at the beginning of May 1921 and martial law was proclaimed. On the morning of 5 May, a well-armed force of some 400 Arabs attacked the Jewish settlement of Petah Tiqva. A Bristol F2b from 14 Squadron was sent to disperse the attackers by flying low over them, until an Indian cavalry unit could intervene. Four bombs were dropped in front of the raiding party which caused them to withdraw, before they were dispersed by the cavalry. The next day, Arabs from the nearby village of Tulkarem were preparing to attack the Jewish settlement at Hadera. A Bristol F2b from 14 Squadron was able to prevent the attack for a while by dropping bombs and firing in front of

the Arabs, but when the aircraft had to refuel, the raiders took advantage of the absence to start their attack. By the time the aircraft returned to Hadera the Arabs had infiltrated the southeast quarter of the settlement and were in the process of looting and burning the buildings, but the aircraft caused panic amongst the attackers who began to flee. At this point another aircraft and an armoured car arrived on the scene and the two aircraft, together with the armoured car, were able to ensure that the attackers were completely routed.

THE DARDANELLES

At the end of World War I, Ottoman Turkey had been divided amongst the victorious Allies.

The straits of the Dardanelles were declared a neutral zone and were administered jointly by Britain, France and Italy, while much of western Anatolia was granted to Greece. The immediate result of the latter edict of the Treaty of Sèvres was the Greco-Turkish War, which was fought from 1919 until the sacking of Smyrna (İzmir) by the Turkish forces in September 1922. The army of Kemal Ataturk then swung northwards towards the Dardanelles and the small British military contingent at Chanak (Çanakkale). French and Italian forces had withdrawn and the Turkish army seemed poised to overwhelm the British positions. Reinforcements were swiftly despatched, most particularly by the RAF; on 26 September Fairey IIID seaplanes arrived from Malta on HMS *Pegasus* followed the next day by

A Fairey IIID floatplane towed by a motor pinnace at Constantinople. The aircraft, which were normally based in Malta, were amongst the first arrivals to reinforce the beleaguered British force at Çanakkale in September 1922. (Jarrett)

Right: A Sopwith Snipe 7F.1 of 25 Squadron flies over Constantinople (Istanbul) during the Chanak Crisis. The squadron remained in Turkey for a year before returning to the UK. The Snipe, which was originally intended as a replacement for the Sopwith Camel, continued to serve in Iraq with 1 Squadron until 1926. (Flintham)

Below: Bristol F2b aircraft of 4 Squadron prior to flying off the deck of HMS *Argus* during the Chanak Crisis. The pilots had no previous experience of operating from the deck of an aircraft carrier. (Jarrett)

203 Squadron equipped with the Gloster Nightjar on HMS *Argus*. Both of these units were based at Kilya Bay, just across the straits from Çanakkale. On 30 September 1922, 56 Squadron equipped with the Sopwith Snipe and 208 Squadron with the Bristol F2b arrived from Egypt and were based at San Stefano (Yeşilköy) near Constantinople. On 11 October, 4 Squadron equipped with the Bristol F2b arrived having flown their aircraft off HMS *Argus*. This was the first occasion that any of the pilots had operated from an aircraft carrier, but nevertheless, all the aircraft made it safely to Kilya Bay. They were followed the next day by 25 Squadron equipped with the Sopwith Snipe and 207 Squadron flying the DH9A bomber which were delivered to San Stefano by HMS *Ark Royal*. By 10 October, the crisis was averted due to careful diplomacy, but the rapid arrival of the

RAF (thanks to the RN) must have been a clear indication of the seriousness of the British resolve. Some units returned to their usual bases in the December, but most remained in Turkey until the summer of 1923.

INDEPENDENT STILL

Despite the efforts of some in the Admiralty and the War Office, the RAF remained an independent service in the years immediately after World War I. The service might have become a shadow of its former wartime self, but it was still active, albeit thinly stretched, across the Empire and in its short existence had demonstrated the effectiveness of air power both in the environment of total warfare and also the role of colonial policing.

The RAF squadrons remained in Turkey through the harsh winter of 1922/23. Here the Bristol F2b Fighters of 4 Squadron are covered in snow at Kilitbahir (across the Dardenelles from Çanakkale). (Jarrett)

CHAPTER 2

POLICING THE EMPIRE

1923-1938

One of the main outcomes of the Cairo Conference, which was convened in March 1921 to decide British policy in the Middle East, was the adoption of the concept of 'Air Control.' This idea proposed that most of the British Mandates in the Middle East could be policed effectively by a relatively small number of RAF aircraft instead of a large number of army troops. By using the speed, range and firepower of the aeroplane, the size of army garrisons which were being employed for the task could be reduced considerably. At a time when both the Admiralty and the War Office were questioning the need for a separate air service, the policy of Air Control provided the RAF with justification for its continued independence. It also suited the Treasury, which was impoverished after a costly war.

AIR CONTROL

The main principle of Air Control, as opposed to air support of army operations, was that of minimum force. Often the mere presence of an aeroplane – at a time when such machines were still a novelty outside Europe – might be enough to dissuade potential troublemakers; at other times an energetic 'beat up' or, more properly a 'show of force,' might also be effective without having to resort to the use of weapons. If guns or bombs had to be used, it would only be after warnings had been given, usually by leaflet, so that the population had the

In many ways, the Westland Wapiti epitomized the RAF of the 1920s and 1930s. While experimental aircraft captured the public imagination with high speeds, great altitudes and long ranges, the bulk of RAF squadrons patrolled the skies of the Empire in obsolescent biplanes of mediocre performance. (Flintham)

chance to vacate the area. Suitable targets were then attacked, such as fortified buildings or agricultural infrastructure, for example stock pens or irrigation systems. The theory was that troublemakers' energy could be diverted from insurrection towards repair work. Thus, the routine of Air Control was one of regular and often monotonous patrols over difficult country, but occasional flash-points brought the need for more active intervention.

Over the next year, the RAF formally assumed full responsibility for the security of Mesopotamia/ Iraq, Transjordan, Aden and Palestine and at the end of 1922 more than two-thirds of the RAF's front-line units were based overseas. This figure is slightly distorted because of the units deployed to Turkey in response to the Çanakkale crisis, but there were just four-and-a-half squadrons in the 'Inland Area' of the UK: 2, 24, 29 and 100 Squadrons, plus

a flight of 56 Squadron. The remaining five UK-based units comprised the 'Coastal Area,' which included 203 and 205 Squadrons at Leuchars where they made up the air component for aircraft carriers, two flying boat squadrons (3 Squadron at Gosport and 230 Squadron at Calshot) and a single torpedo bomber unit, 210 Squadron, at Gosport. The remaining strength of the RAF was based in the Middle East or India. Of these, two squadrons were in Egypt (47 Squadron at Helwan and 216 Squadron at Heliopolis), one in Malta (267 Squadron at Kalafrana) and one in Palestine (14 Squadron at Ramleh) which also covered Transjordan. Eight squadrons were based in Iraq and a further six in India.

Although Air Control reduced the call on army manpower, there was still a need for ground troops to support the aircraft. A number of army

The crew of a Rolls-Royce 1920 Pattern Mk I armoured car relaxing in the Iraq desert. The armoured car companies were an integral part of the system of Air Control in Palestine, Transjordan and Iraq. The vehicle was built using a Silver Ghost chassis, and was armed with a water-cooled Vickers .303in machine gun. The type remained in service long into World War II. (Pitchfork)

battalions were retained in theatre for this purpose, but much of the work was carried out by locally recruited levies (for example in Transjordan, aircraft worked closely with the Transjordan Field Force and the Arab Legion). Additionally, the newly-formed RAF Armoured Car Companies (ACC), equipped with Rolls-Royce armoured cars, provided another mobile and powerful supporting force. Based at Amman, with a section at Ramleh, 2 ACC covered Palestine and Transjordan, while 3, 4, 5 and 6 ACCs were based in Iraq.

Meanwhile, in India the campaign in Waziristan against the Mashuds continued into 1923, reaching its conclusion in the autumn. On 23 and 24 September, 31 Squadron was reinforced by heavy bombers from Risalpur and all aircraft carried out intensive bombing of the village of Zazhe Oba and surrounding settlements. The targets were switched to the villages of the Ghuri Khel tribe on 25 September and operations against these continued until 5 October. After a further 'show of force' flypast

on 21 October, the tribal leaders indicated that they would cease fighting and an uneasy truce in Waziristan started on 28 October 1923.

IRAQ

After an attempted raid into northern Iraq by the Turkish army was foiled in the late summer of 1922, a second concentration of Turkish troops was reported in early 1923. A strong force, including air support, was dispatched to deal with them, and after bombing attacks by Vickers Vernons of 45 Squadron, the Turks withdrew once more. However, with the sizeable British contingent in the northwest of the country, the Kurdish leader Sheikh Mahmoud Barzanji now saw the opportunity to start an insurrection against British rule. The swift response to Mahmoud included the airlift by a combined force of Vernon aircraft from 45 and 70 Squadrons of two companies of

A Fairey IIID of 267 Squadron, which was part of the air contingent on HMS *Ark Royal* in the early 1920s. During the 1920s and early 1930s, the aircraft embarked on Royal Navy (RN) aircraft carriers, and their associated flying and technical personnel, were provided by the Fleet Air Arm of the RAF. This arrangement remained in place until 1937, when control of the FAA was transferred to the Admiralty. (Flintham)

Two DH9A aircraft of 14 Squadron, which was dual-based at Ramleh, Palestine and Amman, Transjordan. Aircraft from the squadron and armoured cars from 2 Armoured Car Company (ACC) prevented an invasion of Transjordan by a large force of Akwhan in August 1924. Note the spare wheel carried just forward of the wing on both aircraft, in case of damage when landing in remote areas of desert. (Flintham)

Indian infantry from Kingarban to Kirkuk between 21 and 28 February 1923. The villages between Kirkuk and Mahmoud's capital Sulaymaniyah were then bombed over the next days. Meanwhile, the columns which had originally intended to fight the Turks returned to Kurdistan, along with the Sopwith Snipes of 1 Squadron and DH9A aircraft of 30 and 55 Squadrons. While these latter squadrons kept up reconnaissance and offensive action against Kurdish dissidents, the bomber/transport units were kept busy ferrying supplies and personnel to the frontline and evacuating the sick and wounded from it. This campaign was the first time that the RAF carried out a mass airlift of troops and the first large-scale systematic resupply operation by air. By May 1923, 6,000 troops had converged on Sulaymaniyah and Mahmoud fled into Persia.

However, Sheikh Mahmoud reappeared in Sulaymaniyah in May the following year and declared a *jihad* or holy war against the British. RAF aircraft were once again swiftly deployed to the area: 6, 8 and 30 Squadrons flew to Kirkuk,

while 45, 55 and 70 Squadrons were detached to Kingarban. After due warning, the RAF bombed Sulaymaniyah on 27 and 28 May 1924 and then continued to harass Mahmoud's supporters until the army reoccupied Sulaymaniyah and restored peace two months later.

The south of the country was marginally more stable, but it was plagued by raids by the Akhwan, a savage religious militia controlled by Ibn Saud, the ruler of the Nejd region. In September 1923, raids in the region of Ad Diwaniyah were seen off by a mixed force of Snipe fighters of 1 Squadron and DH9As bombers of 8 Squadron working with a company of armoured cars. The following month, a revolt at As Samawah was quickly contained by the Vernons of 45 and 70 Squadrons and DH9As of 84 Squadron. Over the next year, a series of small rebellions in the region were also quelled by air control.

The Akhwan were also active in northwest Arabia and in July 1924 a force of some 5,000 Akhwan were reported massing on the border with Transjordan. They entered the country on 12 August and headed towards Amman. The next morning the Akhwan were stopped and then routed by the combined force of DH9As from 14 Squadron operating from Amman (reinforced later in the day by a section of Bristol F2bs from Ramleh) and the armoured cars of 2 ACC.

INDIA - PINK'S WAR

Trouble broke out in Mohmand country to the north of the Khyber Pass in May 1924, with a revolt by the Abdur Rahman Khel tribe. Between 25 and 28 May, Bristol F2bs aircraft of 5 and 28 Squadrons bombed the fortified towers in villages in the Spli Toi valley. In July a larger force, comprising the Bristol F2bs of 5 Squadron and a flight from 28 Squadron, plus two flights of DH9As provided by 27 and 60 Squadrons, was

placed under command of Wing Commander (Wg Cdr) A.A. Walser MC, DFC. Bombing operations started against three villages in the Mohmand area, dropping larger 112lb and 230lb bombs, which were more effective against buildings than the usual 20lb weapons. Poor weather limited operations and on 28 July three Bristol F2bs crashed after flying into thunder clouds. Nevertheless, the revolt was, at least temporarily, suppressed.

After a comparatively quiet year in Waziristan, trouble broke out once more in early 1925, agitated again by the Abdur Rahman Khel tribe who had refused to accept the government's terms the previous year. This time it was decided to put down the rebellion by use of aircraft operating independently of ground troops. To achieve this, Wg Cdr R.C.M. Pink CBE was given command of a force comprising eight DH9As from 27 and

A Bristol F2b aircraft returning from a raid on the Jelal Khel during 'Pink's War' on the northwest frontier of India in 1925. The type was used by 5, 20 and 31 Squadrons during the short campaign, while 27 and 60 Squadron operated the DH9A. The successful demonstration by Wg Cdr R.C.M. Pink that air power could secure the submission of dissident tribes in remote areas caused the Indian Army to re-think its attitude to the potential of the aeroplane. (Jarrett)

60 Squadrons, operating from Miranshah fort, and Bristol F2bs from 5 and 20 Squadrons based at Tank. Operations started on 25 February with leaflet-dropping to warn the rebels that their villages would be bombed if they did not surrender. Unsurprisingly, the rebels did not take this opportunity to do so and bombing operations started on 9 March. Targets were systematically attacked during the rest of the month and an air blockade prevented rebel gangs from moving freely within the area. At the end of March the DH9A units were redeployed to Miranshah to make way for a flight of Bristol F2bs from 31 Squadron, which started flying night-bombing sorties from Tank on 4 April. The bombing programme continued by day and night through the remainder of April, until the rebel leaders capitulated on 1 May 1925. The short campaign was successful and caused remarkably few casualties on both sides: a handful of rebels were killed or wounded. The RAF lost just one aircraft to ground fire, although sadly the crew, Flying Officer (Fg Off) N.C. Hayter-Hames and Fg Off E.J. Dashwood, were both killed.

NORTHERN IRAQ

Despite his defeat the previous year, Sheikh Mahmoud made a third appearance in northern Iraq at Sulaymaniyah in the spring of 1925. Two villages that had given support to Mahmoud's insurgents were bombed by aircraft of 6 and 30 Squadrons on 17 April 1925. Operations continued into the summer months, culminating in a five-day battle between government forces and about 900 insurgents to the northeast of Sulaymaniyah, which started on 20 June. Heavy air support, mainly delivered by 6 Squadron, helped to rout the rebels and Mahmoud escaped once more into Persia. The RAF then carried out follow-up operations during the next month to destroy a number of villages that had supported Mahmoud. However, despite these punitive raids, Mahmoud still enjoyed some popularity and he

attempted yet another insurrection during the spring of 1926. This time 30 Squadron provided most of the firepower in another long engagement between 17 and 19 June, which once again ended in defeat for the rebels.

DEVELOPMENTS AT HOME

During the mid-1920s, the RAF in the UK underwent a modest expansion of front-line squadrons. While the operational squadrons overseas soldiered on with wartime aircraft types, such as the Bristol F2b and the DH9A, the home units enjoyed more modern equipment such as the Armstrong-Whitworth Siskin and Gloster Gamecock fighter aircraft and the Fairey Fox bomber. One innovation in 1924 was the formation of the Auxiliary Air Force (AAF) and the Special Reserve (SR), which were envisaged as a reserve force akin to the Territorial Army (TA). In the event of mobilization, the regionally-based reserve units would provide a basis for any expansion of the RAF's front-line strength. The AAF units were, with the exception of the adjutant who was a regular officer, manned entirely by reservists and in many ways, they were as much a social club as they were a flying and fighting force. The SR units were slightly different, in that their manning was made up of roughly half regulars (including the Commanding Officer) and half reservists. The first AAF squadrons to form in 1925 were 600 (City of London) and 601 (County of London), followed by 602 (City of Glasgow) and 603 (City of Edinburgh) Squadrons. All of these units were equipped with the DH9A. The SR squadrons also started to form the same year, commencing with 502 (Ulster) Squadron equipped with Vickers Vimys.

Arguably, the main role of the RAF at home was to provide the training, supply and administrative support for the operational units abroad. The RAF College and the RAF Apprentice School, which had been established at Cranwell and Halton respectively, provided the new service with a core of high quality

PIONEERING FLIGHTS

officers and technical personnel. Additionally, the RAF Pageants (later renamed RAF Displays) held annually at Hendon served an important role in generating public support for an independent RAF.

Other events that caught the public imagination were the record-breaking long-distance flights carried out in the late 1920s. Despite their publicity value, the real purpose of these flights was to extend the reach of RAF as technology improved: the ability of aircraft to deploy swiftly to anywhere in the Empire was a fundamental principle of air power. The first notable flight was by a section of three DH9As of 47 Squadron which were flown from Helwan to Kano, Nigeria (and back) between 27 October and 19 November 1925.

The flight was a remarkable achievement because much of the 5,200 miles flown was over inhospitable and largely uncharted jungle. The following year, Wg Cdr C.W.H. Pulford OBE led a specially formed flight of four Fairey IIID aircraft from Cairo on 1 March 1926 towards Cape Town. The aircraft routed via Wadi Halfa, Khartoum, Malakal, Mongalla, Kisumu, Tabora, Abercorn, N'dola, Livingstone, Buluwayo, Pretoria and Bloemfontein, reaching Cape Town on 12 April. At each of the stopping points, the crews attended diplomatic functions and participated in exercises with local troops. The 'Cairo to the Cape Flight' became an annual event for regular squadrons from Middle East Command and was subsequently carried out by 47 Squadron in 1927 and 1928, by 45 Squadron in 1929 and 14 Squadron in 1930.

In July 1926, two Supermarine Southampton flying boats flew from Plymouth to Aboukir, opening

In 1925, de Havilland DH9As of 47 Squadron carried out a long-range flight from Helwan, Egypt to Kano, Nigeria. This remarkable flight over inhospitable terrain was the first of a number of long-range expeditionary flights mounted by the RAF in the 1920s. (Jarrett)

the way for a much longer 'cruise' the following year. In October 1927, four Southampton II flying boats left Felixstowe for Australia; routing via Karachi and Singapore, the aircraft reached Perth on 7 June 1928. Over the next months, the flight flew anti-clockwise around Australia, before leaving for Singapore. From Singapore, the aircraft carried out another cruise to Hong Kong and back, eventually returning to Seletar, Singapore in December 1928. The unit then remained at Seletar where it was re-designated as 205 Squadron.

A serious attempt to set world records was made with the procurement in December 1928 of a Fairey Long-Range Monoplane. On 24 Apr 1929, Squadron Leader (Sqn Ldr) A.G. Jones-Williams MC and Flight Lieutenant (Flt Lt) N.H. Jenkins OBE, DFC, DSM took-off from Cranwell and flew to Karachi, covering 4,130 miles in 50 hours 38 minutes of non-stop flying. Although they had sufficient fuel for another 6 hours when they reached Karachi, it was late in the day and they did not have

sufficient fuel to make the next landing site. In the knowledge of being the first to fly non-stop from the UK to India, they abandoned the record attempt and landed at Karachi, rather than face a crash landing in unfamiliar terrain in the dark. Unfortunately, the same crew was killed the following year when they flew into the Atlas Mountains during another record attempt (Cranwell to Cape Town).

Another event which caught the public imagination in the late 1920s was the Schneider Trophy air race. The trophy, awarded to the fastest pilot to fly around a closed course, was contested by teams from Italy, France, the USA and the UK and would be kept permanently by any team which won the competition on three consecutive occasions. Prior to 1926, the RAF had depended on the largesse of the aircraft manufacturers to provide suitable aircraft: in that year, there was no British entry, but the Treasury was persuaded to fund future RAF participation under the auspices of the Marine

A year after the formation, personnel of 602 (City of Glasgow) Squadron, Auxiliary Air Force (AAF) were photographed in front of a DH9A at Renfrew in 1926. The unit was amongst the first RAuxAF units to form; eventually 17 squadrons would be formed, taking the numbers 600 to 616. Special reserve squadrons were numbered 500 to 504. (Pitchfork)

Left: The Fairey Long Range Monoplane which was flown for an attempt on the world long-distance record with a flight from London to Karachi in April 1929. Powered by a Napier Lion XIA engine, the aircraft had a fuel capacity of over 1,000gal and cruised at 110mph. Unfortunately, the aircraft crashed in Tunisia during another record attempt later in 1929. However, a second aircraft captured the record by flying non-stop from Cranwell to Walvis Bay in 1933. (Pitchfork)

Below: Probably best known as the type flown by Alcock and Brown to cross the Atlantic, the Vickers Vimy served in Egypt with 216 Squadron during the 1920s. (Jarrett)

A Supermarine S5 seaplane at Calshot Spit, near Southampton on 7 June 1927, being prepared for trials prior to the Schneider Trophy race to be held in Venice, Italy that year. (Central Press/Hulton Archive/Getty)

Aircraft Experimental Establishment (MAEE) at Felixstowe. As a result, the RAF was able to field a strong team which won the 1927 Schneider Trophy, which was held in Venice. The fastest time over the course was achieved by Flt Lt S.N. Webster, flying a Supermarine S5 seaplane. The competition in the following year was cancelled due to the death of Jacques Schneider, the founder of the competition. However in 1929, at Calshot, the RAF won the competition for a second consecutive time. This time the winner was Fg Off H.R.D. Waghorn in a Supermarine S6.

CHINA, INDIA & ARABIA

Meanwhile, the events in the rest of the world kept the front-line units busy. In Waziristan, Mohmand insurgents attacked clans loyal to the Indian government in June 1927. As a result, 5 and 20 Squadrons carried out bombing raids against a number of villages in Mohmand country on 6 and 7 June. These attacks killed around 40 rebels, but quickly suppressed the insurgency.

Violence erupted in Shanghai in early 1927 when the Chinese Nationalist Party carried out a purge of Communists in the city. The Shanghai Defence Force (SDF) was formed from army and naval units which were hastily deployed to China to protect the lives and property of British citizens there. The Bristol F2b aircraft of 2 Squadron were despatched to Shanghai to provide air support, arriving on 1 June. Flying from the racecourse, which was very small and poorly-suited to air operations, 2 Squadron flew photo-reconnaissance sorties over the next three months, mainly to provide the SDF with up-to-date maps. The squadron left Shanghai in early September.

In late 1927, the Akhwan were again threatening trouble on the border region of Iraq, when a large

Above: Two DH9A aircraft of 30 Squadron over southern Iraq. During operations in early 1928 by Akforce against the Akhwan in southern Iraq, these aircraft were deployed forward to provide reassurance to the inhabitants living in an area west of An Najaf that they would be protected. (Flintham)

Left: On 14 October 1927, four Supermarine Southampton II flying boats (S1149 to S1152) carried out a 27,000-mile far east cruise. This aircraft was captained by Flt Lt C.G. Wigglesworth AFC. The expedition, led by Gp Capt H.M Cave-Browne-Cave DSO, DFC, spent two years flying from Felixstowe to Singapore via Australia and Hong Kong. (Flintham)

A Vickers Victoria V over northern India. Eight of these aircraft, from 70 and 216 Squadrons, carried out the evacuation of nearly 600 British and other nationals from Kabul during the winter of 1928/29. Powered by two Napier Lion XI engines, the aircraft could carry 22 passengers. It was superseded in service by the Vickers Valentia, although many were, in fact, re-engined Victorias. (Flintham)

force of some 5,000 Akhwan led by Faisal ed Dowish were reported to be in the area. A series of violent raids started on 5 November when the 21 occupants of a police post at Busaira were slaughtered. Two sections of armoured cars and a flight from 84 Squadron were deployed forward to Abu Ghar in the desert to the west of Basra in an attempt to contain the insurgents, but more raids continued through December, including an incursion into Kuwait. As a response to the continued Akhwan threat, a mixed force of aircraft and armoured cars, known as Akforce, established its headquarters at Ur on 8 January 1928. The unit's fighting strength comprised nine DH9A aircraft from 84 Squadron plus two sections of armoured cars from 1 ACC deployed to As Sulman and a further nine DH9As from 55 Squadron and two sections of cars at Busaiya. For the bombing and transport support, 70 Squadron equipped with Vickers Vernon and Victoria was also based at Ur. Akforce operations began on 11 January, with leaflet-dropping to warn the Akhwan to move back at least four days' march away from the frontier region. A flight of DH9As from 30 Squadron was also deployed forward to reassure tribes to the west of Najaf that they would be protected.

Unfortunately, and despite some encouragement from 'warning bombs,' the leaflets had little effect and on 27 January the Akhwan carried out another major raid into Kuwait. One group of the insurgents was located and attacked by 55 Squadron aircraft two days later; the next day two formations each of six aircraft searched the area for the remainder of the Akhwan force. A large raiding party was found first by aircraft of 84 Squadron, who relayed the position by radio to the 55 Squadron patrol. Both formations attacked the insurgents, but one DH9A was shot down during the engagement. Intelligence sources then reported another imminent raid on Kuwait in mid-February, but poor weather between 16 and 18 February hindered aerial reconnaissance. The raid finally took place on 19 February 1928. On the same day, Akforce aircraft located the main Akhwan headquarters and bombed it; shortly afterwards the main body of Akhwan was located and during the day it was attacked by three waves of aircraft. Another DH9A was lost during this action.

On 24 February three Victoria bombers and 12 DH9As attacked enemy positions at Es Safa and another nearby encampment. Five days later

Akforce was reinforced by the arrival of 30 Squadron at Shaibah. However, the crisis was almost over: a political settlement was reached with Ibn Saud, the king of the Nejd, and the Akhwan withdrew. Between January and March 1928, Akforce aircraft had flown more than 7,000 hours.

ADEN

In preparation for the assumption of Air Control of Aden and its hinterland, 8 Squadron was moved to Aden in February 1927. This substitution of garrison troops by a single squadron of aircraft generated a cost saving of 30 percent of the annual budget for the garrison. Later in the year, their ageing DH9A aircraft were replaced with the Fairey IIIF and these were soon in action against Yemeni insurgents. After the fall of the Ottoman Empire, the Imam of Yemen laid claim to the whole of southwest Arabia. His claim was backed by a well-trained army of 6,000 Zaidi troops, commanded by Turkish officers and NCOs, which invaded the British Protectorate and occupied the town of Dhala. The British garrison in

Aden had insufficient troops to be able to expel the invaders and a long stalemate ensued. Matters came to a head in February 1928 when two sheikhs, who had treaties with Britain, were abducted and the British authorities were forced to take action. After due warning, the Zaidi headquarters at Qataba was bombed on 21 February and again on each of the next two days. Air operations continued over the next five months, and although little damage was done and few casualties were caused, the Zaidis were forced onto the defensive. The squadron's aircraft also carried out attacks on the fort at Dhala to assist the Emir of Dhala in the re-occupation his town during July; by mid-August the Zaidis had been ejected from areas under British protection and the Imam agreed to stop further incursions.

In January 1929, trouble broke out among the Subehi tribe in the southwest corner of the Arabian Peninsula: in fact, it was an annual event, but this time warnings were dropped and the villages were bombed. The grain and animals owned by the tribe were kept in a *zariba* – a compound surrounded by entangled dry thorn bushes – which proved to be extremely vulnerable to incendiary bombs. A three-

During the Palestine Uprising of August 1929, four DH9A aircraft of 14 Squadron were sent from Amman to Ramleh to aid the ground forces. The aircraft carried out daily patrols of the hostile areas and intervened in several incidents where the police or army were unable to control gangs looting shops and buildings. (14 Squadron Association)

month long bombing campaign by 8 Squadron to destroy these *zariba* was enough to persuade the Subehi to submit to government authority.

KABUL AIRLIFT

An uprising in Afghanistan by rebels opposed to the introduction of liberal 'western' customs into Afghan life by King Amanullah in late 1928 left many expatriate civilians trapped at the British legation in Kabul between the opposing sides. Plans were made to evacuate them, and four Victoria aircraft from 70 Squadron (based at Hinaidi in Iraq) were despatched to India, a distance of some 2,500 miles. The first Victoria flew from Risalpur to Kabul on 23 December 1928, accompanied by three DH9As from 60 Squadron, which were carrying luggage. Over the next few days RAF aircraft transported 71 women and children from Kabul through the mountains of the Himalayan foothills to Peshawar, before winter weather temporarily halted operations. When flights started again on 30 December, the pilots reported 4in of snow on the ground at Kabul and intensely cold weather

conditions in the mountains. Despite these hardships the evacuation continued, as weather conditions and rebel activity permitted, through the next two months. There was a lucky escape from disaster on 29 January, when a Victoria flown by Flt Lt R. Ivelaw-Chapman and Fg Off Davies suffered an engine failure en-route to Kabul, but the pilots skilfully managed a forced landing onto a small plateau which ended in a 2,000ft precipice. By early February there were eight Victorias, from both 70 and 216 Squadrons, involved in the operation. The airlift was completed on 25 February 1929, by which time 586 individuals of 11 different nationalities had been flown from Kabul to India. The operation was the first ever large-scale airlift.

1929 PALESTINE UPRISING

Palestinian resentment at the increasing Jewish immigration throughout the 1920s escalated into lawlessness and violence in August 1929. A section of four DH9As from 14 Squadron were immediately dispatched to Ramleh on 23 August to carry out a reconnaissance of Jerusalem and the next day a battalion of the South Wales Borderers was flown in from Cairo in Vickers Victoria transports of 216 Squadron. More troops followed by train a day later. Over the following days naval ships arrived, including HMS *Courageous*, which brought a battalion of the South Staffordshire Regiment from Malta as well as its complement of Fairey Flycatcher aircraft. The RAF also reinforced Palestine with Bristol F2bs from 208 Squadron, DH9As and Fairey IIIFs from 45 Squadron (both normally based in Egypt) and armoured cars from Iraq.

Aircraft carried out numerous patrols each day to reconnoitre the hotspots around Palestine and to check the border crossing points along the Jordan Valley for possible insurgents. On 26 August, four DH9As from 14 Squadron based at Ramleh came across a looting party of 50 Arabs confronting the police at Haifa. The aircraft opened fire, killing two of the gang and dispersing the rest. Similar direct interventions by aircraft occurred over the next few days.

By now the RAF presence in Palestine had been considerably reinforced and on Friday 30 August a show of force was mounted over the Mosque of Omar in Jerusalem, where a large crowd gathered daily for mid-day prayers. Eight DH9As from 14 Squadron, four Fairey IIIFs from 45 Squadron, a Bristol F2b from 208 Squadron and three Fairey Flycatchers from HMS *Courageous* arrived over Jerusalem at low level to dramatic effect just as the crowd emerged from the Mosque. There was another large demonstration flight by nine DH9As from 14 and 45 Squadrons accompanied by six Fairey Flycatchers for the benefit of the residents of Semakh, Tiberius, Safed and Metula two days later. By the beginning of September, the British authorities were beginning to regain control within Palestine, although it was another fortnight before the disturbances had completely died down.

NORTHERN IRAQ

In northern Iraq, Sheikh Mahmoud made a last attempt to incite a Kurdish uprising in September 1930. He was countered by units of the recently-formed Iraqi army, supported by Westland Wapiti IIA aircraft of 30 and 55 Squadrons, operating from Mosul and Kirkuk respectively. In the last two weeks of September the Wapitis bombed rebel positions, including the village of Surdash. Anti-insurgency operations continued over the winter months, reinforced by more Wapitis from 84 Squadron and Victorias of 70 Squadron, and culminating in a sustained bombing campaign against all villages which had harboured supporters of Mahmoud. As a result, Mahmoud lost his popular support and he eventually surrendered to an RAF force in May 1931. However, his place as a thorn in the side of the government of Iraq was soon filled by Sheikh Ahmad Barzan, who had been leading a low-level insurrection in central Kurdistan since the late 1920s. Operations against Ahmad by the Iraqi army started in December 1931. Once again, the army was supported by Wapitis of 30 Squadron, this time operating from Diana, to the northeast of Erbil. On 9 December, the Iraqi column met strong resistance near Barzan and was forced back. Warning notices were dropped on Barzan, which was then bombed, although no serious damage was done. Ground operations re-started in March 1932, but once again they met with determined resistance. When Kurdish rebels ambushed the column on 3 April, the five Wapitis of 'C' Flight 30 Squadron carried out continuous attacks on the rebels throughout the day until they were driven off at dusk. For the rest of the month, and on through May, bombing attacks were carried out by the aircraft of 30, 55 and 70 Squadrons. In early June 1932, Sheikh Ahmad crossed the border into Turkey, where he surrendered to the Turkish authorities.

During the 1920s, air control had been largely successful in pacifying large areas of the Middle East. Major rebellions had been defused and the concept of international borders in an area which, in the days of the Ottoman Empire, had no borders, was successfully introduced. However, the old traditions of inter-tribal raiding proved hard to eradicate, and by 1930 much of the work of the RAF squadrons in Palestine, Iraq and Aden was

A Westland Wapiti IIA of 30 Squadron, based at Mosul. Known to service personnel as the 'What-A-Pity,' the type replaced the DH9A in Iraq and India in the late 1920s, but continued in service until the late 1930s. It also equipped many of the RAuxAF squadrons in the UK. The Wapiti was designed to re-use many of the parts of the DH9A, including the wings, thus reducing the need for spares. (Flintham)

in policing these local tribal disputes. The British Mandate for Iraq ended in October 1932, but RAF units remained in the newly-independent country to ensure its security in the short term.

WAZIRISTAN

In May 1930, troubled flared once more in Mohmand country, this time incited by the Hadji of Turangzai who started a rumour that the British Raj no longer existed. As a result, Bristol F2b aircraft of 5 and 20 Squadrons, DH9As of 27 and 60 Squadrons and the Wapitis of 11 and 39 Squadrons were involved in virtually continuous operations through the summer. On 12 May 1930 aircraft of 27 and 60 Squadrons dispersed a large rebel group which had laid siege to the fort at Datta Khel. Daily bombing operations over the next two months enforced a curfew on much of the region to stop mass gatherings and there was a large formation demonstration flight on 27 May 1930 to show that the Raj was still very much in existence. The majority of the Mohmand rebels submitted to

the government in mid-July, although operations in Waziristan continued through August. In September 1930, the garrison at Chitral was replaced. Chitral was an independent principality, an untypically peaceful state within a troubled region, protected by troops of the Indian army. The garrison was replaced every two years and the relief column had to travel through the wilds of Waziristan in order to reach the principality. The tribes of Waziristan saw the column as 'fair game' for ambushes and sniping, so the column often had to fight all the way to Chitral and back. Aircraft played a vital role in the operation, being used to reconnoitre the road ahead of the column and also engage snipers or rebel bands. Along the road, picquet (picket) posts signalled to the aircraft using two long strips of white canvas. The strips were placed side by side if the road area was clear; if there were enemy present, the strips were laid in a 'V' with the apex indicating the direction of the threat. If the picquet post came under attack, the strips were laid as a 'T' pointing in the direction of the attackers. During September 1930, the Wapitis of 11 and 39 Squadrons supported the Chitral relief column. Apart from forward reconnaissance and close air support for the column, the aircraft were also used to drop supplies to the troops during the march.

In early June 1930, the aircraft of 39 and 60 Squadrons had been called in to help to disperse a large lashkar of 'Red Shirts' which was heading towards Peshawar to take part in anti-British demonstrations. The Red Shirts were members of the non-violent civil protest organization 'Khudai Khidmatgan,' which was attracting much support in northwest India. Much of 1931 and early 1932 was spent monitoring the movements of Red Shirt groups; however, the more traditional violent uprisings also continued in Mohmand country in the spring and summer of 1932. Aircraft of 5, 20, 27, 39 and 60 Squadrons were all involved in bombing operations over Waziristan during this time. In September, the Chitral relief column was supported by Hawker Harts of 11 and Wapitis of 60 Squadrons. The following year the major effort of the 27 and 60 Squadrons was directed against the

Khan of Kotkai, who started agitating trouble in Afghanistan in March. When the village of Kotkai was eventually identified (it had been wrongly plotted on the maps) it was bombed by Wapitis of 27 and 60 Squadrons and the Harts of 11 and 39 Squadrons. The Khan's rebellion was suppressed in August.

FASTER, HIGHER, FURTHER

After successful participation in the Schneider Trophy in 1927 and 1929, Britain was poised to win the trophy in perpetuity. There was no competition in 1930, because more time was needed to enable competitors to develop their aircraft. Unfortunately, this coincided with the withdrawal of Air Ministry funding for the project, but RAF participation was saved by the generous gift of £100,000 by Lady Lucy Houston, DBE. Neither the Italians nor the French were ready for the competition in 1931, leaving the RAF to win by default. Nevertheless, the RAF took the

A formation of Vickers Wellesley bombers from the Long Range Development Unit (LRDU) which flew non-stop from Ismailia, Egypt to Darwin, Australia in 1938. (Charles E. Brown/RAF Museum/Getty)

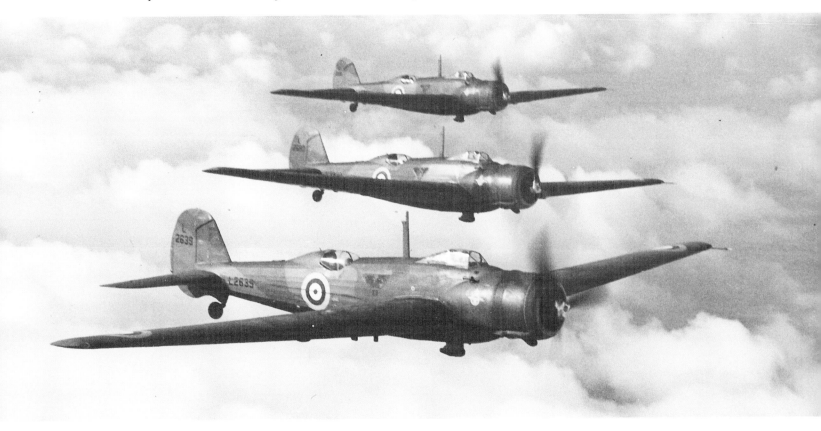

Supermarine S6B (serial number S1595) was flown by Flt Lt J.N. Boothman when he won the Schneider Trophy Race on 12 September 1931, flying at an average speed of 340mph; the same aircraft was flown on 29 September by Flt Lt G.H. Stainforth to achieve the World Speed Record of 407.5mph. (Hudson/ Topical Press Agency/ Getty)

Above: Bristol Bulldog II fighters from 17 Squadron. The type formed the bulk of the RAF fighter strength throughout the 1930s. During the Abyssinian crisis, the Bulldog-equipped 3 Squadron was deployed to Port Sudan. (Museum of Flight/CORBIS/Getty)

Right: A formation of Supermarine Scapa flying boats of 204 Squadron, based at Alexandria in 1936. The aircraft was originally known as the Southampton IV and was powered by two Rolls-Royce Kestrel engines. (Charles E. Brown/RAF Museum/Getty)

competition seriously and the winning Supermarine S6B flown by Flt Lt J.N. Boothman completed the course at a record average speed of 340mph. Two weeks later the speed record was broken again, also in a S6B, this time flown by Flt Lt G.H. Stainforth, who achieved an average speed of 407mph.

Research into high-altitude flight also resulted in the setting of world records later in the decade. Flying from Cranwell in September 1936, Sqn Ldr F.R. Swain set a record of 49,967ft in a Bristol 138 experimental aircraft. This record was broken by the Italians the following year, but just a month later, in June 1937, another Bristol 138 flight by Flt Lt M.J. Adam set a new record of 53,937ft.

Long-distance records were also achieved by RAF aircraft. Following the flights with the Fairey Long-Range Monoplane in the late 1920s, the RAF established the Long-Range Development Unit (LRDU) at Upper Heyford, Oxfordshire in 1938. In November of that year, three Vickers-Armstrong Wellesley light-bomber aircraft of the LRDU, led by Sqn Ldr R. Kellett, set off from Ismailia, in Egypt, to fly the 7,162 miles to Darwin in Australia. One Wellesley was forced to land at Koepang, West Timor (although it had by that

stage already exceeded the extant record), but the other two aircraft landed at Darwin after 48 hours of non-stop flying time.

1935 ABYSSINIA CRISIS

An international crisis, provoked by a border dispute between Ethiopia and Italian Somaliland in 1934, culminated in the invasion of Abyssinia by Italian troops in October 1935. The British government chose not to intervene directly, but a substantial naval task force, including the aircraft carriers HMS *Glorious* and HMS *Courageous* and their combined complement of nine squadrons, had sailed for the Mediterranean in August. Although Abyssinia was surrounded by British-administered territories, the only RAF presence in the region was provided by 8 Squadron equipped with Vickers Vincents at Aden and 47 Squadron equipped with the Fairey Gordon in Sudan. In order to protect British interests, the RAF presence in the Middle East and Africa was boosted by the rapid deployment of 13 UK-based squadrons into the theatre. Aden was reinforced by the Hawker Hart bombers of 12 Squadron and

A Vickers Vildebeest of 36 Squadron, based in Singapore. The standard torpedo bomber of the RAF during the 1930s, the type remained in service in the Far East until 1942. (Flintham)

the Hawker Demon fighters of 41 Squadron, while the Bristol Bulldog fighters of 3 Squadron were sent further up the Red Sea coast to protect Port Sudan, where they were joined by 47 Squadron. Malta, which enjoyed a strategically close proximity to Italy, was reinforced with Vickers Vildebeest torpedo bombers from 22 Squadron to support the fleet and was protected by the Hawker Demon fighters of 74 Squadron. Both 35 and 207 Squadrons, flying the Fairey Gordon, were sent to Ed Damar, near Atbara, Sudan to provide a striking force and the Hawker Harts of 33 and 142 Squadrons were sent to Mersa Matruh, close to the Egyptian border with the Italian colony of Cyrenaica. The air defence of Egypt was also augmented by 29 Squadron flying the Hawker Demon at Al Amiriyah, near Alexandria. Meanwhile the flying boats of 204 Squadron (equipped with the Supermarine Scapa), 210 Squadron (Short Rangoon) and 230 Squadron (Short Singapore III) were deployed to Aboukir, Gibraltar and Alexandria respectively. Additionally, three new Short Singapore III flying boats which were being delivered to 203 Squadron at Basra were diverted to reinforce Aden. Most of the units remained at their deployed locations for the next year before returning to their home bases. The exception was 33 Squadron, which had detached aircraft for operations in Palestine during 1936 and

remained in Egypt after the crisis settled. Although the RAF had not been called upon to fight, the service had demonstrated the ability to deploy rapidly if needed to reinforce British interests around the world.

INDIA – THE FAQIR OF IPI

On 31 May 1935, a major earthquake shook Quetta, which was the home of 5 and 31 Squadrons. There were casualties amongst RAF personnel, including some deaths, and the aircraft of both units were also severely damaged. The other RAF squadrons in India provided aid to Quetta, including flying in medical personnel and supplies. In July, the Hadji of Turangzai was active again in Mohmand country. Heavy fighting ensued when Indian army troops were despatched to quell the insurrection, supported by the aircraft from 11, 27, 39 and 60 Squadrons. Aircraft were used to break up rebel lashkars, particularly those who were attempting to destroy the newly-completed Gandab road. From 9 July until 26 September air blockades were used to isolate rebels and limit their movement. These blockades consisted of a continuous relay of aircraft, operating either singly or in pairs, each flying consecutive two-hour patrols. The tribes eventually submitted in late October, after air blockades prevented

The early 1930s saw streamlined and more powerful aircraft entering service. The Hawker Hart, powered by a Rolls-Royce Kestrel engine, could out-perform most fighters of the day. Apart from being the standard day-bomber used by the RAF home squadrons, the type also equipped overseas units, including 11 Squadron (here), based at Risalpur in northwest India. (Flintham)

them from carrying out any agricultural activities.

Unfortunately, as the influence of the Hadji of Turangzai waned in late 1935, that of another rebel leader, the Faqir of Ipi, steadily increased. Support for the Faqir grew through 1936 amongst the Tori Khel tribe of the lower Khaisora valley and in November 1936 two columns of troops were sent into the region to restore order. The bulk of the RAF's task to support the columns fell to 5 and 27 Squadrons flying the Westland Wapiti, while 20 Squadron equipped with Hawker Audax light bombers oversaw the biennial relief of Chitral. However, all of the squadrons in India became involved, in one way or another, in the Waziristan operations and on 31 December 1936, the Wapitis of 60 Squadron were tasked to destroy the fort at Arsal Kot. The fort was a challenging target, not least because of its small size of just 132yds by 66yds; however, the formation led by Flt Lt Cannon with Corporal (Cpl) Cronin scored several direct hits with 230lb bombs which destroyed the top two-thirds of the fortified tower, rendering the whole building unusable. The operations in Waziristan against the Faqir of Ipi, which continued into 1937 and on through most of that year, were notable because of

the close co-operation between the army and the RAF. General Sir Robert Archibald Cassels GCB, GCSI, DSO, the Commander-in-Chief (C-in-C) India commented in his report that 'continuous pressure of air action by day and night, played an important part in obtaining the surrender of the tribes. It secured the surrender of hostages and kidnapped persons, and on occasion the mere threat of such action proved wholly effective. Columns were invariably accompanied by close-support aircraft whose co-operation was of the highest tactical value. In addition, bomber transport aircraft were used extensively to transport military personnel and stores and for the evacuation of casualties, thereby saving long and trying journeys by ambulance transport. The Tori Khel eventually submitted in September 1937 and other neighbouring tribes followed the next month.

1936 PALESTINE UPRISING

During the 1930s the immigration of Jews into Palestine, fuelled by fascist anti-Semitism in Europe, increased exponentially. This was matched

Equipping three squadrons in the UK and three squadrons in the Middle East during the 1930s, the Fairey Gordon was a development of the IIIF. The aircraft is from 14 Squadron and operating over TransJordan. (14 Squadron Association)

Many Vickers Valentia transports were converted from the Vickers Victoria, although this particular aeroplane was originally built as a Valentia. The type, which saw service with 70 and 216 Squadrons in the Middle East and 31 Squadron in India, could carry 22 troops in the transport role, but it also be deployed as a bomber aircraft. (Flintham)

by simmering resentment amongst the local Arab population in Palestine against what they saw as an invasion of their land. In April 1936, inter-communal violence broke out, accompanied by a general strike by Arab workers. The army presence in the region was increased to four battalions and the Hawker Hart light bombers of 6 Squadron were sent to Ramleh; meanwhile the Fairey Gordons of 'C' Flight of 14 Squadron had deployed to a forward operating base at Jisr El Mejamie, on the Jordan. In the following months, as the insurrection grew, Palestine was reinforced by Hart light bombers of 33 Squadron operating from Gaza and Audaxes of 208 Squadron from Ramleh. Air transport and re-supply was provided by Vickers Valentias of 216 Squadron, which could cover the distance from Egypt to Palestine in 3 hours, as opposed to the alternative 14-hour journey by train. The armoured cars of 2 ACC were also heavily involved in ground operations throughout the Palestine revolt.

Four air contact zones were established, based on the areas of responsibility of the army battalions, within which aircraft were kept at readiness on the ground, and army convoys included mobile wireless vehicles known as 'Roadex.' If air support was required, the Roadex would transmit a 'XX' call with its callsign and co-ordinates. This would be picked up by the relevant RAF detachment, which would then launch a pair of aircraft to the given co-ordinates. Aircraft flew in pairs to provide each other with cross-cover. Once the aircraft reached the Roadex, further communication was by pre-arranged signals by Very light or Aldiss light. The guerrillas usually knew the country well and made effective use of any available cover, such as olive trees, to conceal themselves from the air. As a result, the aircraft had to fly low (around 500ft above the ground) in order to have any chance of detecting them, and at this altitude crews were frequently subjected to accurate small arms fire. The detachment from 14 Squadron covered the 'Jordan Air Contact Zone,' comprising the western part of Transjordan, including Jerusalem, while the other zones were covered by 6, 33 and 208 Squadrons.

Left: In the days before reliable Radio/Telecommunication (R/T) equipment could be carried in aircraft, the main method of communication between ground forces and aircraft was by written message. Here a Hawker Audax of 208 Squadron picks up a message in 1936. (Pitchfork)

Below: A four-engined Short Singapore III flying boat of 203 Squadron, which was based at Basra. During the Spanish Civil War, the type was used to operate anti-piracy patrols from Malta to protect British shipping in the Mediterranean. (Flintham)

Two Gloster Gladiators of 605 Squadron over Kent in 1939. Although it had been largely replaced by the Hurricane and Spitfire by the outbreak of World War II, the type continued in service with some front-line units until 1940. (Charles E. Brown/RAF Museum/Getty)

The 'XX' calls answered by Harts of 6 Squadron included a major action on the Nablus–Tulkarm road on 3 September, during which an aircraft was shot down. Apart from reacting to 'XX' calls from army units, routine patrols were flown, particularly at dawn and dusk. Some night patrols were also flown, dropping flares which had a useful deterrent effect on would-be night raiders. Aircraft were also used to drop leaflets on villages. In October responsibility for the security of Palestine was passed from the Air Ministry to the War Office, which by now had increased the strength of the army in Palestine to eight battalions. Martial Law was also declared that month and violence by small local groups and criminal gangs tailed off. Both 33 and 208 Squadrons returned to Egypt at the end of the year, as did 6 Squadron, although two flights remained as a semi-permanent detachment at Ramleh.

After a relatively quiet start to the year, the rebellion flared again in late 1937. The arrival of insurgent leaders from Syria and Iraq brought with it better organization of the rebellion, which was now made up of larger groups of armed rebels. On 31 January 1938, an army column was pinned down by about 100 rebels near Umm Al Fahm, and five Hawker Hardy light bombers from 6 Squadron carried out bombing and strafing attacks on rebel positions until dusk. On 4 March, another large band of insurgents, this time 400 strong, was located near Yamun, where it was engaged by army troops supported by Hardy light bombers of 6 Squadron. Once again, the RAF reinforced Palestine, this time with Harts from 211 Squadron, which had only recently arrived in Egypt, and Gloster Gladiators from 80 Squadron. By now the tactic of the 'Air Pin' had become well-established: a village would be cordoned by aircraft flying continuous patrols around its perimeter. The aircraft would shoot anyone who attempted to leave, while army patrols entered the village to search it. On 15 September aircraft from 6, 80 and 211 Squadrons successfully attacked a 500-strong rebel group near Deir Ghassana.

Meanwhile 14 Squadron, now equipped with the Vickers-Armstrong Wellesley light bomber, operated in support of troops of the TJFF and Arab Legion to secure the border crossings into Palestine from Syria and Trans-Jordania. On the night of 12 October 1938 six Wellesleys, two of which were loaded with flares and four with bombs, flew in the light of a full moon against rebel positions to the north of the Sea of Galilee, dropping thirty-two 20lb bombs; during this engagement one of the aircraft was hit by ground fire in four places. The Wellesleys were also used for night patrols to enforce the curfew in the area of Lake Hule, dropping flares, and, on occasions, bombs. Additionally, 14 Squadron carried out daily coastal reconnaissance sorties, searching for ships trying to land either smuggled weapons or illegal immigrants.

REORGANIZATION & EXPANSION AT HOME

After the failure of the Conference for the Reduction and Limitation of Armaments in Geneva over the period 1932–34, conflict in Europe looked increasingly possible. In the following years, the Government authorized a number of expansion plans for the RAF, beginning with 'Scheme A' in 1934. Scheme A envisaged growth to 960 aircraft employed by 84 squadrons by early 1939; just four years later, 'Scheme L' proposed an expansion to nearly 2,400 aircraft operated by 141 squadrons by 1940. The rate of expansion was phenomenal: for example, between July and September 1936 eight new squadrons were formed, bringing the strength of the Metropolitan Air Force (the UK-based units) to 79 squadrons. At that stage, a further 2,500 pilots were needed by April 1937, so civilian flying schools were co-opted into the flying training system. A massive programme of airfield construction was also started, to ensure that the RAF had sufficient airfields suitable for operations with modern aircraft. Reserve forces were to play an important part in the expansion plans too, making up 13 squadrons under Scheme A and 20 under Scheme L. In 1936, the Special Reserve was merged into the AAF and a new RAF Volunteer Reserve (RAFVR) was also formed. Rather than manning specific flying units, as was the case with the AAF, the RAFVR was based at airfields or towns, where it provided a pool of trained pilots who could be posted to front-line units as the need for reinforcements arose.

The organization of the Metropolitan Air Force was also consolidated in 1936 into separate Commands with specialized roles. These were Bomber Command, Fighter Command, Coastal Command and Training Command. The following year the Fleet Air Arm, which operated from aircraft carriers,

The last biplane heavy bomber to serve with the RAF, the Handley Page Heyford equipped 11 front-line squadrons from 1933 until 1939. The aircraft had a maximum speed of 142mph and could carry a bomb-load of 1,600lb over 920 miles.

The Fairey Hendon II night bomber first entered service in 1936, but only equipped 38 Squadron, which had previously operated the Handley Page Heyford. Despite its more streamlined appearance, the type offered little improvement in performance. In 1938, the squadron was re-equipped with the Vickers Wellingtons.

was transferred from the RAF to the RN. In parallel with the expansion of the service, the RAF home commands also began to be re-equipped with more modern aircraft in the late 1930s: biplanes which had served throughout the 1920s and the early 1930s were replaced with monoplanes, although sometimes there was little differential in performance. For example when 38 Squadron based at Mildenhall replaced its 'stately' looking Handley Page Heyford with the Fairey Hendon bomber in November 1936 the new monoplane was just over 10mph faster than its predecessor and offered only a slight improvement in range for the same bomb load. Furthermore, many of the operational squadrons of the overseas commands continued to soldier on with obsolescent biplanes.

INDIA - THE FAQIR OF IPI & THE MADDA KEHLS

Amongst the units equipped with obsolescent biplanes in 1938 were those in India, where the Westland Wapiti, Hawker Hart and Hawker Audax

continued to be used for operations against the Faqir of Ipi. In early 1938, the Fakir had taken refuge amongst the Madda Khel tribe in the Tochi Valley; although this location meant that he was cut off from the rest of Waziristan by high mountain ranges, he nevertheless sought to incite anti-British action and he gathered a rebel force of some 1,000 men to attack the scout post at Datta Khel. Between March and June, 5, 11, 20, 27, 39 and 60 Squadrons were all involved in operations over Madda Khel country, either by directly supporting ground troops, enforcing proscribed areas or carrying out punitive bombing attacks. In May, 5 Squadron was tasked with enforcing the proscribed areas while the combined forces of 11, 39, 27 and 60 Squadrons, some operating from the forward airfield at Miramshah, bombed recalcitrant villages.

In late 1937, another religious agitator had become active in Waziristan: Shami Pir was a Syrian, with pro-Nazi affiliations, but his intention was to overthrow the government of Afghanistan. He set out with a rebel force for Kabul on 20 June, but was discovered by Audax light bombers from

20 Squadron flying an armed reconnaissance patrol. The aircraft attacked and dispersed the insurgents and the immediate threat to Afghanistan was defeated.

In the meantime, the Faqir of Ipi had been evicted by the Madda Khels, but he was able to take up residence in the Kharre district, where he continued his subversive activities. The Wapitis of 27 and 60 Squadrons carried out an intensive six-week bombing campaign against villages hosting the Faqir during July and August. Although the pace of operations slowed in the autumn, RAF aircraft were kept busy in support of ground forces, both against the Faqir of Ipi and in the general policing of the tribal areas.

MORE REORGANIZATION & EXPANSION AT HOME

The Munich Crisis of September 1938 emphasized the real risk of war in Europe. RAF units in all theatres were put onto a war footing: aircraft were camouflaged and where necessary squadrons were dispersed to wartime operating bases. One major policy change in November was the adoption of another Expansion Scheme ('Scheme M') under which the number of bomber squadrons was to be increased to 85 and the number of fighter squadrons to 50.

A CHANGE OF EMPHASIS

The RAF at the end of the 1930s was a very different service to that of the previous decade. For most of the 1920s and the early 1930s the greater part of a small air force was based overseas, policing the Empire in primitive aircraft. By the late 1930s the scope of the policing work had diminished and much of it had, in both Iraq and India for example, been passed on to local air forces. Against a backdrop of the rise of fascism in Europe, the Abyssinian Crisis, the Spanish Civil War and the Munich Crisis, the focus of a much larger RAF was now at home and preparations were being made for a seemingly inevitable war in Europe.

Indian Army troops prepare to board a Vickers Valentia of 31 Squadron for the relief of Chitral. Air transport enabled the relief force to bypass the attentions of the hostile tribesmen, through whose territories they would otherwise have had to march. (Pitchfork)

CHAPTER 3

HOLDING THE LINE

1939-1942

As the end of the decade loomed, the responsibilities of colonial policing remained, although Iraq and the Northwest Frontier of India had quietened over the preceding ten years. However, it was the threat of impending war with Germany that occupied most people's minds. The Munich Crisis had effectively given the RAF a year's grace in which to prepare for war and as the number of front-line units grew under Expansion Scheme 'M', the RAF began to look more like a viable fighting force. However, the majority of its squadrons were still equipped with aircraft that were, at best, obsolescent.

COLONIAL DUTIES

The influx of Jewish immigrants to Palestine continued through 1939 and the Vickers Wellesley bombers of 14 Squadron maintained coastal patrols to give the naval forces warning of approaching ships carrying illegal immigrants. In Palestine itself, bands of Arab dissidents continued to fight Jewish gangs and both sides fought the British authorities. Bands of insurgents from neighbouring Arab countries were also active in Palestine. A Hawker Hardy from 6 Squadron was shot down on 11 March while supporting a TJFF patrol which was engaging insurgents from Syria. The action was joined by another Hardy and a Gloster Gladiator, but little progress was made against the invaders, who had secured ideal defensive positions in a narrow wadi. The ensuing stalemate was broken that evening by Wellesley

Supermarine Spitfire pilots discuss tactics on an airfield 'somewhere in England,' while the ground crew service the aircraft. Although the Spitfire is often considered to be the embodiment of the RAF during the Battle of Britain, there were infact more Hurricanes than Spitfires in service at the time. However, the type was undoubtably a decisive factor in establishing air superiority on all fronts during World War II. (William Vandivert/The LIFE Picture Collection/Getty)

bombers of 14 Squadron dropping 250lb bombs on their positions. In India, 5 Squadron equipped with the Westland Wapiti spent the month of August providing close air support to the column relieving the garrison at Wana, Waziristan, but otherwise the region enjoyed an unaccustomed peace.

OPENING MOVES

Germany invaded Poland on 1 September 1939 and two days later Great Britain responded by declaring war on Germany. On that day, a Bristol Blenheim IV of 139 Squadron carried out a reconnaissance of the German naval bases and discovered a number of naval ships, including the heavy cruiser *Admiral Scheer*, in the Schillig Roads, just outside the port of Wilhelmshaven. Unfortunately, the crew of the Blenheim was unable to report their sighting until they returned to their base so that a combination of bad weather and darkness prevented the striking force from locating the ships. However, the reconnaissance was repeated the next day, 4 September, and a force of 15 Blenheim IVs (five aircraft each from 107, 110 and 139 Squadrons) set off to attack the *Admiral Scheer* and the cruiser *Emden* in dock at Wilhelmshaven. At the same time, nine Vickers Wellingtons (from 9 and 149

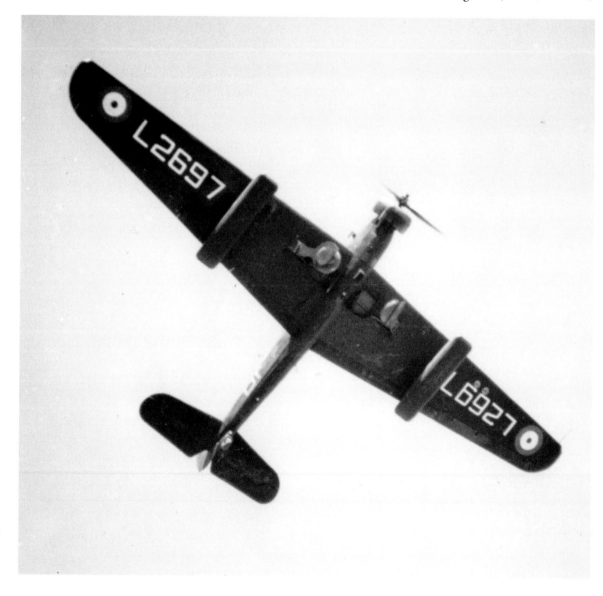

Colonial policing duties continued despite the impending war. In 1939, 14 Squadron equipped with the Vickers Wellesleys flew operations against insurgents in Transjordan. The aircraft is fitted with under-wing panniers which carry bombs. (14 Squadron Association)

Squadrons) flew to Brunsbüttel, at the mouth of the River Elbe, where two German battleships had been reported. Neither attack was successful: five Blenheims and two Wellingtons were lost and the German ships suffered only superficial damage.

The next missions by Bomber Command comprised armed reconnaissance in strength over the German coastal waters. A successful mission by 12 Handley Page Hampdens on 26 September was followed three days later by another sortie by 12 Hampdens of 61 and 144 Squadrons. These aircraft found two destroyers and bombed them, but were they intercepted by German fighters and five Hampdens were shot down. During the next two months poor weather over the Heligoland Bight frustrated further missions.

The Armstrong-Whitworth Whitley, which equipped 4 Group, had the longest range of any aircraft type in Bomber Command service, but as it was also the slowest type, the Whitley was considered to be too vulnerable to attack by fighters for use on daylight operations. Instead, they were to be used solely for night bombing. In fact, the type was first used to drop propaganda leaflets over German cities, starting with Bremen and the Ruhr on the first night of the war, by aircraft of 51 and 58 Squadrons. After a break in activities, the leaflet drops were resumed in mid-September and from then on, the aircraft ranged far over Germany: on 1 October 1939, Whitleys of 10 Squadron dropped leaflets on Berlin and on 27 October aircraft of 51 Squadron carried out similar raids on Munich and Frankfurt. In contrast to the dangers of operating in daylight, the aircraft did not suffer from the attentions of German fighters or anti-aircraft defences.

In early December 1939, the weather had cleared sufficiently for bomber operations to resume over Heligoland Bight. On 3 December, a force of

The Vickers Wellington B Is of IX Squadron were amongst the first RAF aircraft to see action when they attacked German battleships in the Elbe estuary on 4 September 1939. The Wellington, which remained both in production and RAF service throughout the war, formed the backbone of the RAF bomber force in the UK and the Middle East. (Flintham)

The Lockheed Hudson progressively replaced less suitable types such as the Avro Anson as a maritime patrol aircraft. On 8 October 1939, three Hudsons from 224 Squadron became the first RAF aircraft to shoot down a *Luftwaffe* aeroplane. (© IWM COL 183)

24 Wellingtons from 38, 115 and 149 Squadrons attacked shipping near Heligoland. Although the formation was engaged by fighters, no aircraft were lost. However, this success was short-lived: on 14 December, 12 Wellingtons of 99 Squadron lost two of their number to anti-aircraft fire over the Schillig Roads and another three were shot down by fighters. Four days later 22 Wellingtons of 9, 37 and 149 Squadrons found no suitable targets during their armed reconnaissance, but lost 12 of their number to fighters, with another three aircraft badly damaged. Clearly this rate of attrition could not be sustained, especially in view of such meagre

results, and this was the last major operation carried out by the 'heavy' bombers of Bomber Command in daylight.

COASTAL COMMAND

Despite Great Britain being a pre-eminent naval power, and despite the experience of anti-submarine operations during World War I, Coastal Command entered World War II woefully under-equipped. Nevertheless, standing patrols in the form of a continuous 'daisy chain' of aircraft flying from Montrose to the limit of endurance for the Avro Anson (some 50 miles short of the Norwegian coast) were mounted from 24 August 1939 in order to close off the North Sea to German vessels. Unfortunately, the patrols were initiated just too late to detect the departures of the heavy cruisers *Admiral Graf Spee* and *Deutschland*.

The obsolescent Anson was progressively replaced by the Lockheed Hudson, which proved to be much more suitable for long-range patrols. The Hudson was also better armed: on 8 October 1939, three Hudsons from 224 Squadron led by Flt Lt A.L. Womersley claimed one of the first RAF aerial victories when they shot down a Dornier Do18 operating over the Skagerrak.

DEPLOYMENT TO FRANCE

The British Expeditionary Force (BEF) deployed to France in September 1939 and took up defensive positions in northeast France, near the Belgian border. The air component supporting the BEF comprised four squadrons of Westland Lysander army co-operation aircraft (from 2, 4, 13 and 26 Squadrons), four squadrons of reconnaissance aircraft (15 Squadron with the Fairey Battle and 18, 53 and 59 Squadrons with the Bristol Blenheim) and two squadrons of Hawker Hurricanes (85 and 87 Squadrons) to provide fighter cover. The Battles of 15 Squadron were soon replaced by Blenheims of 57 Squadron. The air component was based on airfields in the vicinity of Lille, but its close proximity to the border with neutral Belgium meant that its units could not carry out any offensive action. However, the Blenheim squadrons were used for photographic reconnaissance sorties along the German Westwall (Atlantic Wall) defensive system.

The light bombers of 1 Group, Bomber Command were unable to reach central Germany from their peacetime bases in the UK, so the group was sent en-masse to France to form the Advanced Air Striking Force (AASF). Flying from bases in the Rheims area, it was intended that the eight squadrons of Battles and two squadrons of Blenheims would, much like the Independent Force of 1918, be able to prosecute independent operations and could carry

A Fairey Battle of 103 Squadron, part of the Advanced Air Striking Force (AASF) in France. When the fighting began, the obsolescent Battle proved no match for the German defences and by the summer of 1940, most of the AASF squadrons had been annihilated. (Flintham)

A Spitfire Mk I of 602 *City of Glasgow* Squadron. The first *Luftwaffe* aircraft to be shot down over the UK was a Heinkel He111 bomber which was intercepted by Blue Section, 'B' Flight from the squadron on the morning of 16 October 1939. (Pitchfork)

the war into Germany. Two Hurricane squadrons (1 and 73 Squadrons) were to provide fighter cover for the AASF. Like the air component, initial operations by the AASF consisted of reconnaissance flights over the westernmost parts of Germany. Unfortunately, these sorties proved to be costly: two out of three Battles from 88 Squadron on reconnaissance over Aachen were shot down by fighters on 20 September and ten days later four out of the five aircraft of 150 Squadron were also shot down by fighters over Saarbrucken. Flights by Battles over Germany were curtailed after these incidents. The Hurricanes of the air component and the AASF also encountered German aircraft periodically. On 30 October, a Dornier Do17 reconnaissance aircraft was shot down by Pilot Officer (Plt Off) P.W. Mould of 1 Squadron flying a Hurricane; by April 1940, Fg Off E.J. 'Cobber' Kain of 73 Squadron had shot

down five enemy aircraft, making him the RAF's first 'ace' of the war. In January 1940, British Air Forces France (BAFF) was established to provide central command of both the air component and the AASF.

FIGHTER COMMAND

Meanwhile the *Luftwaffe* (German air force) also began to take an interest in British naval activity. Reconnaissance aircraft probed the naval dockyards at Rosyth and the anchorage of the Home Fleet at Scapa Flow. On the morning of 16 October 1939, two Heinkel He111 aircraft carried out a reconnaissance flight over Edinburgh and Rosyth and that afternoon a force of 12 Junkers Ju88 bombers attacked warships in the Firth of Forth. The bombers were intercepted by Supermarine

A Vickers Wellington Mk IA Directional Wireless Installation (DWI) aircraft of I General Reconnaissance Unit (GRU). The aircraft was fitted with a 35ft diameter electro-magnet (degaussing) covered with a balsa wood fairing to clear German magnetic sea mines from coastal waters. (Flintham)

Spitfires of 602 and 603 Squadrons, which shot down two of the German aircraft. Reconnaissance and bomber sorties by the *Luftwaffe* continued sporadically through the winter and, despite some gaps in radar coverage, many of these were successfully intercepted by RAF fighter aircraft. Amongst German losses were a number of Heinkel He111 aircraft, shot down by 603 Squadron on 22 and 28 October and 7 December.

Fighter aircraft also carried out offensive action: on 28 November 1939, 12 Blenheim IFs of 25 and 601 Squadrons carried out a low-level raid at dusk against the German seaplane base on the island of Borkum, where they strafed five seaplanes and a number of coastal patrol vessels.

Luftwaffe reconnaissance aircraft continued to probe the defences of all naval installations in Scotland and bombers attacked convoys in the North Sea. Fighter Command continued to intercept many of these aircraft and, for example an He111 was shot down by Hurricanes from 43 Squadron on 3 February 1940 while attacking shipping off Whitby. German aircraft also dropped magnetic mines in coastal waters, but from January 1940 many of these were cleared by Wellington IA Directional Wireless Installation (DWI) aircraft operated by 1 General Reconnaissance Unit (GRU) from Manston. The DWI equipment consisted of a large circular electromagnet which caused the mines to explode when they were overflown by the aircraft.

On 15 February 1940, a patrol of three Hudson bombers from 220 Squadron located the *Altmark*, a German oil tanker and supply ship, off the coast of Norway. The *Altmark*, which was transporting 299 prisoners from ships sunk by the 'pocket battleship' *Admiral Graf Spee*, attempted to seek

The Handley Page Hampden overcame its disastrous debut as a day bomber to play an important part in the night bombing offensive, eventually equipping 14 squadrons in Bomber Command. Another seven Coastal Command units also operated the type as a torpedo bomber. (RAF Official Photographer/ IWM/Getty)

The Wellington and Hampden, and the Armstrong Whitworth Whitley (above) were the medium bomber types operated by Bomber Command during the first years of the war. These aircraft are from 78 Squadron. (Fox Photos/Hulton Archive/Getty)

refuge in the Jøssingfjord. But the aircraft had alerted HMS *Cossack*, which entered the fjord on 16 February and rescued the prisoners.

After a *Luftwaffe* bombing raid on Scapa Flow on 16 March, the British government demanded that the RAF carry out some form of retaliation. Three days later, Bomber Command carried out the first night bombing raid on the seaplane base at Hörnum on the island of Sylt. A total of 30 Whitley and 20 Hampden bombers took part in the raid and although many crews claimed direct hits on the target, subsequent photo-reconnaissance revealed that little damage had been done.

NORWAY

On 7 April 1940, the crew of a Coastal Command Hudson reported that the German battleships *Scharnhorst* and *Gneisenau* were heading north after leaving Wilhelmshaven. Unfortunately, an attack by 12 Blenheim bombers of 107 Squadron achieved no hits and a follow-up mission by two squadrons of Wellingtons could not locate the ships in deteriorating weather. Fearing that the ships might be attempting to break out into the Atlantic, a full-scale search of the North Sea and the Norwegian coast was ordered for Coastal Command aircraft the next day. Weather conditions remained poor, but a Short Sunderland of 204 Squadron located the cruiser *Admiral Hipper* and escort which were heading for Trondheim. In fact, the German naval activity was in support of an invasion of Norway and by the evening of 9 April much of southern Norway was under German control. A number of reconnaissance flights over Bergen confirmed the presence of two light cruisers, *Köln* and *Königsburg*, and a force of 12 Wellingtons from 9 Squadron and 115 Squadron were dispatched to bomb the ships; however, neither vessel was damaged in the attack. On 12 April, six out of a force of 12 Hampdens from 44 Squadron and 50 Squadron were shot down by fighters when they attempted to bomb a German ship at Kristiansand. Unfortunately, many of the airfields being used by the *Luftwaffe* were beyond the range of most RAF bomber types, but the airfield at Stavanger could be reached and was bombed on 11 April and again on 14 April. From then on, RAF aircraft also began to be used to lay mines in the Elbe estuary and in addition, over the next seven days Bomber Command aircraft flew 200 sorties against airfields used by the *Luftwaffe* in Norway and Denmark.

On 12 April 1940, British forces landed at Åndalsnes and two days later at Namsos, but they had to wait a further ten days before they had any air support. This arrived during the evening of 24 April when 18 Gloster Gladiators from 263 Squadron, flown off the aircraft carrier HMS *Glorious*, landed on the frozen surface of Lake Lesjaskog, situated between Trondheim and Lillehammer. Unfortunately, the presence of the aircraft was soon discovered by the *Luftwaffe*, which bombed the lake and by the following evening ten of the aircraft had been put out of

action. Over the next two days, the remaining Gladiators carried out useful work, flying reconnaissance sorties and intercepting *Luftwaffe* bombers, but their numbers rapidly dwindled until all had been completely wiped out by 26 April. A general evacuation of British forces from southern Norway commenced on 28 April. Bomber Command attacked airfields at Stavanger, Oslo and Aalborg; on 30 April a night raid on Stavanger was flown by 28 Wellingtons and Whitley bombers. These efforts limited the ability of the *Luftwaffe* to interfere with the evacuation, which was also covered by Blenheim IV long-range fighters of 254 Squadron.

FRANCE

The German invasion of Belgium and the Low Countries on 10 May 1940 was accompanied by a ferocious air campaign against Allied airfields. The BAFF fighter presence, already increased by the addition of 607 Squadron and 615 Squadron, was further reinforced by 501 Squadron on 10 May, followed by 3, 79 and 504 Squadrons; a total of ten Hawker Hurricane squadrons deployed

A Gloster Gladiator of 263 Squadron in Norway during the campaign of April 1940. The aircraft were deployed on 24 April, but were overwhelmed by *Luftwaffe* forces and all had been destroyed by 26 April. (Flintham)

to France. Although these squadrons fought hard and effectively, with pilots flying up to six sorties a day, they were heavily outnumbered and were unable to stop the overwhelming might of the *Luftwaffe*. One wave of eight Fairey Battles and another wave of 24 Battles were sent to attack German military columns advancing through Luxembourg. These missions were flown at 250ft to avoid *Luftwaffe* fighters, but at that height the slow-flying aircraft were extremely vulnerable to ground fire: a total of 13 Battles were lost, for negligible results. Six Bristol Blenheim IF long-range fighters from 600 Squadron, operating from Manston, carried out a strafing attack on German aircraft and *Fallschirmjäger* (parachute troops) at the Dutch airfield at Waalhaven, but once again losses were heavy as five of the Blenheims were shot down by German fighters. Another attack on Waalhaven airfield by Blenheim bombers was more successful and this was followed with a night raid by 36 Wellington bombers. Also that night, nine Whitley bombers were dispatched to attack roads and railways near Geldern, Goch, Kleve and Wesel. During the day, the BEF had advanced to take up a defensive line on the River Dyle in central Belgium and the Blenheim squadrons of the air component had carried out reconnaissance sorties to locate the main thrusts of the German army. Two main thrusts had been identified: one through Luxembourg and the Ardennes and the other centred on Maastricht, where German glider-borne *Fallschirmjäger* had captured the bridges across the River Maas (Meuse) and the Albert Canal as well as Fort Eben Emael. The following day eight reconnaissance sorties were flown by Blenheims over Maastricht, but the *Luftwaffe* continued to attack Allied airfields; 114 Squadron lost all of its aircraft in such an attack. A force of eight Fairey Battles from 88 Squadron and 218 Squadron were dispatched against a German column in Luxembourg, but only one aircraft returned from the mission. Bomber Command aircraft were also involved in the day's actions: Blenheim long-range fighters from 21 Squadron and 110 Squadron attacked troops in

the Maastricht area in the afternoon and that night, 36 bombers attacked the transport infrastructure around Mönchengladbach.

By 12 May 1940, the BEF had established positions along the Dyle and the BAFF concentrated operations against the German thrust through Maastricht which was directly threatening the BEF. Nine Blenheim bombers from 139 Squadron carried out a dawn raid on the bridge over the Albert Canal at Vroenhoven on the western outskirts of Maastricht, but the bridge was not hit and seven aircraft were shot down by *Luftwaffe* fighters. A follow-up raid by 24 Blenheim bombers from 15 Squadron and 107 Squadron was similarly unsuccessful but despite a fighter escort by Hurricanes of 87 Squadron, ten Blenheims were lost. In a final attempt to destroy the canal crossings, five Fairey Battles from 12 Squadron were sent to bomb the bridge at Vroenhoven and another nearby bridge at Veldwezelt. Although the bridge at Veldwezelt was slightly damaged, all five aircraft were shot down. A force of 15 Fairey Battles also attacked German troops near Sedan and despite losing six aircraft, the action helped to delay, albeit temporarily, the German advance. That evening another force of Blenheim bombers from 21 Squadron and 82 Squadron bombed German troop positions to the west of Maastricht, an action which also succeeded in slowing the German advance.

The following day the Blenheims were not used, in an attempt to husband the resources of the RAF in France. However, seven Battles from 226 Squadron were sent to stop German tanks advancing from Breda towards Antwerp. Operating at low level, they could not find any German forces and instead elected to bomb a disused factory building in the southwest suburbs of Breda and thereby block the main road with rubble. It was during this day the Germans had forced a crossing of the River Meuse near Sedan and had broken through the French defences. On the morning of 14 May, a patrol of eight Battles from 103 Squadron, escorted by Hurricanes of 73 Squadron, found and bombed German pontoon bridges over the Meuse

near Sedan with some success. Subsequently four Battles of 150 Squadron also bombed the bridges. That afternoon, all bombers available to the BAFF were sent against bridges and troops in the Sedan area. The first wave of 19 Battles (five from 12 Squadron, eight from 142 Squadron and six from 226 Squadron) encountered stiff opposition from anti-aircraft fire as well as *Luftwaffe* fighters and 11 Battles were shot down. The second wave formed by 11 Battles of 105 Squadron and four from 150 Squadron, with two Blenheims from 114 Squadron and six more from 139 Squadron also suffered heavily: ten Battles and five Blenheims were lost. The final wave of Battles (ten from 88 Squadron, eight from 103 and seven from 218 Squadron) lost nine of their number. After suffering such

catastrophic losses, no further missions were mounted by the BAFF, but 30 Blenheims from 21, 107 and 110 Squadrons of Bomber Command carried out an attack in the evening with the loss of seven aircraft. The BAFF Hurricane force had also suffered heavily losing 27 aircraft during the day, but they claimed 38 *Luftwaffe* aircraft destroyed.

DEVELOPMENTS IN NORWAY & FRANCE

A second expedition by Allied troops to Norway had landed at Harstad in late April. On 22 May, a re-equipped 263 Squadron flew its Gladiators from HMS *Furious* to Bardufoss, about halfway between

A Bristol Blenheim IV long-range fighter of 248 Squadron over the North Sea in 1940. However, the majority of Blenheims were used as light bombers, equipping some 21 squadrons in Bomber Command, including some of those allocated to the AASF. (RAF Official Photographer/IWM/ Getty)

Narvik and Tromsø. They were joined four days later by Hurricanes of 46 Squadron, which been flown off HMS *Glorious* to Skånland. The aircraft carried out intensive operations against *Luftwaffe* bombers over the next few weeks, including, after the ground campaign faltered, covering the evacuation of Allied forces during the first week of June. The squadrons left Norway on 7 June and landed on HMS *Glorious*. Unfortunately, all the aircraft and many of the crews were lost when the carrier was attacked and sunk by *Scharnhorst* on 8 June 1940.

By now the airfields of BAFF were at risk of being overrun. The Air Component was withdrawn to England, from where it could continue to operate more securely and no less effectively, and by 21 May only a handful of Westland Lysanders of 4 Squadron remained in France. Meanwhile the AASF had consolidated its remaining aircraft into six squadrons of Battles: the four remaining aircraft of 105 and 218 Squadrons were redistributed and the nine Blenheims of 114 and 139 Squadrons were transferred to the reconnaissance units of the Air Component. The Battle and Hurricane squadrons had also withdrawn to airfields in the Champagne area near Troyes, from where the Battles were used for night bombing. However, Bomber Command attempted once more to operate by daylight over Belgium: on 17 May, 12 Blenheims from 82 Squadron set out to attack German troops near Gembloux, south of Brussels, but despite a fighter sweep, they were intercepted by 15 Messerschmitt Bf109 fighters and 11 of the Blenheims were shot down.

By 26 May the BEF had started to withdraw towards Dunkirk. With the battlefront in range of fighters based in southern England, the RAF was able to establish a degree of local air superiority over the Calais area. The AASF Battles continued their task of night interdiction, supplemented by Bomber Command's heavy bombers; Blenheim night fighters of 604 Squadron patrolled over the Channel ports. With sufficient cloud cover or fighter escort, Blenheim bombers were now able to operate by day against enemy troops approaching the frontline. During the evacuation from Dunkirk, between 27 May and 4 June, the RAF operated at maximum effort to protect the troops within the Dunkirk perimeter, however the fighter patrols were frequently overwhelmed by numbers. On 27 May Spitfires from 74 and 610 Squadrons and Hurricanes of 65 and 145 Squadrons fought hard to stop *Luftwaffe* bombers from reaching Dunkirk, but were outnumbered two-to-one by the escorting fighters. The number of fighter patrols was increased further, sometimes by up to four squadrons, so that there would be a continuous presence over Dunkirk. Over the nine days of the Dunkirk evacuation RAF fighters flew nearly 3,000 sorties in support of the operation as well as a further 650 bombing and 170 reconnaissance sorties.

The three fighter squadrons of the BAFF continued to fight, covering the withdrawal of other units of the BEF towards Nantes. On 7 June, two more Hurricane squadrons, 17 and 242 Squadrons, were sent to France to reinforce the fighter strength. However, by then the Battle of France was lost: the French requested an armistice on 17 June and it was formally signed five days later. The BAFF Hurricane units were all recalled to the UK on 18 June, once the evacuation at Nantes had been completed.

ITALY DECLARES WAR

When Italy declared war on Britain on 10 June 1940, the British response was immediate. After refuelling in the Channel Islands, 36 Whitleys of 10, 51, 58, 77 and 102 Squadrons set off to bomb Turin and Genoa on 11 June, although only 13 aircraft reached their targets because of storms and severe icing over the Alps. Eight Wellingtons from 99 and 149 Squadrons, which had been based forward at Salon, near Marseille, were prevented from taking off by the French authorities that night, but they did fly on 15 June. Unfortunately, once again the weather intervened and only one aircraft attacked its target. The following night four of nine Wellingtons made successful attacks from Salon.

However, it was in the Middle East and East Africa that the Italian threat was felt most acutely:

only comparatively light British forces in Egypt stood between the Italian army in Libya and the Suez Canal, and further south in Eritrea the powerful Italian air and naval forces at Massawa presented a direct threat to shipping in the Red Sea en-route to or from the Suez Canal. Eight Blenheims from 45 Squadron carried out an attack on El Adem airfield, near Tripoli, on the morning of 11 June destroying a number of Italian aircraft on the ground. A follow-up attack was carried out in the afternoon by Blenheims of 55 and 113 Squadrons, which, like 45 Squadron, were based at Fuka. Meanwhile in Eritrea, the Wellesleys of 47 Squadron flying from Erkowit and 223 Squadron from Summit attacked the airfields at Gura and Asmara respectively and the Wellesleys of 14 Squadron, operating from Port Sudan, carried

out a dusk attack on the naval oil storage facility at Otumlo near Massawa. The following day it was the turn of the Blenheim squadrons at Aden: nine Blenheims from 8 Squadron attacked the airfield at Assab in southern Eritrea and eight aircraft from 39 Squadron bombed the airfield at Dire Dawe in Ethiopia. That day also saw further raids on Gura and Asmara by 47 and 223 Squadrons and in Libya nine Blenheims from 113 Squadron bombed ships in Tobruk harbour.

Over the next few months the bomber squadrons in Sudan and Aden carried out interdiction sorties against Italian forces in Eritrea. The Gladiators of 'K' Flight 112 Squadron, based at Port Sudan, and 94 Squadron at Aden also took their toll on Italian aircraft. These units also operated in conjunction with South African Air Force (SAAF) squadrons

A Whitley V of 58 Squadron takes off at dusk. The unit was part of the force that bombed Turin and Genoa the night after Italy declared war in 1940. (RAFM)

which were based in Kenya. The Blenheim IVF long-range fighters of 203 Squadron, operating from Aden, were mainly used for convoy escort duties, covering the southern part of the Red Sea; the northern part was covered by Wellesleys (and later Blenheims) of 14 Squadron, which also flew bombing and coastal reconnaissance work over Eritrea. Over Libya, too, the RAF kept the pressure on the Italians, with regular bombing attacks by the Blenheim squadrons; the Gladiator squadrons (33, 80 and 112 Squadrons) also contested air superiority with the Italian Air Force.

THE BATTLE OF BRITAIN

Air attacks on coastal shipping increased as more *Luftwaffe* units moved to forward bases in France. From early June, there were almost daily combats over convoys in the English Channel between RAF fighters and *Luftwaffe* bombers escorted by Messerschmitt Bf109 and Bf110 fighters. Southern England was now in range for German bombers and on the nights of 5 and 6 June 1940 a force of around 30 bombers attacked airfields and air defence installations on the east coast of England. However, this development was short-lived: there were no further raids over the next week while the German forces concentrated on the last days of the campaign in France. On 18 June, the day after the French collapse, a force of 18 Blenheims escorted by 24 Hurricanes successfully attacked *Luftwaffe* aircraft on the ground at Merville airfield and similar operations followed over the next five days against Schipol, Amiens, Rouen and Eindhoven. On 18 June, the *Luftwaffe* also recommenced its night attacks, which continued for most nights thereafter. These raids, typically comprising 70 bombers, all attacking widely-spaced targets, caused more nuisance than damage. Blenheim IF night fighters from 23 and 29 Squadrons were launched to intercept the raiders, but initially they enjoyed little success. However, Air Intercept (AI) radars became available from mid-July and the first kill

using AI was by Fg Off G. Ashfield and Sergeant (Sgt) R. Leyland from the Fighter Interception Unit, who shot down a Dornier Do17Z on the night of 22 July.

If the night raids by the *Luftwaffe* could be largely dismissed as a nuisance, the same could be said of the RAF's efforts over Germany. On the night of 15 May 1940, Bomber Command started its strategic campaign against Germany's means of oil supply and production. That night 96 aircraft, comprising a mix of Wellington, Whitley and Hampden bombers attacked a number of targets in the Ruhr industrial area, near Duisburg and Dortmund. Attacks by similar numbers of aircraft against oil- and transport-related targets then continued on virtually every subsequent night: these mainly covered an arc across northern Germany from the Ruhr to Kiel, but also, on occasions extending as far as Mannheim in the south and Berlin in the east. However, despite these efforts very little damage was done to German industry. Another nightly task was that of laying sea mines in the approaches to the main ports in northern France, the Low Countries and Germany; finally, the Channel ports were bombed by Blenheims and Battles, operating at night. During the week following 21 June 1940, Blenheim squadrons in Bomber Command also started a series of daylight 'cloud cover' raids. A force of some 20 would head towards targets in Germany, such as the railway system at Osnabruck or Hamm, but if there was insufficient cloud cover in which to hide from fighters, they were to return to base. However, these tactics proved to be largely ineffectual with few attacks actually being made.

Through the last week of June and the month of July, most of the *Luftwaffe*'s efforts continued against maritime convoys in the English Channel. Although a number of vessels were sunk, it was not a particularly effective anti-shipping campaign, but it did serve to draw RAF fighters into battle. RAF fighters were in action on most days through June and July and, for example on 10 July, four squadrons (74 Squadron with Spitfires and 32, 56 and 111 Squadrons with Hurricanes) intercepted 24 Do17

In 1940, the Hawker Hurricane Mk I formed the backbone of Fighter Command. The first monoplane fighter to enter service with the RAF, the type was powered by a 1,030hp Rolls-Royce Merlin engine and armed with eight Browning 0.303in machine guns. The type was involved in heavy fighting over France and Norway and 34 Hurricane-equipped squadrons were deployed during the Battle of Britain. (Hulton Archive/Getty)

A total of 19 Spitfire-equipped squadrons were involved in the Battle of Britain. A Spitfire Mk I of 611 *West Lancashire* Squadron makes a low pass over the squadron dispersal area. The unit was part of 12 Group, which was responsible for the defence of the Midlands during the battle, and provided a second line of defence after the front-line units of 11 Group. (Popperfoto/Getty)

An American pilot from 71 'Eagle' Squadron fires the guns of his Hurricane into the butts to check harmonization. Three Eagle squadrons (71, 121 and 133) were formed between September 1940 and July 1941: all were manned by US-born volunteers, many of whom had enlisted in the Royal Canadian Air Force (RCAF) in order to fight for the British. A total of 11 US pilots flew in the Battle of Britain and some 250 served in Eagle squadrons until the units were absorbed into the USAAF in September 1942. (Popperfoto/Getty)

bombers, escorted by 30 Bf109 and Bf110 fighters, which were attempting to bomb a convoy. However poor weather limited the *Luftwaffe*'s efforts for much of the second half of July and the beginning of August. Even so, during the period from 10 July to 10 August, the RAF lost 96 aircraft and the *Luftwaffe* lost 227, giving a good indication of the ferocity of the combat over the English Channel. One consequence of the fighting over the Channel was the establishment of the Air Sea Rescue (ASR) service at the end of July, using RAF marine craft and Lysanders to rescue downed aircrew.

Amongst the tasks allocated to Coastal Command aircraft was that of escorting convoys, for protection against submarines or against long-range patrol aircraft. In the Western Approaches the longer-range Sunderlands and Whitleys, which had

replaced some of the Ansons, could carry out this duty, but shipping in much of the eastern Atlantic was still beyond the range of land-based air cover. The basing of 98 Squadron equipped with the Fairey Battle in Iceland in July 1940 proved prescient, for although the Battles were singularly unsuitable for maritime work, the precedent had been set for longer-range aircraft eventually to be based there and to reach further into the mid-Atlantic. Bristol Blenheims of Coastal Command were used to attack German airfields in Norway, although not always with great success: on 9 July, 12 Blenheims from 21 and 57 Squadrons attacked the airfield at Stavanger, but seven of the aircraft were shot down. Apart from convoy escort, the Blenheims, along with Hudsons and Whitleys, were used for coastal reconnaissance around the eastern rim of the North Sea and a newly-formed specialist unit, 1 Photographic Reconnaissance Unit (PRU), ranged over Norway, Germany and France with camera-equipped Spitfires. One particular responsibility for these aircraft was to monitor the build-up in the Channel ports of troop-carrying barges, which were intended to convey the German invasion force to England.

After delays because of inclement weather, the main German attack on the UK opened on 12 August 1940. An initial simultaneous strike by Bf110 fighter-bombers on four Chain Home (CH) radar stations was followed by large formations of Junkers Ju88 bombers, heavily escorted by Bf109 and Bf110 fighters, which attacked the CH station at Ventnor, as well as the airfields at Manston, Lympne and Hawkinge. Despite being intercepted

by RAF fighters, the main bomber raids caused considerable damage to their targets. That evening was the turn of Bomber Command to strike back at Germany: 11 Hampdens from 49 and 83 Squadrons successfully bombed the aqueducts on the Dortmund–Ems Canal near Munster, denying its use for transporting invasion barges to the coast. The following morning two daylight raids were conducted by Blenheims against enemy-held airfields at Jersey (by 114 Squadron) and Aalborg (by 82 Squadron). Unfortunately, 11 of the 12 aircraft from 82 Squadron were shot down. The *Luftwaffe* continued its attacks in the afternoon with large formations of Junkers Ju87, Ju88 and Do17 bombers, which were, as usual, heavily escorted by fighters. Although severe damage was done to the docks at Southampton and the Coastal

Flt Lt E.S. Lock DSO, DFC* was the highest scoring RAF fighter pilot during the Battle of Britain. By the time he was killed by ground fire during a fighter sweep over France in August 1941, Eric 'Sawn-off' Lock, from Shropshire, had shot down 26 enemy aircraft and had become a household name as the leading 'fighter ace' in the RAF. (J.A. Hampton/Hulton Archive/Getty)

Command airfield at Detling, most of the raids missed their objectives after the bombers were split up by the Hurricanes of 43, 56, 87, 111, 151, 213, 238, 257 and 601 Squadrons and Spitfires of 74, 152 and 609 Squadrons. A night raid by He111 bombers against the Spitfire factory at Castle Bromwich that evening was little more successful. That night, too, Bomber Command dispatched 32 Whitleys from 10, 51, 58 and 102 Squadrons to bomb aircraft factories in Milan and Turin.

There was less activity on 14 August, with just two raids by *Luftwaffe* bombers, but 15 August marked the heaviest attacks yet made on mainland Britain by the *Luftwaffe*. In the first major raid of the day a large formation of 60 Ju87 dive-bombers attempted to bomb Hawkinge and Lympne airfields. They were intercepted over Hawkinge by Hurricanes of 501 Squadron and Spitfires of 54 Squadron and that attack was largely ineffective, although Lympne was put out of action for two days. The next attack was delivered from the North Sea, by 63 He111 bombers escorted by 21 Bf110 fighters, which had taken off from bases in Norway. The formation was first intercepted over the Farne Islands by Spitfires from 72 Squadron and later Spitfires of 41 Squadron and Hurricanes from 79 and 605 Squadrons. The *Luftwaffe* formation suffered heavy losses, including one third of the Bf110 escorts, and it was completely broken up. As the bombers headed back to Norway, they were engaged by a flight of Blenheims from 235 Squadron which were on a shipping strike, and a Blenheim accounted for another He111. The day's third raid also came from across the North Sea, this time made up of 50 unescorted Ju88 bombers from Aalborg. Despite being intercepted by Spitfires of 616 Squadron and Hurricanes of 73 Squadron, who shot down seven, the raiders were able to attack the bomber airfield at Driffield where they destroyed ten Whitleys on the ground. Meanwhile, in the south, another strike by high-speed Bf110 fighter-bombers wrought considerable damage at Martlesham Heath. This was shortly followed by 88 Do17 bombers closely escorted by more than 130 Bf109 fighters, supported in turn by a further fighter sweep of more than 60 Bf109 fighters, which approached Deal in mid-afternoon. This large formation was intercepted by Spitfires of 64 Squadron and Hurricanes of 111 and 151 Squadrons, but with such a powerful escort, the bombers were almost invulnerable and they were able to deliver a devastating attack against the Short Brothers seaplane factory at Rochester. Two more raids by Ju87 and Ju88 bombers, over the Isle of Wight and further to the west at Portland, were met by eight RAF fighter squadrons, while in the last raid of the day Bf110 fighter-bombers and Do17 bombers attacked Croydon and West Malling respectively before being caught by Hurricanes of 32 Squadron. By the end of the day, the *Luftwaffe* had done very little damage to any of Fighter Command's airfields and

Spitfire Mk Is of 610 *County of Chester* Squadron on patrol during the summer of 1940. Based at Biggin Hill, Kent the squadron saw combat over Dunkirk and also as a front-line unit during the Battle of Britain. (Past Pix/SSPL/Getty)

the RAF claimed to have shot down 182 German aircraft. Although the actual figure was 76 aircraft, it was, nevertheless, an impressive total.

The next day brought more heavy raids throughout the day, which saw a total of 15 squadrons from Fighter Command in action. Although the *Luftwaffe* made successful attacks on a number of airfields, albeit at a high cost in aircraft lost, once again very few of these were fighter bases. There was some respite on 17 August, with no major raids, but the *Luftwaffe* did return in force on 18 August. Attacks on Biggin Hill and Kenley were intercepted by Hurricanes of 32 and 111 Squadrons and Spitfires of 64, 610 and 615 Squadrons. While little damage was caused at Biggin Hill, Kenley was extensively hit and the sector operations room was put out of action temporarily until it could be re-established locally in a disused butcher's shop. A short time later, a large force of Ju87 and Ju88

dive bombers appeared over the Isle of Wight. The Ju88 force bombed the airfields at Gosport, Ford and Thorney Island, but the Ju87 formation concentrated on the CH station at Poling. Here they were intercepted by the Hurricanes of 43 and 601 Squadron and Spitfires of 152, 234 and 602 Squadrons, who shot down 16 of the 28 Junkers Ju87s. This was the last occasion that the Ju87 was used during the Battle of Britain. Another evening raid was successfully broken up by RAF fighters before it could do any damage and by the end of the day 71 *Luftwaffe* had been shot down for the loss of 27 RAF aircraft.

For the next five days the weather intervened, curtailing the German offensive, but 24 August marked the start of 14 days of daily large-scale raids. These were concentrated against the airfields of Fighter Command and although the airspace was hotly contested each day by RAF fighters,

A Short Sunderland I flying boat of 95 Squadron undergoing servicing at Pembroke Dock, Wales. In early 1941, the squadron moved to Freetown, Sierra Leone to provide anti-submarine cover for the shipping routes off west Africa. (Hulton-Deutsch/Corbis/Getty)

much destruction was wrought at North Weald (24 August and 3 September), Debden (26 August), Hornchurch (24 and 30 August and 2 September) and Biggin Hill (30 August and 1 September). On the night of 24 August, a number of *Luftwaffe* aircraft bombed London, with the result that Bomber Command was ordered to carry out a retaliatory raid on Berlin the next night. A force of 12 Hampdens from 61 and 144 Squadrons, 14 Whitleys from 51 and 78 Squadrons and 17 Wellingtons from 99 and 149 Squadrons bombed targets in Berlin on the night of 25 August and further raids followed on subsequent nights.

On 7 September, the *Luftwaffe* switched its focus from the UK's air-defence system to bombing London itself. On the afternoon of that day a single raid of almost 1,000 aircraft attacked dockyards, gasworks and power stations in London, followed by more attacks through the night. The following day was relatively quiet, until the evening, when *Luftwaffe* night bombers resumed the assault on London. Bomber Command aircraft were also active that night over the Channel ports, where they attacked concentrations of invasion barges: on 8 September, these attacks were prosecuted by 76 aircraft including Battle, Blenheim, Whitley and Wellington bombers. Over the next few days the intensity of *Luftwaffe* attacks on Britain decreased, influenced largely by the weather,

but on 15 September two large air armadas were dispatched to bomb London. In both cases, they suffered serious losses when they were intercepted by strong forces of nearly 200 RAF fighters and they were unable to deliver their attacks. On this day, the RAF claimed to have shot down 185 *Luftwaffe* aircraft and although, once again the real figure was somewhat lower (56 aircraft), the losses were enough to dissuade the Germans from further large-scale daylight bombing. For the remainder of the month, daylight operations by the *Luftwaffe* were limited to high-level fighter sweeps in the hope of drawing RAF fighters into combat, but there were also some daylight bombing raids on London, Southampton and Bristol. However, night bombing by both sides continued unabated: *Luftwaffe* bombers raided dockyards at Merseyside and London and the RAF intensified the campaign against the invasion barges, launching nearly 200 aircraft on the night of 17 September and maintaining the effort each night until the end of the month.

MALTA & GREECE

Until June 1940 there were no fighters permanently based in Malta, but four Gladiators were acquired from the Fleet Air Arm (FAA) early that month. These aircraft were ready to face an attack by the Italian Air

The Martin Maryland was used as a photo-reconnaissance aircraft by 431 Flight from its base on Malta. The unit played a vital role in the preparations for the attack on ships of the Italian fleet, moored in Taranto, by Fleet Air Arm aircraft in November 1940. (RAFM)

A Spitfire Mk VB of 222 Squadron based at North Weald. Deliveries of this version began in early 1941 and the improvements introduced included a 1,440hp Rolls-Royce Merlin 45 series engine and improved armament comprising two 20mm cannon and four .303in Browning machine guns. (IWM/Getty)

A section of three Wellington Mk ICs of 37 Squadron, one of three long-range bomber units in the Middle East in late 1940. Eventually the force would grow to 12 squadrons. The Mk IC was also used successfully as a torpedo bomber over the Mediterranean. (Flintham)

Force on 11 June and they continued to defend the island against the daily attentions of Italian aircraft based in Sicily for the rest of the year. The seaplane station at Kalafrana also became a forward operating base for the Sunderlands of 228 and 230 Squadrons from Alexandria and within three days of this arrangement 230 Squadron had sunk two Italian submarines. Malta was further reinforced during the next few months with Hurricanes of 261 Squadron and three Martin Maryland reconnaissance aircraft, which became 431 Flight. The island was also used as a base for Wellingtons, firstly for Egyptian-based aircraft to bomb southern Italian ports, including Naples, on the night of 31 October, and secondly for 148 Squadron, which formed on the island in December 1940. On 10 and 11 November, the Sunderlands of 228 Squadron and the Marylands of 431 Flight carried out the reconnaissance necessary for a successful strike by FAA Fairey Swordfish against the Italian fleet at Taranto. German forces arrived in the Mediterranean theatre in early January 1941 and *Luftwaffe* aircraft operating from Sicily started

bombing attacks against Malta from 9 January. RAF Wellingtons replied to these by bombing the Sicilian airfields on 12 and 15 January.

When Italy invaded Greece in late October 1940, the Blenheim IF aircraft of 30 Squadron and Gladiators of 80 Squadron were sent from Egypt to reinforce the Greek Air Force. These were soon followed by the Blenheims of 84 and 211 Squadrons, which flew interdiction sorties against targets near the Adriatic ports of Durazzo and Valona. In that time, the Gladiator pilots of 80 Squadron claimed to have shot down 42 Italian aircraft for the loss of only six of their own aircraft.

THE BLITZ & THE OFFENSIVES IN LIBYA & ERITREA

In late 1940 the *Luftwaffe* campaign against Great Britain consisted mainly of sporadic but widespread small-scale raids by fighter-bombers during daylight hours and a concerted bombing campaign against

London and the major industrial centres at night. London was a frequent target for night attacks, but other targets attacked between October 1940 and May 1941 included Birmingham, Coventry, Swansea, Southampton, Hull, Glasgow, Belfast, Newcastle, Plymouth and Portsmouth. Initially Fighter Command's night fighter force, few in number and poorly equipped, enjoyed little success against the night bombers. More squadrons were formed and some of the day squadrons were re-rôled so that at the beginning of 1941 there were eight specialist night units equipped with the Bolton-Paul Defiant (85, 96, 141, 151, 255, 256, 264 and 307 Squadrons) and four with Bristol Beaufighters (25, 29, 219 and 604 Squadrons). These aircraft were also equipped with an Air Intercept (AI) radar. The last large-scale night raid by the *Luftwaffe* was against London on 10 May.

After advancing into Egypt in September 1940, the Italian army had stopped after a short distance at Sidi Barani. Over the next few months the British forces in Egypt prepared to eject them. The RAF, which had been diluted by sending aircraft to Greece, was reinforced by two Wellington squadrons (37 and 38 Squadrons) and the Hurricanes of 73 Squadron, which arrived via Takoradi in West Africa. The Blenheims of 11 and 39 Squadrons were recalled from Aden and those of 45 Squadron from Sudan, restoring the air forces available in Egypt to their 'pre-Greece' levels. The offensive started with air attacks on the Italian airfields at El Adem by Blenheims on 4 December, Castel Benito by Wellingtons on 7 December and Bennina by Blenheims on the same day. The ground campaign started at dawn on 8 December, supported by aircraft including the Hurricanes of 33 Squadron, which carried out strafing attacks against Italian transport 50 miles inside Libya. By 16 December the Italians had been pushed back into Libya, but buoyed with success, and in the face of a full-scale Italian retreat, the British and Dominion forces carried on into Cyrenaica, pushing the Italians back beyond El Agheila.

A Boulton Paul Defiant of 151 Squadron. During the early days of World War II, the type proved to be a failure as a day fighter, but was used successfully as a night fighter, eventually equipping 13 squadrons. (Corbis/Getty)

Red Sea convoy protection occupied the Blenheims of 8 Squadron operating from Aden during the autumn of 1940. The squadron still had a flight of Vickers Vincents on charge and these were needed for policing duties during an insurrection by disaffected tribes in the north of the protectorate during October. In Eritrea, Kassala was retaken on 18 January 1941 and the Blenheims of 14 Squadron and Wellesleys of 47 and 223 Squadrons supported the army's advance towards the natural stronghold at Keren. During the Battle of Keren, which opened on 15 March, all three squadrons' aircraft bombed Italian troop and artillery positions on the battlefield. Keren fell on 27 March and the campaign in East Africa ended in early April.

ON THE OFFENSIVE

As the 'Blitz' over Britain continued into the first half of 1941, Fighter Command's night fighter force adapted and improved. Ground Control Intercept (GCI) sites were established and the monthly number of night fighter kills increased from just three enemy bombers in January 1941 to 96 by the end of May. One Blenheim fighter unit, 23 Squadron, flew in the night intruder role, patrolling enemy airfields in France and engaging *Luftwaffe* aircraft as they returned from missions. The day fighter squadrons also flew offensive sweeps over France (known as 'Rhubarbs'); these were periodically interspersed with large-scale fighter escorts for Bomber Command Blenheims in operations known as 'Circuses.' In early 1941, a typical circus might comprise six Blenheims escorted by around 70 fighters. However, neither rhubarbs nor circuses proved to be effective in their aim of shooting down *Luftwaffe* fighters and it was the RAF's fighter losses that increased: by the end of 1941, four RAF fighters were being lost for every German aircraft shot down. Meanwhile, Bomber Command continued its offensive activities: every night the Hampden, Wellington and Whitley squadrons as well as some Blenheim units targeted Germany's oil production and transportation. The

Blenheim day bomber and Coastal Command units were also used for daily anti-shipping patrols off the Dutch, German and Norwegian coasts.

In the year since the start of the war, the RAF had more than doubled its squadron strength. Some of the extra manpower came from displaced Europeans and a significant amount came from the Dominions. Poles, Czechs and Frenchmen had fought in the Battle of Britain and Canadians, Australians and New Zealanders served both in RAF units and in squadrons from their own countries' air forces. In North Africa, the RAF was reinforced by SAAF squadrons and in the Far East the Royal Australian Air Force (RAAF) provided squadrons for the defence of Singapore.

GREECE, LIBYA, IRAQ, CRETE & SYRIA

The presence of German army units in Bulgaria in early 1941 resulted in the dispatch of a British Expeditionary Force (BEF) and further RAF units from Egypt to Greece: the Blenheims of 11 and 113 Squadrons and Hurricanes of 33, 112 Squadrons and Lysanders (plus a flight of Hurricanes) of 208 Squadron arrived in Greece in March. A detachment of Wellingtons from 37, 38 and 70 Squadrons was also sent to join them. The Greek campaign was short-lived after the German invasion of Yugoslavia on 6 April. Despite the best efforts of the Blenheim and Wellington crews, an opportunity to destroy German columns at the choke point in the Monastir Gap between 7 and 11 April was frustrated by poor weather. The *Luftwaffe* took its toll of aircraft, too: on 13 April, all six of a formation of Blenheims from 211 Squadron was shot down and two days later all of 113 Squadron's Blenheims were destroyed on the ground at Niamata. British forces started an evacuation to Crete on 21 April and the last Hurricanes left three days later.

The German *Afrika Korps* retook El Agheila at the end of March 1941 and swiftly pushed the British forces, which had been weakened by

having to reinforce Greece, back to the Egyptian border. The garrison at Tobruk held out against attack and it was bypassed by the *Afrika Korps*; the Hurricanes of 6 and 73 Squadron remained at the airfield for the first month and were able to establish air superiority over the enclave, defending the garrison against *Luftwaffe* bombing attacks and, along with the Blenheims of 45 Squadron, attacking the investing forces. The Hurricanes were withdrawn in April, but retained a forward operating base at Sidi Barani. The loss of Cyrenaica put Tripoli beyond the range of bombers based in Egypt, so the Wellingtons of 148 Squadron were moved forward again to Malta. Another arrival in Malta at the end of April was 21 Squadron, whose Blenheims were pressed into service for anti-shipping strikes.

When a coup on 3 April 1941 in Iraq installed Rasid Ali, a pro-German agitator, in power, the British forces acted swiftly: 400 troops of the King's Own Royal Regiment were flown from Karachi to Shaibah by Vickers Valentias and Douglas DC2s of 31 Squadron. However, the RAF station at Habbaniya, base to 4 Flying Training School (FTS), was besieged by the Iraqi Army. The FTS's training aircraft comprising Hawker Audaxes, Fairey Gordons and Airspeed Oxfords were modified to carry 20lb bombs and divided into four bombing squadrons. A flight of Gladiators and ten Wellingtons from 37 Squadron were sent from Egypt to reinforce Habbaniya and ten Wellingtons from 70 Squadron were despatched to Shaibah. At dawn on 2 May the 4 FTS aircraft, supported by the Wellingtons, made a pre-emptive strike on the besieging Iraqis. Over the next four days a fierce battle raged. The force at Shaibah was further reinforced by more Wellingtons from 37 Squadron as well as Blenheim fighters of 203 Squadron. The transport aircraft of 31 Squadron were used to airlift troops from Shaibah to Habbaniya and to evacuate families

A Bristol Bombay transport aircraft of 216 Squadron. Some 50 were built and most saw service in the Middle East. The Bombay could carry 24 troops and also be used as a bomber.

A Bristol Beaufort in service with 217 Squadron. The type was the main torpedo bomber used by the RAF and equipped five squadrons in the UK and three in the Middle East. (Hulton Archive/Getty)

and dependents on the return leg. The Wellingtons were replaced by Blenheims from 84 Squadron and Hurricanes and more Gladiators from 94 Squadron and there was further reinforcement of troops flown in by 216 Squadron's Bristol Bombays. Armoured cars of 2 ACC were also sent as reinforcements. After a short campaign the Iraqi revolt was put down and the pro-British government was restored on 1 June.

The German invasion of Crete started on 20 May 1941 and airborne forces were soon able to establish a bridgehead at the airfield of Maleme on the west of the island. All RAF aircraft had been recalled from Crete in the second week of May, so it was left to the Blenheims of 14, 45 and 55 Squadrons, operating at the extremes of their range from Egypt, to bomb the enemy positions and aircraft during the day. At night, it was the turn of the Wellingtons of 37, 38 and 70 Squadrons. All of these units carried out operations over Crete for the next week, but they were unable to stem the flow of German troops and supplies into Crete and the island was evacuated on the nights of 29 and 30 May.

Inspired by German successes, the Vichy French administration in Syria began to court the Germans, with the result that a force was sent to neutralize the French forces in Syria. Ground operations started on 8 June, supported by Hurricanes from 70 Squadron and Blenheims of 11 and 84 Squadrons, later augmented by 45 Squadron. The Blenheims bombed airfields, barracks and military objectives, including a precision attack by the Blenheims of 11 Squadron on the Governor's residence in Beirut. After a short but hard fought campaign, the Vichy surrendered on 14 July.

BATTLESHIPS, U-BOATS & BOMBERS

After a two-month cruise in the Atlantic, the German battleships *Scharnhorst* and *Gneisenau* arrived in Brest harbour for repairs on 22 March 1941. Over the next two weeks Bomber Command mounted a number of attacks on the ships, without hitting them. However, in a suicidal attack, a Bristol Beaufort of 22 Squadron, flown by Fg Off K. Campbell, hit and severely damaged *Gneisenau* with a torpedo. *Gneisenau* was further damaged by four direct hits four days later. On 18 May, the battleship *Bismarck*, accompanied by the cruiser *Prinz Eugen*, broke out from Norway. After being caught and unsuccessfully engaged by naval forces, contact was lost seven days later. However, a Consolidated Catalina of 209 Squadron located *Bismarck* on 26 May and the ship was sunk the following day; meanwhile *Prinz Eugen* escaped to Brest. In another development, the cruiser *Lützow* (formerly *Deutschland*) was located on 13 June off the Norwegian coast by a Beaufort of 42 Squadron, which successfully hit the vessel with its torpedo, causing extensive damage.

More raids were flown against the ships in Brest and *Prinz Eugen* was hit (with a single bomb) on the night of 1 July. *Scharnhorst*, which had completed its repairs, left Brest on 21 July, but was located by a reconnaissance Spitfire the following day.

On 24 July, a mass daylight raid on Brest was carried out by a force of 100 Wellington and Hampden bombers, plus three Boeing B-17 Fortress from 90 Squadron. This raid provided some diversion for the 15 new Handley Page Halifax bombers of 35 and 76 Squadrons which bombed *Scharnhorst* in its new dock at La Pallice (La Rochelle), scoring five hits on the ship for the loss of five bombers. As a result, *Scharnhorst* returned to Brest for further repairs.

With the major proportion of the *Kriegsmarine*'s (German Navy) capital ships languishing in Brest, the twin threats facing Allied shipping in the Atlantic were land-based aircraft (and in particular the Focke-Wulf Fw200 Condor) and U-boats. At the beginning of the war, the Royal Navy had taken responsibility for anti-submarine warfare, but as Coastal Command relearnt the lessons of World War I, while also doubling in size and re-equipping with more suitable aircraft, so more of that responsibility could be assumed by aircraft. Basing three coastal squadrons, the Sunderlands of 95 and 202 Squadrons and Hudsons of 200 Squadron, at Banjoul, Gambia in mid-1941 effectively curtailed activities by U-boats off the coast of West Africa. Additionally, the Very Long Range Aircraft, in the shape of the Consolidated B-24 Liberator which entered service with 120 Squadron in June 1941, could operate from Iceland and thereby close the 'Greenland Gap' between air cover from land-based aircraft flying from the mainland UK and Newfoundland. The introduction of Air-Surface Vessel (ASV) radar also improved the ability of Coastal Command's aircraft to locate U-boats on the surface. Beaufighters, first issued to 252 Squadron in late 1940, were also an effective counter against German aircraft. Protection from long-range patrol aircraft would be eventually provided by escort carriers, but an interim measure was the introduction of Catapult Aircraft Merchant Ship (CAM ship), merchant vessels which carried a single Hurricane which could be launched, with the aid of a rocket-assisted catapult, to intercept enemy aircraft. After engaging the enemy, the Hurricane would ditch in the sea. There were nine operational

A Douglas Havoc I (also known as the 'Moonfighter') night intruder of 23 Squadron. The aircraft was originally delivered to the RAF as Boston II light bomber. The Havoc was used to patrol over *Luftwaffe* airfields at night, and attack enemy aircraft as they returned to their home base. (23 Squadron Archive)

launches of Hurricanes from CAM ships between August 1941 and July 1943, resulting in eight kills as well as a number of enemy aircraft being successfully driven off.

Daylight raids by the Blenheims of Bomber Command continued through the second half of 1941, including attacks against Bremen on 4 July and Rotterdam on 16 July and, by 54 aircraft drawn from 18, 82, 107, 114, 139 and 226 Squadrons escorted by Westland Whirlwinds of 263 Squadron, on two power stations near Cologne 12 August. However, while these attacks achieved some success, they did so at an unsustainable loss rate of over 20 percent. The night bomber force was less vulnerable to German defences, but its accuracy was questionable: an investigation published in August 1941 by Mr D.M. Bensusan-Butt reported the shocking statistic that of

all aircraft tasked against a target, on average only 20 percent of crews would manage to drop their weapons within five miles of the actual target. Indeed, post-raid photographs by 1 PRU aircraft of Mannheim and Gelsenkirchen confirmed that little damage was being done to the intended targets. Perhaps the only result of night bombing in 1940–1941 was to ensure that the Germans had an efficient night fighting capability by the time that Bomber Command ramped up its offensive in the following years.

RUSSIA

Two squadrons of Hurricanes (81 and 134 Squadrons) were sent to Russia in September 1941 to show solidarity with the Soviets against the

Germans and to assist in the defence of Murmansk. After flying from HMS *Argus*, the Hurricanes operated from Vaenga airfield from 11 September until 18 October and shot down a number of *Luftwaffe* aircraft. The Hurricanes were then handed over to the Soviet Air Force.

OPERATION *CRUSADER* & NORTH AFRICA

In the days leading up to the start of Operation *Crusader* in North Africa on 18 November 1941, Wellingtons from Middle East Command bombed the port areas in Benghazi and Tripoli, while the Blenheim squadrons attacked airfields and storage dumps. Hurricanes and Curtiss Tomahawks had already achieved air superiority over the battlefront, which had prevented *Luftwaffe* reconnaissance aircraft from observing evidence of an imminent offensive and now gave RAF aircraft some degree of freedom to operate over the battlefield. These included six Wellingtons from 109 Squadron which were equipped with electronic jamming equipment which was intended to interfere with the *Afrika Korps'* tank radio nets. Apart from providing escorts for Blenheims, the fighter aircraft also doubled as fighter-bombers, attacking troops and transport in the enemy's immediate rear areas. Because of the difficulties co-ordinating Close Air Support, once the ground offensive began the Blenheims generally operated against targets 50 miles beyond the advance. On 25 November, repeated attacks by Blenheims succeeded in repelling a counter-thrust by 21.Panzer Division in the area of Sidi

Hawker Hurricanes of 134 Squadron at Vaenga airfield, Murmansk in autumn 1941. The aircraft were flown by RAF pilots for two months before being handed over to the Soviet Air Force. (Sheppard)

Curtiss P-40 Tomahawks, being ferried on the 'Takoradi Route' from West Africa to Egypt. The aircraft were shipped to Takoradi in crates, then assembled and flown across Africa. Four RAF squadrons in the Desert Air Force equipped with the Tomahawk served in the ground-attack role.

Omar. By Christmas the *Afrika Korps* had pulled back to Ajdedabia and Cyrenaica was once more in Allied hands.

After the successful re-conquest of Cyrenaica at the end of 1941, the tables were turned in January 1942. Having been resupplied by sea, the *Afrika Korps* started a surprise counter-offensive on 21 January. Despite being diluted from supplying squadrons to reinforce the Far East, the RAF aircraft were able to establish air superiority over the battlefield but the momentum of the German

advance carried them forward. By 14 February the 8th Army had withdrawn to a defensive line at Gazala, to the west of Tobruk.

In the first months of 1942 Malta was the target for heavy bombing by the *Luftwaffe*. By March the German raids frequently numbered more than 200 bombers and in that month over 2,000 tons of bombs were dropped on the island. The defenders were able to shoot down a respectable number of raiders, but on occasions their own losses meant that on some days only a handful of aircraft remained

serviceable. On 20 April, 47 Spitfires were flown into Malta from the USS *Wasp* and the following month another 62 arrived. The German attacks started to slacken in mid-May.

SINGAPORE & BURMA

In late 1941, the RAF presence in Malaya comprised three Squadrons of Blenheims (27, 34 and 62 Squadrons), 243 Squadron with Brewster Buffaloes, two Squadrons of Vickers Vildebeests (36 and 100 Squadrons) and 205 Squadron with Catalinas. These units were reinforced by four RAAF squadrons equipped with Buffaloes and Hudsons and by 488 Squadron RNZAF, also equipped with Buffaloes. In addition, 60 Squadron, equipped with Blenheims, and 67 Squadron with Buffaloes were based in Burma near Rangoon.

The Japanese attack on the US fleet at Pearl Harbor on 7 December 1941 marked the start of the war in the Far East, but it was only one of a number of simultaneous strikes across the Pacific Rim. The previous day a Hudson of 1 Squadron RAAF detected two large Japanese convoys heading towards Malaya, but the convoys could not be found by later reconnaissance sorties. On 8 December, Japanese troops started landing near Kota Bharu on the northwest coast of Malaya. At dawn and in heavy tropical rain, the Vildebeests of 36 and 100 Squadrons attempted to attack a Japanese cruiser but were unsuccessful. However, the landing ships were attacked through the day by RAAF Hudsons as well as Blenheims from all four RAF squadrons in the region. The Allied airfields were also subject to heavy assault by Japanese aircraft and many of the Allied aircraft were destroyed on the ground. Singapore city was also bombed. On the following day, a much-depleted force of Blenheims attacked the airfield at Singora (Songkhla) on the eastern coast of Thailand, where considerable damage was wrought amongst Japanese aircraft. A follow-up

A Bristol Blenheim IV of 14 Squadron over the Western Desert. The light bombers of the Desert Air Force proved very effective in supporting the army during the Operation *Crusader* offensive in late 1941; they were also instrumental in holding back the *Afrika Korps* long enough for the army to regroup during the forthcoming German offensive. (14 Squadron Association)

A Handley Page Halifax
Mk II of 405 Squadron,
RCAF being prepared
for a bombing mission
over Germany. The
type was the second
four-engined bomber
to enter RAF service,
the first being the Short
Stirling. Over 6,000 of
the type were built and
saw wartime service
with Bomber Command,
Coastal Command
and in the Middle East.
(Hulton Archive/Getty)

raid was itself disrupted by a Japanese air raid at Butterworth which destroyed all but one of the Blenheims on the ground. The remaining Blenheim flown by Sqn Ldr A.K.S. Scarf carried out its mission alone.

Over the next fortnight, the handful of remaining aircraft fought fiercely with the Japanese forces advancing relentlessly on Singapore. In mid-December, the first reinforcements from the Middle East arrived in the shape of five Blenheims. Meanwhile, part of the Japanese force in Thailand had swung northwards into Burma. Like Singapore, Rangoon also began to be subjected to a concerted bombing campaign by Japanese aircraft, but attacks against the Burmese capital were met by the Buffaloes of 67 Squadron and also the Curtiss P-40s of the American Volunteer Group, also known as the 'Flying Tigers.'

A force of 50 Hurricanes, including those of 258 Squadron, arrived in Singapore in January 1942 and these first saw action on 20 January when they shot down eight bombers over Singapore; unfortunately, subsequent raids were escorted by Mitsubishi A6M Zero fighters, which were superior in performance to the Hurricane. A number of Hudsons also arrived and these were taken on by 62 Squadron. On 21 January, further Japanese landings were reported at Endau, approximately 100 miles north of Singapore. Nine Vildebeests from 100 Squadron and three from 36 Squadron carried out a torpedo attack on the Japanese ships, but lost five of their number and a second raid by nine Vildebeests and three Fairey Albacores resulted in the loss of another seven aircraft. The Japanese had also landed in Burma in mid-January. However, an attempt by the Japanese to gain air superiority over Rangoon was

Opposite: A flight of Brewster Buffalo fighters of 243 Squadron flying over Singapore harbour in late 1941. The US-built Buffalo was hopelessly outclassed in combat by the Japanese Mitsubishi A6M Zero-Sen. (RAFM)

Below: Fund-raising schemes were set up in Great Britain and across the Empire to raise money to assist in the purchase of new military aircraft. Bristol Blenheim, serial number Z6372, was paid for by the Gold Coast Spitfires Fund; after being flown across Africa on the 'Takoradi Route' it was delivered to 60 Squadron in India.

A Short Stirling Mk I from 7 Squadron. The type was the first four-engined bomber to enter service with the RAF. Eventually 12 squadrons would be equipped with the Stirling, but it lacked performance and was never as operationally successful as the Halifax or Lancaster. (RAFM)

thwarted by the combined efforts of 67 Squadron and the Flying Tigers.

Further reinforcements from the Middle East arrived at the end of January 1942: Burma was bolstered by two squadrons of Blenheims (45 and 113 Squadron) and three of Hurricanes (17, 135 and 136 Squadrons). By now the handful of aircraft in Singapore had been withdrawn to Sumatra, where they were joined by 84 and 211 Squadrons with Blenheims and by 232, 242 and 605 Squadrons, which had flown their Hurricanes off HMS *Indomitable*. From a jungle airfield at 'P2' near Palembang successful attacks were flown against Japanese invasion force on 14 and 15 February, and although this action temporarily halted the landings near Palembang, it only delayed the inevitable. Sumatra was evacuated on 18 February and the much-reduced force of 18 serviceable Hurricanes, 12 Hudsons, six Blenheims and two Vildebeests moved to Java. Here the defence of

Batavia (Jakarta) continued until 6 March, when resistance in Java capitulated.

BATTLESHIPS AGAIN

Late on 11 February 1942, the *Scharnhorst*, *Gneisenau* and *Prinz Eugen* left Brest and over the course of the next day sailed through the English Channel to Kiel. The German Navy was fortunate in crossing two standing patrol lines by Hudsons while the aircraft were on their outbound leg or while their ASV equipment was not working, and the presence of the German vessels was not detected until late morning. The weather was poor, with a cloud base of 700ft, and a succession of attacks by aircraft throughout the day failed to achieve any hits. All six FAA Fairey Swordfish, which made the first attack, were shot down and subsequent attacks by Beauforts from 42, 86 and 217 Squadrons were also unsuccessful. Some 240 bombers were also launched

during the course of the day, of which 39 attacked the German flotilla, but none achieved hits. Ironically both *Scharnhorst* and *Gneisenau* were damaged by mines as they neared Kiel: mine-laying was seen as a low priority by Bomber Command and yet it was one of the most effective roles carried out by its aircraft. On 26 February *Gneisenau* was seriously damaged when it was hit by bombs during a raid on Kiel and the ship saw no further action during the war.

Meanwhile the battleship *Tirpitz* was discovered by a Spitfire of 1 PRU, in Åsenfjord near Trondheim. A mission by seven Short Stirlings from 15 and 149 Squadrons and nine Handley Page Halifaxes from 10 and 76 Squadrons on 30 January was foiled by bad weather. Later raids by a mixed force of Halifaxes from 10, 35 and 76 Squadrons and Avro Lancasters from 44 and 97 Squadrons on 30 March, 27 and 28 April fared no better, partly because of weather conditions and partly because of effective smoke screens hiding the ship.

SPECIAL OPERATIONS

From late 1941 the RAF became more closely involved in special operations on continental Europe. Based at Tempsford near Bedford, the Lysanders of 419 Flight,

later renumbered as 138 Squadron, worked with the Special Operations Executive (SOE) and were used for transporting agents to and from occupied France. The unit was expanded to include Whitleys and Halifaxes for parachute dropping and it was joined by the Whitleys of 161 Squadron in early 1942. On 27 February 1942, Whitleys of 51 Squadron were used to drop airborne troops near Saint-Jouin-Bruneval, Normandy for Operation *Biting*, a daring raid to capture the components of German 'Wurzburg' radar located at La Poterie-Cap-d'Antifer.

RE-EQUIPPING BOMBER COMMAND

In early 1942, Bomber Command faced up to its inability to hit point targets at night and instead changed its policy to bombing German cities. This change of policy coincided with the arrival of more capable aircraft and better navigational equipment. The four-engined Stirling and Halifax had entered service in late 1940 with 7 and 35 Squadrons respectively, but it was not until early 1942 that these aircraft were operational in large numbers. The Lancaster also entered service with 44 Squadron in March 1942. This period coincided with the

The Armstrong-Whitworth Whitley Mk II was used for parachute training by the airborne forces. In February 1942, the type was used for the first operations by airborne forces at Tragino, Italy and Bruneval, France. (Flintham)

In late 1941, 88 Squadron was re-equipped with the Douglas Boston III light bomber in place of the Blenheim IV. Over 1,230 Boston III, IV and Vs were used by the RAF in the UK, Middle East and Italy. (Hulton-Deutsch Collection/ Corbis/Getty)

introduction of a radio-based navigation system known as 'Gee,' which could give position fixes accurate to within a few miles up to a range of about 400 miles. With the Master Station at Daventry, this system could theoretically offer reasonable accuracy as far as the cities of the Ruhr. However the first missions on which Gee was used, eight night raids against Essen during March, were no more accurate than previous non-Gee attacks. A raid by 135 aircraft against Cologne on 13 March was more successful, although on a subsequent raid on 5 April, the nearest bombs landed five miles from the target.

The city of Lübeck was attacked by over 200 bombers on 28 March. Lübeck was beyond the range of Gee, but its coastal location made it relatively easy to find. The bombers succeeded in destroying almost half of the city, much of which was composed of ancient wooden buildings, but, like similar raids on Rostock in the following month, this widespread destruction did not have the anticipated effects on either the morale of the civilian population or industrial production.

However, on occasions Bomber Command proved that it could be capable of precision attacks. In perfect weather conditions, a force of 235 bombers attacked the Renault factory at Boulogne-Billancourt near Paris on the night of 3 March. This raid appeared to be a complete success, although production at the factory was restored within four months. Then, on 17 April, six Lancasters of 44 Squadron and another six from 97 Squadron carried out a low-level daylight raid on the MAN submarine diesel-engine works at Augsburg. The raid was an impressive feat of airmanship, but seven of the 12 aircraft were shot down and despite accurate bombing the damage to the plant was minimal.

Offensive sweeps in the form of 'rhubarbs' and 'circuses' continued into 1942. From late 1941, the Bristol Blenheim in Bomber Command was gradually replaced by the Douglas DB-7B Boston III. The first 'circus' operation involving Bostons of 88 Squadron took place on 12 February 1942 and in the subsequent months 'circuses' frequently attacked ports and coastal installations in northern France and the Low Countries. The Bostons were also used, as the Blenheims had been, for anti-shipping strikes, but these were mainly the preserve of the Hudson squadrons in Coastal Command. In the north,

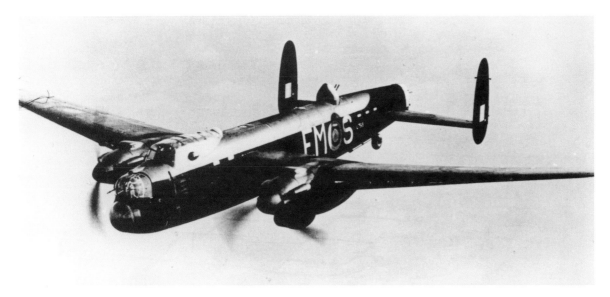

Left: An Avro Manchester Mk IA of 207 Squadron, the first unit to operate the type. Powered by two Rolls-Royce Vulture engines, which proved unreliable in service, the Manchester was not an operational success; however, its failure led to Avro developing the four-engined Lancaster, which was arguably the most successful British-built bomber in World War II. (Flintham)

Below: A Douglas C-47 (DC-3) Dakota of 31 Squadron during the evacuation of Myitkyina in April 1942. The Dakota was, perhaps, the single most important aircraft type during the war in Burma, as it allowed troops and supplies to be transported for long distances over otherwise impassable terrain. (Pitchfork)

48 and 608 Squadrons were responsible for patrolling the Norwegian coast, while 53, 59, 320 and 408 Squadrons covered the coast from the Hook of Holland to the mouth of the Elbe.

BURMA & CEYLON

By the beginning of March 1942, the RAF fighter strength in Burma had been whittled down to three Brewster Buffaloes, 20 Hurricanes and four US-crewed P-40 Warhawks. A small number of Hudsons and nine Blenheims also remained. When the order to evacuate Rangoon was issued on 7 March 1942, these surviving aircraft flew to a temporary airfield at Zigon, about halfway between Rangoon and Mandalay. Here they were split between 'Burwing,' comprising 17 Squadron (Hurricane) and 45 Squadron (Blenheim), which redeployed to Magwe on the River Irrawaddy and 'Akwing,' made up of 67 Squadron (Hurricane) and 139 Squadron (Hudson) which moved to Akyab on the coast. On 20 March, a force of nine Blenheims escorted by ten Hurricanes of Burwing carried out a highly

The Hawker Hurricane IIDs of 6 Squadron were armed with a 40mm cannon under each wing, which gave them the firepower to attack and destroy the tanks and armour of the *Afrika Korps*. The squadron subsequently became known as the 'The Flying Tin Openers.' (Flintham)

successful raid on Japanese aircraft at Mingaloon airfield destroying 16 aircraft. Unfortunately, the enemy quickly responded and both Magwe and Akyab were subjected to heavy bombing attacks which virtually wiped out the RAF presence in Burma. In mid-April, all RAF units were evacuated to India. There was also a mass evacuation of refugees from Magwe, Schwebo and Myitkyina, mounted by the Douglas DC-2s and DC-3 (C-47) Dakotas of 31 Squadron and the 2nd Troop Carrier Squadron USAAF. Between them these units transported 8,600 refugees to India before Myitkyina fell on 8 May. Meanwhile, the Hudsons of 62 Squadron (which had recently been re-numbered from 139 Squadron) carried out two long-range raids on 14 and 18 April, refuelling at Akyab to attack a squadron of Japanese flying boats which had arrived at Port Blair in the Andaman Islands. The long-range flying boats, which posed a direct threat to shipping bound to or from Calcutta, were withdrawn.

After their successful subjugation of Malaya, Singapore and the Dutch East Indies, the Japanese task force, comprising six aircraft carriers, ventured further west into the Indian Ocean. On 4 April they were detected by a Catalina of 413 Squadron, which was able to warn of its approach. Between 5 and 9 April, Japanese aircraft attacked airfields and military installations on the island, including the naval bases at Columbo and Trincomalee. The Japanese raiders were engaged by Hurricanes of 30, 258 and 261 Squadrons as well as Fairey Fulmars from 273 Squadron. On 9 April, a formation of nine Blenheims from 11 Squadron carried out an unescorted attack on the Japanese fleet and although the aircraft managed to straddle the flagship, aircraft carrier *Akagi*, with their bombs, the ship was not hit; five Blenheims were shot down. The Japanese force withdrew and the attack on Ceylon marked the westernmost advance of the Imperial Japanese Navy during the war.

The battered squadrons from Java and Burma were re-equipped in India. The war in the Far East had little significance to the tribes on the northwest frontier and in the summer of 1942, the Blenheims of the reconstituted 34 Squadron were diverted for operations against dissident tribesmen.

MIDDLE EAST

The *Afrika Korps* started an outflanking attack on the 8th Army at Gazala on 27 May 1942. Over the next week, the RAF fought hard over the battlefield. The Western Desert Air Force was composed of two SAAF squadrons equipped with the Boston, 223 Squadron (RAF) with the Martin Baltimore, two SAAF squadrons with the Curtiss P-40 Tomahawk and one SAAF and two RAAF squadrons with the Curtiss P-40 Kittyhawk, 112 and 250 Squadrons (RAF) with the Kittyhawk and 33, 80 and 274 Squadrons (RAF) with Hurricanes. The Boston and Baltimore squadrons bombed German and Italian positions while Hurricanes, Tomahawks and Kittyhawk fighter-bombers were deployed for attacks on enemy transport to the rear of their lines. On 1 June, the Spitfires of 145 Squadron arrived to act as top cover for the fighter-bomber squadrons. Another arrival was 6 Squadron which were equipped with the Hurricane IID, armed with two 40mm cannon intended specifically for attacking enemy armoured vehicles. However, despite the successes of the Western Desert Air Force and a valiant fight by the army at Bir Hakim and Knightsbridge, the armoured might of the *Afrika Korps* managed to break through and by the beginning of July the 8th Army had retreated back to a defensive line at El Alamein. Here, at the first battle of El Alamein, the *Afrika Korps* was halted.

While the 8th Army was fighting in the desert, two badly needed resupply convoys were on passage to Malta. On 10 June, a total of 59 Spitfires were flown to Malta from the deck of HMS *Eagle*. The next day the 'Harpoon' convoy of six merchant vessels and escort ships left the Straits of Gibraltar and on 12 June the 11 merchant vessels making up the convoy 'Vigorous' left Alexandria. Both convoys were subjected to heavy attacks from *Luftwaffe* bombers as they approached Sicily and Crete respectively. Fighter protection for Harpoon was provided by the FAA while that for Vigorous was by Tomahawk and Kittyhawk-equipped squadrons of the Western Desert Air Force. The main threats to both convoys, however, were two Italian naval forces. Vigorous was threatened by a force which included the battleship *Littorio* and the cruiser *Trento*. On 15 June, the Italian warships were attacked at dawn by Beauforts of 217 Squadron, which damaged *Trento*; later attacks carried out by Beauforts of 39 Squadron and also USAAF Liberators operating from Suez damaged *Littorio*. That night, *Littorio* was sunk by torpedo-carrying Wellingtons of 38 Squadron, but in the meantime Vigorous had already turned back to Egypt. By 15 June, Harpoon was being escorted by long-range Beaufighters from Malta, but it was engaged by the second Italian naval group, which sank some of the merchant ships and escorts. An attack on the Italian naval force by two Beauforts and four Albacores from Malta was inconclusive, but it

A Bristol Beaufort II of 39 Squadron over the Mediterranean Sea. The aerials of the air-to-surface vessel (ASV) radar can be seen projecting under the wing. Operating from Malta, Beauforts were successful in sinking a large number of of ships which were loaded with vital supplies for the *Afrika Korps*. (Flintham)

appeared to persuade the Italian warships to disengage from the convoy. Closer to Malta, RAF Spitfires were able to keep enemy aircraft away from the ships and on 16 June the two remaining vessels arrived at Malta.

THOUSAND BOMBER RAID

The planned expansion of Bomber Command had been delayed by the need to provide aircraft to Coastal Command and to the Middle East, but by mid-1942 it was just possible, by using aircraft and crews from the Heavy Conversion Units (HCU), to assemble 1,000 bombers for a single raid. The first 'Thousand Bomber Raid' was against Cologne on the night of 30 May 1942 and was flown by 1,046 aircraft including Wellington, Whitley, Hampden, Stirling, Halifax, Avro Manchester and Lancaster bombers. A third of the aircraft came from training units. The weather conditions were good over the target area and the bomber force completed its attack within a 2-hour time window. Reconnaissance photographs taken the following morning showed that substantial damage had been done to the city and with a loss rate of nearly four percent of the participating aircraft, the operation was deemed to have been successful. Another 'Thousand' raid, this time by 956 aircraft, was ordered against Essen on 1 June, but with cloud cover over the target the results were more scattered. This was also the case with a third raid (the last Thousand Bomber Raid of 1942) by 1,006 aircraft on Bremen on the night of 25 June. However, mounting a 1,000-aircraft raid made large demands on the bomber units and was not yet sustainable. For the rest of the year the almost nightly bomber raids continued but on a much smaller scale.

U-BOATS IN THE BAY OF BISCAY

The geographic position of U-boat bases at Lorient and St Nazaire meant that German U-boats would have to cross the Bay of Biscay in order to reach their operating areas in the Atlantic Ocean. By leaving port at night, they were able to make passage unmolested on the surface. Leaving port in daylight was riskier, but aggressive patrols by Ju88 fighters had given the *Luftwaffe* a degree of air superiority over the bay. However, the campaign against U-boats received a boost in mid-1942 with the introduction of the Leigh Light, which gave aircraft a true 24-hour capability against submarines. The problem facing aircraft on anti-submarine patrols at night in areas such as the Bay of Biscay was that they had no way of knowing if an ASV contact was a U-boat or a fishing vessel. Furthermore, there was a 'dead area' within approximately two miles in which the ASV would lose contact. The answer was for aircraft to home to within two miles of a suspected target and then illuminate it with a powerful searchlight. The first operational use of the equipment was by Wellingtons on 172 Squadron on 4 June 1942, when one of a patrol by four aircraft found and attacked an Italian submarine. Over the rest of the month the five Leigh Light-equipped aircraft found seven U-boats, while Whitleys using conventional tactics in the same area found none. Forcing the U-boats to remain submerged during the early part of their voyage had an immediate impact on their operational capability.

The *Luftwaffe* superiority was also successfully challenged over the Bay of Biscay by 235 and 258 Squadrons, equipped with the Beaufighter, which shot down a number of German aircraft during the summer of 1942.

DIEPPE

An amphibious landing in force by 2nd Canadian Infantry Division took place at Dieppe on 19 August 1942. The RAF committed 41 squadrons of Spitfires, five squadrons of Hurricanes and also 266 and 609 Squadrons equipped with the rocket-firing Hawker Typhoon to provide an 'air umbrella.' Three squadrons of Bostons and Blenheims laid smoke screens to conceal the landings while 88 and 107 Squadrons, equipped

Left: A Wellington Mk VIII of 172 Squadron, the first unit to be equipped with the Leigh Light. The four aerials on the top of the aircraft are the transmitters for the sideways-looking ASV radar; the housing for the Leigh Light is retracted into the belly of the aircraft, under the letter 'A'. (Flintham)

Below: Consolidated B-24D Liberator IIIs of 120 Squadron. The Yagi aerials for the forward-looking ASV radar are clearly visible under the wing. With an operational range of some 2,400 miles (as compared to 1,300 miles for a Sunderland), the Liberator gave Coastal Command a quantum leap in its anti-submarine capability. (RAFM)

with the Boston, carried out attacks on enemy gun emplacements and other defensive positions. These aircraft were supported by cannon-armed Hurricanes. Four squadrons equipped with the North American P-51 Mustang (2, 26, 400 and 414 Squadrons) also attacked ground targets and a force of USAAF Boeing B-17 Flying Fortress bombers attacked the *Luftwaffe* fighter base at Abbeville, putting it out of action for several hours. The RAF maintained air superiority over the battlefield, but at the cost of 106 aircraft lost, for 48 German aircraft destroyed.

CONVOYS

After the Harpoon/Vigorous convoys of June 1942, another attempt to resupply Malta was made when

A Consolidated PBY-5 Catalina flying boat. The type served with nine squadrons in Coastal Command and another 14 based overseas, including Gibraltar, North Africa and the Far East. On 26 May 1941, a Catalina from 209 Squadron on a reconnaissance flight spotted the German battleship *Bismarck* after it had evaded a pursuing force of ships from the Royal Navy.

'Pedestal' sailed two months later. The last ship in the convoy, the tanker *Ohio*, arrived in Malta on 15 August, just as fuel supplies on Malta had become critical. The arrival of more fuel in Malta meant that air operations against Axis shipping and resupply lines could be restarted. On 17 August, a force of six Beauforts of 39 Squadron and nine Beaufighters escorted by eight Spitfires sank the tanker *Rosalino* west of Lampedusa. Over the next 14 days, Beauforts and Beaufighters sank another three tankers which were transporting much-needed fuel to North Africa. As a result, by the end

of August the *Afrika Korps* had only 20 percent of the fuel it needed for sustained operations.

After the disaster of convoy PQ17 in the Barents Sea in early July, it was decided that the next convoy, PQ18, should have more dedicated air cover for protection from German attacks. Nos 144 and 455 Squadrons, equipped with anti-shipping Hampden bombers, and 210 Squadron with nine anti-submarine Catalina flying boats were sent to Russia as the convoy sailed at the beginning of September. The Hampdens operated from Vaenga and the Catalinas from Lake Lakhta, near Arkhangelsk. Four photo-reconnaissance

Spitfires were also dispatched to Russia to monitor the *Tirpitz* during the course of the convoy. After PQ18 arrived at Arkhangelsk on 21 September, all of the remaining aircraft were handed over to the Russians.

The ability to protect convoys against submarines on the western side of the Atlantic was improved by the deployment of 53 Squadron, equipped with the Hudson, to Rhode Island in July 1942. When this task was taken over by the US Navy, the squadron moved further south to Trinidad to counter the U-boat threat in the Caribbean.

THE TURNING POINT

The *Afrika Korps* again attempted to seize the initiative at Alam el Halfa on the night of 30 August. The German troops were bombed by Wellingtons of the Desert Air Force in conjunction with FAA Fairey Albacores which dropped flares over target concentrations so that the Wellingtons could bomb accurately. The following day the Desert Air Force fighters were able to establish air superiority over the battlefield so that not only could Bostons and Baltimores, as well as USAAF North American B-25 Mitchells, attack enemy troops and vehicles, but also air operations by the *Luftwaffe* were severely curtailed. The *Afrika Korps* withdrew from the offensive on 3 September.

The *Luftwaffe* made one last attempt to defeat Malta, starting with heavy bombing raids on 10 October, which continued for ten days. However, these attacks were met by Malta-based Spitfires which gradually took their toll on the German and Italian raiders. During this ordeal, the Malta-based bombers continued to operate every night against Axis shipping.

The second Battle of El Alamein began on 23 October, but in the preceding days, the Desert Air Force had taken advantage of heavy rainfall which had waterlogged the *Luftwaffe* airfields at Fuka and El Daba: these airfields were attacked and some 30 aircraft were destroyed; the supply and servicing infrastructure was also badly damaged. When the battle opened, Spitfires were sent to patrol over *Luftwaffe* airfields. Unlike previous campaigns in which both the quantity and quality of the RAF's aircraft had been suspect, the air forces in Egypt now comprised 96 operational squadrons equipped in the main with modern aircraft. In addition, the establishment of total air superiority over the battlefield enabled the army to keep its intentions hidden from the enemy until the last moment. Even the *Luftwaffe* high-altitude Junkers Ju86P reconnaissance aircraft, capable of flying above 40,000ft, had been forced to withdraw after three of them had been shot down by specially modified Spitfire V fighter aircraft in late August and early September. At night the Wellingtons of 37, 40, 70, 104 and 108 Squadrons were in action against troop concentrations and artillery emplacements, working again in conjunction with Albacores from the FAA. During daylight, the Boston, Baltimore and Mitchell-equipped squadrons kept up continuous pressure on the *Afrika Korps*, until the Germans began to withdraw on 4 November.

IN PURSUIT OF PRECISION

The establishment in August 1942 of a Pathfinder Force (PFF) was an attempt to improve the accuracy of Bomber Command's attacks. The PFF was initially made up from four units which had demonstrated the highest operational effectiveness: 7 Squadron (Stirling), 35 Squadron (Halifax), 83 Squadron (Lancaster) and 156 Squadron (Wellington). During an attack their task was divided into three stages: in the first phase 'finder aircraft' would drop lines of flares in the vicinity of the target area so that under this light the 'illuminator' aircraft, the second phase, would locate the exact target area and drop a concentrated pattern of flares overhead. These flares would enable the 'marker' aircraft in the third phase to drop incendiary bombs accurately onto the target. The resulting large conflagration would then indicate where the main force should drop their bombs. If the ground was obscured by cloud, the target could be 'sky-marked' with further flares. Unfortunately, the new techniques suffered from some teething problems,

Curtiss P-40K Kittyhawk IIIs of 112 Squadron in North Africa. This version of the aircraft was fitted with the 1,600hp Allison V-1710 engine rather than the 1,040hp engine used for the Tomahawk. Eventually, the Kittyhawk equipped five RAF squadrons in the Middle East, as well as one RAAF and five SAAF units in the theatre. (© IWM TR 975)

particularly on the first PFF-marked raid on Flensburg on 18 August 1942, when strong winds blew the markers off the target, but on subsequent raids the levels of accuracy improved.

A number of other techniques were tried in the pursuit of accuracy. A low-level raid was carried out by 94 Lancaster bombers against the Schneider armaments factory at Le Creusot, near Dijon, at dusk on 17 October. Only one aircraft was lost on this mission and all crews reported successful attacks, but later analysis showed that the bombing had not in fact been as accurate as had been claimed: considerable destruction had been caused to French civilian housing outside the factory complex but damage to the factory was light. However, new high-speed aircraft, such as the de Havilland Mosquito, looked like a more promising option for low-level precision operations: four Mosquitoes of 105 Squadron bombed the Gestapo headquarters in Oslo on 25 September. Although four bombs hit the actual building, they passed through it before exploding and devastating houses on the opposite side of the street. While the accuracy of this attack cannot be questioned, it did demonstrate the unsuitability of the weapons used. On 6 December, a

large force of unescorted day bombers comprising 47 Lockheed Venturas of 21, 464 and 487 Squadrons, 36 Bostons of 88, 107 and 226 Squadrons and ten Mosquitoes of 105 and 139 Squadrons attacked the Phillips electronics factory in Eindhoven. In this particular raid, the bombing was very accurate, but the attrition rate of nearly 20 percent of the aircraft involved was unsustainable.

'Rhubarbs' by fighter aircraft continued and the advent of longer-range aircraft meant that fighters could roam further afield. A section of four Mustangs from 268 Squadron were the first Allied single-engined fighters to venture over Germany on 21 October 1942. Flying at low level they attacked industrial targets at Lathen, near Meppen, before shooting up barges on the Dortmund–Ems Canal.

Bomber Command revisited Italy in October, with raids on industrial centres timed to coincide with the offensive at El Alamein. Genoa was attacked by a force of 120 Halifaxes, Stirlings and Wellingtons on the night of 23 October, but cloud in the area resulted in most of the bombs falling 20 miles away near Savona. A daylight raid on Milan the following day by 88 Lancasters was more successful, but of 72

Halifaxes, Stirlings and Wellingtons which followed up that night, only 39 aircraft claimed to have bombed the target and little damage was reported by the Italian authorities.

OPERATION *TORCH*

A largely US force landed in northwest Africa on 8 November, opening a second front on the continent. The RAF participation was limited to a handful of fighter squadrons and four light bomber units, 13, 18, 114, 614 Squadrons, which were equipped with the Bristol Blenheim V. These latter units suffered devastating losses, culminating in an unescorted raid against an airstrip at Chouigui, Tunisia, by 18 Squadron on 4 December during which the entire formation ten aircraft was shot down.

CHANGING FORTUNES

At the close of 1942 the tide seemed to have turned in favour of the Allies: despite the setbacks in the Far East, the victory at El Alamein and the American landings in North Africa pointed towards a brighter future. New aircraft and hard-won combat experience were beginning to make the RAF more effective, too, for despite the expansion of the 1930s, the RAF had entered World War II woefully unprepared and chronically under-equipped. At that time only Fighter Command had had a truly modern aeroplane in the Spitfire, which fortunately was also part of an effective integrated air defence system. Coastal Command had lacked aircraft suitable for role and the overseas Commands had been saddled with obsolete aircraft which, though usable for colonial policing, were wholly inadequate for modern warfare. However, it was Bomber Command, the very embodiment of Trenchard's offensive policy and of the RAF's ability to wage independent war, that had been the least prepared for combat: its aircraft and weapons were totally inadequate for purpose and its crews were poorly trained. Furthermore, while the other Commands quickly – through necessity – adapted to the new situation, often relearning the lessons of the previous World War, Bomber Command seemed reluctant to change its tactics. Three years into the war it was still unable to hit any target consistently and it still seemed to be intent on mounting suicidal operations which achieved little. However, it says much about the quality of RAF personnel that despite these handicaps they did not break under pressure and were able to keep the UK secure against the aggression of Nazi Germany.

Four Supermarine Spitfire VB fighters from 249 Squadron fly over Malta in late 1942. The fighter squadrons on the island fought a ferocious battle with both the Italian Air Force and the *Luftwaffe*. But when Spitfires were delivered they were able to tip the balance of power in their favour. (Flintham)

CHAPTER 4

THE ROAD TO VICTORY

1943-1945

At the beginning of 1943 the RAF was engaged in four major theatres of operations: the Far East, the Middle East, the Atlantic and Europe. Newer aeroplanes, including many US-built types were replacing the obsolescent and generally unsuitable aircraft with which RAF crews had been equipped during the first years of the war. Modernization was coupled to a massive expansion of the service, including flying training schools which provided a growing stream of well-trained aircrews. In the Middle East, the corner had been turned and victory seemed at last to be a distant possibility; the balance of operational fortune would shortly swing in favour of the Allies in the other theatres, too.

NORTH AFRICA

In Egypt, the 8th Army finally broke out from El Alamein in November 1942 and the *Afrika Korps* retreated rapidly back towards Tunisia. Unfortunately, despite having air superiority over the area, the Desert Air Force was unable to capitalize on the German withdrawal and the *Afrika Korps* was able to regroup in defensive positions at the Mareth Line. From mid-March until the final surrender of Axis forces in North Africa the aircraft of the Western Desert Air Force worked closely with land forces. Boston and Maryland bombers carried out softening-up attacks on the enemy frontline and on communications and transport in the rear echelons; meanwhile Kittyhawks and Hurricanes sought out artillery and armour. Spitfires ensured that Allied aircraft

Pilots brief for a sortie in front of a rocket-armed Hawker Typhoon Mk IB at a forward operating base in Northern France during the summer of 1944. Fitted with a 60lb warhead, the 3-inch RP-3 Rocket Projectile (RP) carried by the Typhoon was very effective against German armour. (Getty/PNA Rota)

Above: The ubiquitous Vickers Wellington provided the RAF in the Middle East with a long-range bombing capability. Aircraft from 37 Squadron take off from Shallufa in the Canal Zone. (Flintham)

Right: Ground operations over long ranges in the inhospitable terrain and difficult climate of Burma were only possible thanks to air transport. The workhorse of the RAF transport squadrons in the Far East was the Douglas C-47 (DC-3) Dakota, here in service with 31 Squadron. (Flintham)

enjoyed air superiority over the region and the medium bombers also systematically attacked the enemy-held airfields in northeastern Tunisia. The Axis forces were also cut off from their supply lines by Beauforts, Beaufighters and Wellingtons operating from Malta against shipping convoys, as well as Wellingtons which bombed the Tunisian ports. In April, the *Luftwaffe* attempted to carry out resupply and evacuation by air, but between 5 and 22 April over 400 *Luftwaffe* transport aircraft, including Junkers Ju52 and six-engined Messerschmitt 323 transports were shot down by allied fighters. A total of 24 Junkers Ju52 aircraft were accounted for on 10 April and on 18 April a total of 53 Ju52 transports were shot down. The remaining Axis forces in Tunisia capitulated on 13 May.

ARAKAN

The monsoon season of the second half of 1942 precluded any further action over Burma, but it also gave the RAF squadrons in India breathing space to re-arm. Small-scale Japanese night-time bombing raids on Calcutta in December 1942 caused a disproportionate panic in the city, but the introduction of four radar-equipped Beaufighter night fighters soon restored the balance; this unit expanded to become 176 Squadron. An army offensive into the Arakan region started on 27 December 1942. The Bristol Blenheim V of 11, 42 and 113 Squadrons, the Blenheims of 60 Squadron and the Vultee Vengeances of 110 Squadron, escorted and supplemented by Hurricanes from 67, 79, 135, 136, 146 and 607 Squadrons attacked targets ahead of the ground troops to clear their way. In February 1943, the offensive was expanded to include the first expedition by the 'Chindits' (Long Range Penetration Groups). During their Operation *Longcloth*, the Chindits were supplied by air by the Douglas DC2s and DC-3 Dakotas of 31 Squadron. These aircraft were also involved in the Allied airlift to supply Chinese Nationalist forces, flying over the eastern Himalayas (the 'Hump'). The 31 Squadron aircraft carried out weekly flights to China from

Vultee Vengeance dive bombers of 84 Squadron. Equipping four RAF and two Indian Air Force (IAF) squadrons, the Vengeance was ideally suited to ground-attack operations over Burma. (RAFM)

A Boeing B-17 Fortress IIA of 220 Squadron flies past the Hebrides in May 1943. Some 200 of these aircraft were operated by Coastal Command, mounting anti-submarine patrols into the mid-Atlantic from Chivenor, Benbecula, Iceland and the Azores. (RAF Official Photographer/ IWM/Getty)

Dinjan, where they were protected by the Curtiss Mohawks of 5 Squadron. Operation *Longcloth* ended in April and the Arakan offensive ended in a withdrawal by British and Indian forces in May 1943, before the start of the next monsoon season.

Although ground operations were curtailed by the monsoon, limited air operations continued and in particular the garrison at Fort Hertz, which was behind enemy lines in northeastern Burma, was kept resupplied by air.

The summer monsoon season in the Far East provided an opportunity for the RAF units in the theatre to re-equip with more modern aircraft. In particular, the Spitfires of 81, 136, 152, 607 and 615 Squadrons enabled the RAF to take the initiative in the air and establish air superiority over the Japanese air force. The Blenheims of 11, 34, 42, 60 and 113 Squadrons were replaced by Hurricane fighter-bombers, which were far more suitable for close air support of troops than the previous type. The Vengeance dive bombers of 45, 82, 84 and

110 Squadrons and Beaufighters of 27 and 177 Squadrons also swiftly proved their effectiveness against Japanese lines of communication in the rear areas. Perhaps the most important development in a theatre where movement over long distances was hampered by steep terrain and thick jungle was the expansion of the transport fleet: Dakotas of 62, 194 and later 117 Squadrons joined those of 31 Squadron, making large-scale air movement of troops and supplies a reality. During the course of 1943 the weekly task of an air transport squadron had increased sevenfold.

U-BOATS & COASTAL SHIPPING

The campaign against U-boats in the Atlantic and the Bay of Biscay intensified through the first half of 1943. The Bay of Biscay became a battleground between Coastal Command's aircraft and German submarines and aircraft. Equipped with the more capable ASV III and IV radars, Sunderlands, Catalinas, Whitleys, Wellingtons and Hampdens were successful in forcing U-boats to remain submerged during daylight. These patrols were particularly effective because they were focussed on the routes known to be used by U-boats while transiting from their bases in northern France. At night, the patrols were continued by Leigh Light-equipped Wellingtons of 172 Squadron (later joined by 407 and 612 Squadrons). In March 1943, a total of 52 U-boats were detected in the Bay of Biscay and just over 50 percent were attacked, with one confirmed kill; the following month aircraft found almost 100 submarines and attacked 64, sinking seven. The *Luftwaffe* contested the air over the Bay of Biscay with Ju88 and Focke-Wulf Fw190 fighters, but these were countered by fighter sweeps by Beaufighters of 143, 248 and 235 Squadrons.

By May 1943 there were five squadrons of Very Long Range (VLR) Liberators (53, 59, 86, 120 and 224 Squadrons) which were able to cover the convoy routes in the mid-Atlantic, while closer to land the convoys were escorted by Sunderland, Catalina, Halifax and Fortress aircraft. The response from Admiral Dönitz was to order the U-boats to operate using *Rudeltaktik* (pack attack by animals) tactics known as 'Wolfpacks' and to attack at night when the air cover had departed, for the longer-range aircraft still had no night capability. Even so, the combined efforts of the convoy escort and anti-submarine aircraft working together was taking a relentless toll on the U-boat force. A total of 41 U-boats were sunk in the month of May 1943, which is often regarded as the turning point in the 'Battle of the Atlantic.'

Anti-submarine aircraft also operated from Gibraltar: Hudsons of 48 and 223 Squadrons and Catalinas of 292 Squadron carried out daylight patrols while the Leigh Light-equipped Wellingtons of 179 Squadron operated at night. These aircraft could cover the eastern Atlantic from the Iberian coast and also the western Mediterranean.

The Consolidated B-24 Liberator was one of the most important aircraft to be operated by the RAF during World War II. In the role of the Very Long Range (VLR) aircraft, the Liberator enabled the RAF to close the 'Mid-Atlantic Gap' in air cover for convoys, thus playing a vital role in the winning of the Battle of the Atlantic. This example is a Liberator GR V with an ASV radar mounted in a ventral housing. (RAFM)

By early 1943, the Avro Lancaster was equipping an increasing number of squadrons within the Bomber Command heavy bomber force. This is a Lancaster B I operated by 50 Squadron which was based at Swinderby, Lincolnshire in 1942. (Hulton Archive/Getty)

Almost from the start of the war, aircraft from both Coastal and Bomber Commands had routinely attacked German shipping off the coasts of northern Europe and Norway. However, the Hudsons, Hampdens and Blenheims were particularly unsuitable for such operations and in the three years between April 1940 and March 1943, 107 ships had been sunk at a cost of 648 aircraft lost. In contrast in the same period, dropping of mines in coastal areas, which was seen at Command-level as being a low-priority task, accounted for 369 ships, for 329 aircraft lost. The introduction of the high performance Beaufighter offered a more effective aeroplane with which to carry out anti-shipping strikes and a Strike Wing of three Beaufighter squadrons (143, 236 and 254 Squadrons) was established at North Coates in late

1942. The Wing's first operation in November 1942 did not go well, but after further training another operation was mounted on 18 April 1943. This operation by 21 Beaufighters escorted by Spitfires and North American P-51 Mustangs was successful and marked the start of sustained Beaufighter anti-shipping operations.

THE BOMBING CAMPAIGN

Just as effective anti-shipping operations became a reality with the introduction of the Beaufighter in Coastal Command, so the arrival of the de Havilland Mosquito in Bomber Command had enabled the RAF to carry out precision bombing attacks. On 27 January 1943, a force of nine Mosquitoes from 105 and 139 Squadrons took part in a low-level daylight raid on the Burmeister and Wain submarine engine factory in Copenhagen. This was followed three days later by two raids, each by three aircraft from the same squadrons, on Berlin. These latter attacks successfully disrupted the celebrations of the tenth anniversary of the Nazis' rise to power. A third similar raid was carried out by ten Mosquitoes of 139 Squadron against the molybdenum mine at Knaben in Norway. Over the next few months these two squadrons carried out daylight attacks on railway marshalling yards at Nantes, Tours and Trier. A less successful raid was an attack on the power station at Amsterdam on 3 May 1943 in which all 11 of the attacking force of Lockheed Venturas from 487 Squadron RNZAF were shot down.

At the Casablanca conference in January 1943, the RAF was charged with the general destruction of German industry by night, while the bombers of the 8th Air Force (USAAF) concentrated on more specific industrial targets. By then Bomber Command had expanded to over 50 squadrons, 35 of which were equipped with 'heavy' types such as Stirling, Halifax and Lancaster bombers, many of which were equipped with the Gee navigation system. Another radio-based precision navigation system, 'Oboe', which was fitted to the Mosquitoes of 105 Squadron, enabled the PFF to perfect its techniques for target marking. Later both 109 and 139 Squadrons were also equipped with Oboe and transferred into the PFF. A campaign against the industrial area of the Ruhr valley, using the new target marking techniques, started with an attack on Essen on 5 March. The initial markers, comprising eight Oboe-equipped Mosquitoes, dropped yellow Target Indicator (TI) flares at 15 miles to run to the target and red markers on the aiming point in the centre of the Krupp industrial complex in Essen; they were followed by 22 'backers up' which dropped green TIs as well as

The high performance of the Mosquito B IV gave Bomber Command the capability to attack targets with greater accuracy than could be achieved by a heavy bomber or the previous generation of medium bomber aircraft. (Popperfoto/Getty)

incendiaries onto the red markers. Three waves, each made up of a different bomber type, then followed: firstly Halifaxes, then a mix of Stirlings and Wellingtons and then finally, Lancasters. In all, 367 aircraft attacked the target with encouraging results. Essen was bombed the following week and again on 3 and 30 April. Similar attacks were carried out on other industrial cities in the Ruhr area: Duisburg was bombed five times, including large attacks on 26 April and 12 May, Düsseldorf was bombed on 25 May and 11 June and Wuppertal on 29 May.

Amongst these area attacks, in a remarkable feat of airmanship, 19 Lancasters of 617 Squadron carried out a night time low-level precision attack on three dams in the Ruhr valley on 16 May. Two of the dams were breached, but the critical Sorpe dam was undamaged and eight of the aircraft were lost; however, perhaps the most important legacy of the raid was the concept pioneered by Wg Cdr G.P. Gibson DSO* DFC* of a 'Master Bomber' controlling each individual attack by VHF radio to ensure its accuracy. Ten days later another remarkable daylight raid was carried out by 14 Mosquitoes of 105 and 139 Squadrons which successfully bombed the Carl Zeiss optical systems factory at Jena near Leipzig.

SICILY, ITALY & THE BALKANS

In the last days of the North African campaign, Allied aircraft had already started softening up targets in Sicily and Italy. USAAF bombers and the Wellingtons of 37, 40, 70, 104, 142 and 150 Squadrons bombed industrial targets around Naples and Bari as well as airfields in Sicily, Sardinia and southern Italy and the lines of communication around Palermo and Catania. The garrison at Pantelleria Island was subjected to a short but effective bombardment between 7 and 11 June and both Pantelleria and Lampedusa were taken by Allied forces on 12 June. Meanwhile Airspeed Horsa and US-built Waco Hadrian gliders had been towed from UK to North Africa by Halifaxes and Armstrong-Whitworth Albermarles of 295 and 296 Squadrons. These were used on the evening of 10 July to land airborne troops on Sicily prior to the main seaborne invasion the following day. Seven Halifaxes of 295 Squadron and 27 Albermarles of 295 and 296 Squadrons were involved in the operation. Meanwhile Wellingtons bombed targets near Syracuse, Caltagirone and Catania and the Hurricanes of 73 Squadron attacked enemy searchlight units. The main landings were covered by Spitfires during the day and Beaufighters of 108 Squadron at night time, while night intruder Mosquitoes of 23 Squadron operated against German and Italian airfields. On 13 July, the Spitfires of 1 (SAAF), 92, 145, 417 (RCAF) and 601 Squadrons started to operate from a forward base at Comiso and that evening Albermarles and Halifaxes

Trolleys loaded with 250lb bombs are prepared for loading into a Douglas Boston of 88 Squadron. The type served with four bomber squadrons in Bomber Command as well as three night intruder squadrons and a further four bomber squadrons with the Desert Air Force in Italy. (Fox Photos/Hulton Archive/Getty)

towed 17 gliders to assault the bridge at Primosole near Catania. Throughout the campaign in Sicily, the Wellingtons assigned to the Northwest African Strategic Air Force bombed targets in Italy including railway marshalling yards at Salerno, Naples and Foggia, while the torpedo-armed Wellingtons of 36 Squadron, operating in loose formations of three aircraft, patrolled the seas each night, hunting for Axis shipping. The attentions of these aircraft, as well as Beauforts and Beaufighters operating from Malta had effectively shut down German and Italian coastal shipping in the region. Bomber Command aircraft also carried out raids against Milan, Genoa and Turin during the first 14 days of August. The Germans evacuated Sicily on 17 August 1943. Following the fall of Sicily, Mussolini was overthrown and the Italians negotiated an armistice, which was announced on 8 September. At dawn the following day, Allied troops landed at Salerno. The landings were covered by Allied aircraft including Spitfires based in Sicily; over the

next few days the *Luftwaffe* attempted to intervene, but Allied aircraft had established air superiority over the landings and 221 German aircraft were shot down. The *Luftwaffe* was subsequently limited to operating at night time. Allied bombers continued operations against the transport infrastructure in the rear areas and fighter-bombers sought targets of opportunity immediately behind the frontlines.

The surrender of Italian forces left a vacuum in the Greek islands garrisoned by Italian troops and both British and German forces moved to seize possession. The Germans were able to secure Rhodes quickly, but the Special Boat Service (SBS) landed on Kos on 13 September and paratroops were dropped on the island by Dakotas of 216 Squadron the following day. The *Luftwaffe* in the Aegean and Balkans was strongly reinforced over the next week. Kos was attacked by German aircraft on 17 September, but the raiders were met by stiff resistance from by 2901 and 2909 Squadrons of the RAF Regiment, which had deployed

A Liberator of 108 Squadron delivering supplies to partisan forces in Yugoslavia. Such missions, involving low-level drops in mountainous terrain, were extremely hazardous.

from Palestine to provide air defence of the island. Meanwhile, German airfields around Athens were attacked by Liberator, Halifax, Wellington and Hudson bombers. Unfortunately, Kos did not remain in British hands for long: the Germans successfully captured the island on 3 October 1943.

Allied troops had taken much of southern Italy and by 1 October Naples was in Allied hands and the Germans had evacuated Sardinia. During the advance from the Salerno beachhead, a system for close air support of troops known as 'Rover David' had been established. This technique involved a radio-equipped Forward Air Controller (FAC) directing fighter-bombers, waiting in a 'cab rank' above the battlefield, onto targets close to friendly forces on the frontline. By the autumn the frontlines had become static, with the Germans established on the defensive Gustav Line, which ran from roughly 30 miles north of Naples on the west coast to roughly 30 miles south of Pescara on the east coast.

Liberators of 108 Squadron had started dropping supplies to partisans in Yugoslavia in May 1942. Their work had been taken up by 148 Squadron, which had been formed for special duties with Liberators and Halifaxes. With Allied aircraft now able to operate from southern Italy more direct support of the partisans was possible and on 24 October, Kittyhawks from 112, 250, 260 and 450 (RAAF) Squadrons attacked German ships landing troops near Dubrovnik. Aircraft from the Mediterranean Allied Tactical and Coastal Air Forces (MATAF and MACAF) were also tasked against shipping, storage facilities, radio stations, oil storage, bridges and gun emplacements along the Adriatic coast.

THE BOMBING CAMPAIGN CONTINUES

Bomber Command's strategic aim was modified slightly in mid-1943 to destroy the German aircraft industry rather than general industry, so the targets were chosen from amongst those

Spitfire VC and IX aircraft of 232 Squadron at an advanced landing ground at Serratelle near Salerno in October 1943; these aircraft had covered the amphibious landings at Salerno the previous month.
(Fg Off L.H. Abbott/ IWM/Getty)

A Vickers Warwick I of 269 Squadron carrying a lifeboat under the fuselage. Some 350 of these aircraft, which was originally designed as a replacement for the Wellington, were used instead for Air Sea Rescue (ASR) operations. (Flintham)

cities which contained factories associated with the manufacture of aircraft parts. On 20 June, 60 Lancasters, including those from 9, 50, 97, 408 and 467 Squadrons, attacked the Zeppelin factory at Friedrichshafen, using the Master Bomber technique. After the attack, the aircraft continued to Blida, Algeria. Three days later they flew back to the UK, bombing the Italian naval base at La Spezia on the return leg. Raids against industrial cities in the Ruhr continued, but a series of attacks

on Hamburg commenced on 24 July. The city was out of range of the Gee and Oboe networks, but its location near the coast on the River Elbe meant that it could be located easily using the new H2S mapping radars which were fitted to many of the bombers. Hamburg was visited on the nights of 24, 27 and 29 July by a force of about 740 aircraft which delivered around 2,400 tons of bombs on each occasion. These raids were the first to use 'Window,' made up of strips of aluminium foil, to

A Bristol Beaufighter X of 455 Squadron fires a salvo of RP-3 Rocket Projectiles. The Strike Wings in Coastal Command were very effective against German coastal shipping by using a mixture of torpedo and rocket-armed aircraft. (Pitchfork)

disrupt German air defence radars. USAAF bombers also attacked during the daylight hours of 25 July and the final raid was made by a smaller force of Lancasters on the night of 2 July. Although massive damage was done to the urban areas, industrial production was restored relatively quickly.

Nightly attacks continued through the next months, including bombing the research station at Peenemünde on 17 August and further raids on Berlin, Mannheim, Hanover, Kassel and Düsseldorf. An attack on Düsseldorf on 3 November was the operational debut of another electronic navigation aid, 'G-H,' which incorporated a transponder on the aircraft. Other electronic equipment was also used to help to protect the bomber crews: these included the Bolton-Paul Defiants of 515 Squadron

using 'Moonshine,' and later 'Mandrel' to confuse and jam German early warning radars. Meanwhile, the Beaufighters (and later, Mosquitoes) of 141 Squadron equipped with 'Serrate,' which homed onto air-intercept radar signals, accompanied the bomber stream and operated against *Luftwaffe* night fighters.

COASTAL COMMAND

The pressure on U-boats both in the Bay of Biscay and the Atlantic continued through the second half of 1943. A second Leigh Light-equipped Wellington squadron, 304 Squadron, increased Coastal Command's night anti-submarine capability over

A High Speed Launch (HSL) Type 3; a total of 69 were built and used by the Air Sea Rescue service from late 1942. Powered by three 500hp Napier Sea Lion petrol engines, the 68ft vessel was capable of up to 28kt. (Charles E. Brown/RAF Museum/Getty)

the Bay of Biscay. During August a total of 56 U-boats were sunk by combined naval and air forces in the Atlantic and in October, 20 U-boats which were operating within range of aircraft based in Iceland were sunk in a 14-day period.

In north European coastal waters the anti-shipping Strike Wing at North Coates was proving to be very effective. A typical strike would comprise 12 torpedo-armed Beaufighters escorted by 16 defence suppression Beaufighters, armed with Rocket Projectiles (RPs) and cannon. A second wing was formed at Leuchars in early 1944 with 455 (RAF) and 489 (RNZAF) Squadron Beaufighters.

The PRU continued with its reconnaissance of enemy-held Europe: camera-equipped Spitfires flying at 42,000ft ranged as far as Gdinya, Berlin, Vienna, Budapest and Belgrade, sometimes landing in Italy or North Africa to refuel before returning to base. Coastal Command's Air Sea Rescue force had also expanded to include Supermarine Walrus flying boats

(of 276, 277, 278, 281 and 282 Squadrons) as well as Hudsons (of 279 and 280 Squadrons) equipped with air-droppable lifeboats. Another vital task carried out by Coastal Command was that of meteorological ('Met') reconnaissance. Initially these were carried out by independent Met Flights, but by late 1943 the units had been expanded to squadron strength: 517, 518, 519, 520 and 520 Squadrons operated Halifaxes and Fortresses flying daily Met sorties into the Atlantic to obtain observations of winds and temperatures. On occasions, during the course of their observations the aircraft were also involved in combat against both enemy aircraft and submarines.

By January 1944, U-boats had abandoned operations as large packs and had instead opted to act individually or in small groups. Most of their activity took place at night time off the west coasts of Ireland and Scotland, so Leigh Light patrols were switched from the Bay of Biscay to this area. However, a continuous 24-hour patrol line was set up blocking

A Leigh Light mounted under the wing of a Liberator GR VI of 224 Squadron. In early 1944, the unit was based at Milltown, on the Moray Firth, Scotland to counter U-boats operating from bases in Denmark and Norway. (Pitchfork)

access into the English Channel from the west so that U-boats could not interfere with the forthcoming landings in Normandy.

PREPARATIONS FOR D-DAY

A bombing campaign against Berlin started on 18 November 1943. On that night 402 aircraft attacked the city and over the next four months 16 major raids were mounted against Berlin. The heaviest of these was on 15 February 1944, when 561 Lancasters, 314 Halifaxes and 16 Mosquitoes delivered over 2,600 tons of bombs, but they did so at a significant loss rate of over 6 percent. Well beyond the range of Gee, Oboe and G-H, Berlin was also difficult to detect using H2S radar. Navigators were therefore forced to rely on the technique of dead reckoning, but aircraft such as Lancasters, with much better performance than their predecessors, flew at altitudes that were affected by jet stream winds, phenomena which were little understood at the time. As a result of these factors, navigation during the 'Battle of Berlin' was challenging

and bombing accuracy suffered accordingly. On the last raid which took place on 24 March the markers were blown off the target area by the winds and very little damage was done by the 811 aircraft which were tasked for the mission. The loss rate of heavy bombers at this time was typically about 4 percent, but on some missions, it was much higher: the 44 Lancasters and 34 Halifaxes shot down on the raid on Leipzig on 19 February represented over 9 percent of the 823 attacking aircraft.

On the night of 8 February 1944, a force of 12 Lancasters from 617 Squadron bombed the Gnome et Rhône aircraft engine factory at Limoges. With no target defences and with the benefit of bright moonlight, the formation leader, Wg Cdr G.L. Cheshire DSO** DFC was able to mark the target exactly from low level and the subsequent attack was extremely accurate. A number of daylight precision raids were also carried out by Mosquitoes in early 1944. On 18 February, the wall at Amiens prison was breached by Mosquitoes from 21, 464 (RAAF) and 487 (RNZAF) Squadrons which were escorted by Typhoons of 174 and 198 Squadrons and on 11 March the Gestapo headquarters

A Supermarine Walrus II amphibian picks up a pilot from his dinghy. Seven squadrons operated this type in the ASR role and many aircrew owed their lives to the bravery of the Walrus crews. (Keystone/Getty)

A Hawker Typhoon
Mk 1B of 175 Squadron
being loaded with 250lb
bombs in preparation
for a mission over
northern France.
Using a combination
of cannon, bombs and
rockets, the Typhoon
squadrons of the 2nd
Tactical Air Force
attacked German
armour, vehicles and
trains in the run-up to
D-Day; subsequently
the type provided
close air support for
Allied troops during the
Normandy campaign.
(Fox Photos/Getty)

building in The Hague was bombed by six Mosquitoes from 613 Squadron.

From March, Bomber Command's heavy bombers were included in the 'Transportation Plan,' which involved the destruction of the transport infrastructure in northern France so that the German army would find it difficult to redeploy or reinforce when Allied forces landed in France later in the year. Targets included the marshalling yards at Trappes, in the western suburbs of Paris, which was bombed by on 6 March, and these missions incurred significantly fewer losses than raids on Germany. Nevertheless, large-scale raids continued against German cities. Stuttgart was attacked on 1 and 15 March, Frankfurt on 18 and 22 March, Essen on 26 March and Nuremberg on 30 March. On this last raid, about 120 of the 795-strong attack force mistakenly bombed Schweinfurt some 50 miles away and there was minimal damage to Nuremberg itself.

In May, as part of the 'Transportation Plan,' bridges in northern France were also targeted, but the lessons of previous operations against bridges had been learnt: a careful analysis of these operations indicated that rocket-firing Typhoons and bomb-dropping Spitfires were best suited against these targets. The Typhoons and Spitfires also targeted railway locomotives and rolling stock and, along with the heavy bombers, they also began attacks in early May on German coastal radar installations and naval fire control sites. In order not to give away the location of the beaches selected for amphibious landings, two 'out of area' targets were attacked for every target that was in the invasion area. On 2 June 1944, Typhoons of 198 and 609 Squadrons attacked targets near Dieppe, followed by a night attack by heavy bombers in the same area. Two days later Spitfires of 441, 442 and 443 (RCAF) Squadrons bombed Cap d'Antifer and the heavy bombers attacked sites near Cherbourg; on 5 June, Typhoons of 174, 175 and 245 Squadrons attacked Cap de la Hague.

ADEN

The Gulf of Aden, at the mouth of the Red Sea, was a choke point for shipping transiting to and from the Suez Canal. In 1944, the Wellingtons of 8 and 621 Squadrons provided anti-submarine cover for shipping sailing through the region. However, the issues of pre-war colonial policing never fully disappeared and in early 1944, the colonial government in Aden

A rare image of a Hawker Hurricane IIB of 258 Squadron over Arakan, Burma in 1943. During the battles of Imphal and Kohima, Hurricane squadrons operated from airstrips within the Imphal perimeter to provide close air support to the ground forces.

was faced with a famine in the Wadi Hadramaut. Six Wellingtons flew food supplies to the airstrip at Al Qatn on 29 April, starting a month-long airlift to deliver over eight tons of milk and 400 tons of grain into the Hadramaut. During this operation, the anti-submarine patrols continued and on 2 May a Wellington from 621 Squadron located the U-boat U-852 off the coast of Somalia. The submarine was then neutralized by depth-charge attacks by aircraft from both squadrons.

RETURN TO ARAKAN

In late 1943 and early 1944, the RAF swiftly established air superiority over northeast India, Burma and the Bay of Bengal. A force of 12 Japanese aircraft which attempted to attack shipping off the Arakan coast were shot down by Spitfires of 136 Squadron on 31 December 1943. On 4 February 1944,

XV Corps commenced the second offensive into the Arakan. Many of the front-line troops were supplied by Dakotas from 62 Squadron, whose aircraft each flew three sorties a day. Wellingtons bombed enemy airfields at night and, along with Liberators of 160 Squadron, they also attacked railway marshalling yards as far away as Bangkok and Moulmein.

After reaching Maungdaw, the XV Corps advance was halted by a Japanese counterattack and by 10 February the British, Indian and African troops found themselves surrounded by the Japanese army. The Japanese were held off by troops in the administrative echelon of 7th (Indian) Division, in a defensive position known as the 'Admin Box.' Completely cut off by Japanese forces, the Admin Box was resupplied by RAF Dakotas and USAAF Curtiss C-46 Commandos, which were able to operate freely thanks to the RAF's command of the air over Burma. In the period between 8 February and 6 March 1944, 2,000 tons of supplies were delivered to troops in the

A Handley Page Halifax II Series I Special in the Middle East. This version of the aircraft had the original high-drag nose turret replaced with a fairing. The type was used in the Mediterranean and Balkans both as a heavy bomber (shown) and also as a special duties aircraft; in the latter role the type was used in support of the Special Operations Executive (SOE). (Flintham)

Admin Box. Meanwhile Vengeances and Hurricanes continued their attacks on Japanese positions. The siege was broken on 22 February and the Arakan offensive continued for a short while before being curtailed so that the forces at Imphal and Kohima could be supported.

A second Chindit expedition, Operation *Thursday*, commenced on the night of 5 March 1944 when a force of over 9,000 troops was transported by air into jungle landing strips behind Japanese lines by Dakotas of 31, 62, 117, and 194 Squadrons. Over the next four months, these troops were supplied entirely by RAF Dakotas, and the C-46 Commando and Douglas C-47 Skytrain transports of the USAAF Air Commando. Many casualties were evacuated from the jungle by light aircraft, but Sunderlands of 230 Squadron also flew evacuation missions from Lake Indawgyi in northern Burma.

A major Japanese offensive had also started in early March 1944. Japanese forces crossed the River

Chindwin and began to advance into India on 8 March, but they were stopped at Imphal and Kohima. However, in halting the Japanese advance, the British and Dominion forces at Imphal found themselves cut off from their usual resupply and reinforcement routes and for 80 days Imphal was kept supplied by air. The 5th (Indian) Division was also air-lifted from Arakan to the central front to the north of Imphal by Dakotas of 194 Squadron and C-46 Commandos of the USAAF. A total of 11 Hurricane-equipped squadrons and four Vengeance-equipped squadrons, initially operating from six airstrips within the Imphal perimeter, flew close air support missions against Japanese forces. Further north, Hurricanes flew some 2,200 sorties in support of the defenders of Kohima between 4 and 20 April and over the same period Vengeance dive bombers also provided direct support as well as attacking Japanese encampments and supply dumps. The Spitfires

A Bristol Beaufighter X of 217 Squadron, operating over the Bay of Bengal from Ratmalana, Ceylon in the summer of 1944. During the previous year, RAF Beaufighters carried out a successful long-range interdiction campaign against the Japanese lines of communication in Burma. (Pitchfork)

of 81, 136, 152, 607 and 615 Squadrons ensured that the Imperial Japanese Air Force could not intervene in the battle. Meanwhile Beaufighters and Hurricanes interdicted and interrupted the Japanese supply lines. Intense fighting, some of it at close quarters, continued at Kohima and Imphal through the next months into June.

ITALY

A second amphibious landing was carried out to the north of the Gustav Line at Anzio on 22 January in an attempt to outflank the German positions, but the forces there were unable to break out from the beachheads until late May, by which time the Germans had already withdrawn northwards. Throughout the early months of 1944 RAF Spitfires and Kittyhawk fighter-bombers, Boston and Maryland medium bombers and Wellington and Liberator heavy bombers had attacked the Italian road and railway infrastructure, as well as carrying out close air support for ground troops and maintaining air supremacy over the battlefield. Rome was liberated on 4 June.

Operating from southern Italy on the night of 8 April 1944, three Liberators and 19 Wellingtons dropped 40 mines into the River Danube near Belgrade. This raid was the first raid in a seven-month campaign by the Wellingtons of 37, 40, 70, 104, 142 and 150 Squadrons with the Liberators and Halifaxes of 178 and 614 Squadrons to

A Martin Baltimore IV of 69 Squadron over Malta. The type was used by the RAF exclusively in the Middle East and Mediterranean theatre, where it was an important part of the light bomber force of the Desert Air Force. (Flintham)

A formation of North American B-25 Mitchell II light bombers from 180 Squadron. The unit attacked the headquarters of Panzer Gruppe West on 10 June 1944. Over 800 Mitchells were delivered to the RAF and after D-Day, those of the 2nd TAF continued to support the Alllied advance through the Low Countries and into Germany. (Popperfoto/Getty)

disrupt barge traffic on the River Danube. Under flares dropped by the Halifaxes and Liberators, the Wellingtons dropped 354 mines during the following month. Eventually the river would be virtually closed to traffic, particularly the vital coal and oil transporting barges, thanks to nearly 1,400 mines dropped by Wellingtons and also to night anti-shipping sorties by Beaufighters of 255 Squadron.

At the beginning of June, the Balkan Air Force was formed, which eventually would include the Spitfires of 32, 73 and 253 Squadrons, Hurricanes of 6 Squadron, North America P-51 Mustangs of 213 and 249 Squadrons, Beaufighters of 39 and 108 Squadrons along with Greek and Yugoslav RAF squadrons, three SAAF squadrons and Italian Co-Belligerant Air Force. The main thrust of these forces was to interdict the railway lines between

Zagreb, Belgrade and Skopje and RAF Spitfires and Mustangs accounted for 262 locomotives in the first month of operations.

D-DAY

On the night of 5 June 1944, some 14 Albermarles from 295 and 570 Squadrons dropped the lead elements of 3rd Parachute Brigade into Normandy; the rest of the brigade followed a short time later in 108 Dakotas provided by 48, 233, 271, 512 and 575 Squadrons. Additionally, six Horsa gliders towed by Halifaxes from 298 and 644 Squadrons delivered two companies of the 2nd Oxford & Buckinghamshire Light Infantry onto a crucial bridge across the Caen Canal. Another 129 aircraft carried 5th Parachute Brigade to its drop zones in Normandy. Overnight, 16 Lancasters of 617 Squadron dropping 'Window' radar jamming material simulated the movement of a large naval armada crossing the English Channel towards Cap d'Antifer and the Stirlings of 218 Squadron performed a similar diversionary task towards Boulogne. Dummy paratroops as well as pyrotechnics designed to simulate small arms fire were dropped by Halifaxes and Stirlings of 138, 149 and 161 Squadrons into northwest France.

The main landings early the following morning were preceded by a barrage by over 1,000 heavy bombers against the German coastal batteries. Massed fighter squadrons ensured Allied air supremacy over the beaches and Mustangs of 2 Squadron carried out fire direction for naval guns. Fighter-bombers were also on call for close air support if necessary. In the evening a force of 256 gliders, closely escorted by 15 squadrons of Spitfires carried supplies to the airborne forces.

The weather was poor over the next four days, but 19 squadrons of Typhoons carried out armed reconnaissance beyond the beachhead area, targeting German motor transport and armoured vehicles. By night the heavy bombers of Bomber Command and the USAAF attacked the railway infrastructure in northern France, while Mosquitoes carried out night intruder operations against road and rail traffic. An airstrip was established at Asnelles on 7 June and was initially used for refuelling and re-arming, but within a few days it became a permanent base for a Canadian Spitfire Wing. On 10 June, a force of 40 Typhoons from 181, 182, 245 and 247 Squadrons plus 61 North American B-25 Mitchells from 98, 180, 226 and 320 (RNLAF) Squadrons carried out a successful attack on the headquarters of the German *Panzergruppe* West.

Throughout the landings, Coastal Command was able to keep German naval forces away from the Allied fleet and the Beaufighters of 144 and 404 Squadrons with the Mosquitoes of 248 Squadron drove off three German destroyers in the Brest area. Additionally, 25 U-boats were attacked between 7 and 11 June. On 15 June, the combined North Coates and Langham strike wings carried out a successful anti-shipping strike off the Dutch coast. Unfortunately, as the year progressed, U-boats were becoming more difficult to detect with the introduction to some submarines of the Schnorkel device which enabled them to remain submerged for longer; but throughout July 1944, a total of 45 were attacked and during the same period seven major anti-shipping strikes were also carried out.

Although originally designed as a bomber, the Armstrong-Whitworth Albermarle was successfully used as a glider tug. The type was used during the airborne assaults on Sicily, Normandy and Arnhem. This aircraft was used by 511 Squadron in the transport role. (Flintham)

Douglas C-47 (DC-3) Dakotas of 267 Squadron were deployed to evacuate over 1,000 partisan casualties from Yugoslavia in August 1944. Some 2,000 of the type were supplied to the RAF and saw operational service in Europe, the Middle East and the Far East. (Flintham)

Interspersed with their night activities, Bomber Command aircraft also carried out daylight raids, starting on 14 June when 221 Lancasters and 21 Mosquitoes bombed Le Havre. A similar-sized force attacked Boulogne the following day. Thereafter, the preparation and launch sites for the Fieseler Fi 103 ('V-1') flying bomb and Mittelwerk Aggregat A4 ('V-2') ballistic missile in northern France were attacked on an almost daily basis. The V-1 had made its debut on 13 June and the first line of defence against these weapons was the Tempests of 3, 56 and 486 Squadrons; Mosquitoes, Spitfires, and from July the Gloster Meteors of 616 Squadron, were also successful against the V-1. The V-1 attacks against southern England continued until September 1944 when the launch sites were overrun by Allied forces.

On 30 June 258 RAF bombers attacked a road junction at Villers Bocage, escorted by nine squadrons of Spitfires, marking the beginning of heavy bomber operations in the Caen area. Oboe equipment was fitted to some Lancasters from early July, enabling the heavy bomber force to drop bombs with reasonable accuracy through cloud. The technique was first used on 11 July against the V-1 site at Gapennes, near Abbeville. RAF aircraft attacked Caen itself on 7 and 18 July. Although the main operational focus for Bomber Command had been in northern France during June and July, small-scale raids on German cities had continued throughout the period; on 23 July, a raid on Kiel by 629 Lancasters, Halifaxes and Mosquitoes was the first large-scale attack on Germany for two months.

During July and August 1944, a number of daylight low-level precision attacks were carried out by Mosquitoes. On 14 July, Mosquitoes from 21, 464 and 487 Squadrons escorted by 12 Mustangs from 65 Squadron bombed the SS barracks in the Chateau de Marieville at Bonneuil-Matours in support of Special Forces operations in that area. The attack was followed up with a further raid on 2 August by Mosquitoes of

107 Squadron on the same SS unit which was now housed in the nearby Château du Fou. On the same day, nine Mosquitoes from 305 Squadron bombed a German sabotage training school at Château Maulny near Angers. Three days previously five Mosquitoes from 613 Squadron had bombed the Château de Trévarez which was being used as a recreation centre for U-boat crews after patrols. On 18 August, 14 Mosquitoes from 613 Squadron bombed a German headquarters in Égletons near Poitiers and on the last day of the month six Mosquitoes from 305 Squadron destroyed a large petrol storage at Nomeny near Nancy.

Although German armour was very effective against Allied tanks, it was also extremely vulnerable to air attack. A counterattack by German tanks on 7 August was defeated by rocket-armed Typhoons which flew nearly 300 sorties that afternoon. The main German withdrawal from the Falaise pocket turned into a massacre of similar proportions to that of the Wadi Fara in 1918. A force of 32 Typhoons from 164, 183, 198 and 609 Squadrons wrought havoc on the German tanks as they attempted to break out near Chambois on 20 August.

A second front opened in France on 15 August with landings by Allied troops in the south of France between Cannes and Saint Tropez. Just as in northern France, the mainly US amphibious operations were supported by tactical air power, including nine squadrons of RAF Spitfires.

KOHIMA & IMPHAL

While the Allied armies in northern France attempted to break out from Normandy, the 14th Army sought to fight its way out of India. On 5 June 1944, the Aradura Spur, three miles south of Kohima, was captured from the Japanese, marking the beginning of the breakout from Kohima. Allied troops from Kohima and Imphal joined up on 22 June and the advance continued, supported by the Hurricane and Vultee Vengeance-equipped squadrons, forcing the Japanese back into Burma. Nearly all supplies had to be flown to the front-line

units and as the monsoon broke the Dakotas of 31, 52, 62, 117, 194, 353, 435 (RCAF), 436 (RCAF) and 357 Squadrons, plus the eight US squadrons of the Combat Cargo Task Force found themselves delivering stores in torrential rain under a 200ft cloud-base. The pressure was maintained on the Japanese rear areas by Beaufighters of 177 and 211 Squadrons which attacked ports and boat traffic on the River Chindwin as well as railway rolling stock. They also ranged as far as the Tenasserim coast in southern Burma, seeking out coastal shipping. Wellingtons also laid mines in the waterways. In a novel role for the aircraft, Hurricanes were also used to spray DDT pesticide to counter insect-borne disease in the vicinity of Tamu in the Kabaw Valley.

Tiddim was recaptured on 19 October, followed a week later by a Japanese strongpoint known as Vital Corner. This latter action had been preceded by a heavy barrage which included artillery and bombing by four Hurricane squadrons. The Liberators of 99, 159, 215, 355 and 356 Squadrons were also used on occasions for 'earthquake' operations to bomb pinpoint targets such as bunkers, often after a flight of nearly 1,000 miles; however, they more usually concentrated their efforts against the railway system deeper in Burma.

In the Far East, the work of the photo-reconnaissance squadrons, 681 Squadron flying Spitfires and 684 Squadron flying Mosquitoes, proved to be even more vital than it was in Europe. The quality of maps of Burma was generally poor, so the photographic survey carried out by the two RAF squadrons and their USAAF counterparts became the main source of accurate mapping.

ITALY & THE BALKANS

Despite the Allied air supremacy over Italy, the German army fought strongly on the ground and was able to conduct an orderly fighting retreat northwards. Over the summer months, Allied tactical aircraft were flying 1,000 sorties a day against lines of communication and the road and railway infrastructure in northern Italy. Operations were mounted into Central Europe from the Italian bases, too, including missions against the oil installations at Ploiești, which were attacked by RAF Halifaxes, Liberators and Wellingtons on the night of 9 August. In the week before that raid, however, Halifaxes from 148 Squadrons and 1586 (Polish Special Duties) Flight had flown long-range missions to Warsaw to drop supplies to Polish forces engaged in the Warsaw Uprising. These units were joined by 614 Squadron (Halifax) and 34 SAAF squadrons equipped with the Liberator: 31 of these had been redeployed from southern France. The Liberators of 178 Squadron also replaced the Halifaxes of 614 Squadron in early September. The first mission to Warsaw was flown on the night of 4 August and the last, by SAAF Liberators, on the night of 21 September; these sorties involved large aircraft flying a low speed and low altitude over a heavily defended area, so losses were high: 31 aircraft were lost from 181 aircraft despatched, including 15 of the 16 crews of 1586 Flight.

The Balkan Air Force continued its work over Yugoslavia, as did the Halifaxes and Liberators of 148 and 614 Special Duties Squadrons, which between them dropped a considerable quantity of arms and supplies to partisan forces. Support to partisans included the evacuation of over 1,000 casualties from Yugoslavia on 23 August: the first sortie was flown by six Dakotas of 267 Squadron, escorted by 18 Mustangs and Spitfires.

The Allied advance through Italy continued northwest until August 1944, when the frontline stabilized along the Gothic Line, running between Pisa and Rimini. On the night of 25 August, Halifaxes and Liberators marked and illuminated railway marshalling yards and canal dock areas near Ravenna, for a force of Wellingtons and by day Baltimores and Bostons flew armed reconnaissance sorties looking for targets of opportunity in the same area. A month later the offensive restarted and Kittyhawks and Spitfires flew close air support missions against gun and mortar positions as well as fortified strongpoints as the army

fought around Rimini. Rimini itself fell three days later, but there was no further breakthrough and the front stagnated along the Gothic Line.

Axis shipping had largely been driven from the Adriatic Sea during 1944 thanks to the attentions of the coastal air force. Marauders of 14 Squadron carried out coastal reconnaissance to locate targets for anti-shipping Beaufighters of 272 Squadron with notable success. The most spectacular achievement of this combination of forces was the sinking of the Italian liner *Rex* on 8 September to prevent it being used to blockade Trieste harbour.

DEFEATING THE U-BOATS

In September 1944, all U-boats based in France, regardless of their preparedness for operations, put to sea to escape Allied forces and to establish new bases in Norway. Between 11 and 26 September, five U-boats were sunk by Liberators of 206, 220, 224 and 423 (RCAF) Squadrons in a sea area stretching from the Azores to the Norwegian coast. As German forces in Norway became ever more reliant on ship-borne supplies, the work of the strike wings at Banff (comprising 143, 235 and 248 Squadrons operating Mosquitoes), Dallachy (comprising the Beaufighter-equipped 144, 404 (RCAF), 455 (RAAF) and 489 Squadrons) and North Coates (Beaufighters of 236 and 254 Squadrons) took on greater strategic importance. Between them, the three wings were effective in restricting shipping off the Norwegian, Danish and German coasts. The Halifaxes of 58 and 502 Squadrons carried out the same role at night.

Limited by the longer distance to the Atlantic Ocean, but equipped with Schnorkel devices, which enabled them to stay submerged and thus be harder to detect, U-boats started to operate in waters much closer to the UK: for example, U-boats were found in the Irish Sea and Bristol Channel, as well as in the northwest and southwest approaches. The number of Wellington Leigh Light squadrons was increased with the transfer of 14 and 36 Squadrons from the Mediterranean. Two US Navy

Liberator squadrons and a Ventura squadron also bolstered the anti-submarine force. In early 1945 Sonobuoys were introduced into service with ten Liberator squadrons, giving them a better chance of locating submerged U-boats.

ARNHEM

In mid-September, the German forces had withdrawn into the Netherlands and later that month a daring attempt was made to push across the natural barriers of the Maas and Rhine rivers, by dropping airborne forces ahead of the main armoured advance to secure bridgeheads. On 17 September 1944 paratroopers of the 1st Airborne Division were delivered to their drop zones near Arnhem by Dakotas of 48, 233, 271, 437 (RCAF), 512 and 575 Squadrons. On the same day, Albermarles of 296 and 297 Squadrons, Stirlings of 190, 196, 295, 299, 570 and 625 Squadrons and Halifaxes of 298 and 644 Squadrons towed a fleet of 320 Horsa gliders as well as 15 heavy-lift General Aircraft Hamilcar gliders to the assault landing grounds. A second 'lift' of troops and equipment in 296 Horsas and a further 15 Hamilcars was carried out the next day. Over the next few days the transport aircraft attempted to keep the airborne troops re-supplied by air, but the area was heavily defended by the German army: a number of transport aircraft were shot down and only a small proportion of the supplies dropped could be retrieved by the British troops. However, RAF Spitfires and Tempests were able to keep *Luftwaffe* aircraft away both from Arnhem and the bridgehead established by 82nd and 101st Airborne Division (US Army) at Nijmegen.

GREECE

By mid-October 1944, the Germans had been driven out of Belgrade and most of the Greek islands were being retaken but strong German garrisons remained in Corfu and in northwest Greece. Night intruder missions by Allied aircraft against airfields around Athens restricted the *Luftwaffe's* freedom of movement in the theatre. During the first week of October the tactical squadrons of the Balkan Air Force concentrated on close air support missions in southern Albania, before resuming the offensive against the railway network. Meanwhile the Wellingtons and Liberators ranged further afield to attack marshalling yards as far away as Linz and Vienna. Unfortunately, by the time that Athens was liberated, the beginnings of a civil war in Greece were already simmering. Violence broke out between the Greek factions soon after British troops arrived in early December 1944 and RAF aircraft were called in to attack positions held by communist ELAS guerrillas. The Spitfires of 73 and 94 Squadrons were used for strafing and bombing, supplemented by rocket-armed Beaufighters from 39 and 108 Squadrons. The situation was stabilized, albeit temporarily, by the end of the month.

THE BOMBING CAMPAIGN CONTINUES

Most of the German naval forces were now concentrated in Norway, including the battleship *Tirpitz*. Berthed in Kåfjord, *Tirpitz* was beyond the range even of Lancasters based in the UK, but in early September aircraft of 9 and 617 Squadrons deployed to the Russian airfield at Yagodnik, near Arkhangelsk, to put them within reach of the ship. On 15 September, 27 Lancasters armed with a mixture of 12,000lb 'Tallboy' bombs and sea mines attacked the *Tirpitz* from Yagodnik. Weapon aiming was difficult because of a very effective smoke screen obscuring the battleship, but sufficient damage was caused for her to be moved to a new berth near Tromsø.

While Allied ground forces advanced across the Netherlands, German forces, including strong shore batteries, on the island of Walcheren on the Scheldt estuary blocked Allied access to the port facilities at Antwerp. Since Walcheren was a polder, lying below sea level, it was decided to flood the island and then mount an amphibious assault to

capture it. On 3 October, Oboe-equipped Mosquitoes marked positions on the sea dykes for 252 Lancasters to bomb. A breach was created and the island began to flood; a follow-up operation by 121 Lancasters four days later widened the breach and on 11 and 12 October large formations of Lancasters bombed the gun emplacements at Breskens, on the southern bank of the Scheldt, as well as gun positions on Walcheren itself, near Flushing. A further breach of the dyke near Westkappelle was made by Lancasters on 17 October. During this period, medium bombers also attacked targets on the island. The amphibious assault was carried out in appalling weather on 1 November, supported by Typhoons. The first Typhoon unit in action over the beachhead was 183 Squadron.

By this stage of the war, thanks to electronic navigation aids, target marking and 'Master Bomber' techniques, Bomber Command was capable of hitting a city-sized target with reasonable accuracy. After the Allied advance through the Low Countries, the RAF's heavy bomber force was switched from bombing tactical targets in support of the land forces back to a strategic campaign against German oil production. The loss of radar stations in Belgium and the Netherlands robbed the German defences of early warning of raids, making daylight missions less vulnerable, so RAF bombers could operate by both day and night. In mid-October, a series of large-scale bombing raids against Duisburg was intended to demonstrate the Allies' overwhelming air superiority. At dawn on 14 October 1944, a force of 957 Lancasters, Halifaxes and Mosquitoes with a fighter escort dropped nearly 3,600 tons of explosives on Duisburg. The attack was followed later in the day by 1,250 USAAF bombers escorted by 749 fighters which bombed targets near Cologne. That night diversionary attacks, including one by 233 Lancasters against Brunswick as well as attacks by Mosquitoes on Hamburg, Berlin and Mannheim, were carried out while the main force of 498 Lancasters, 468 Halifaxes and 39 Mosquitoes revisited Duisburg. Thus, over 2,000 RAF bombers had visited Duisburg in a single day. During the month there were further large raids against Stuttgart (on 19 October), Essen (on 23 and 25 October) and Cologne (on 28 and 30 October).

As well as large-scale attacks by heavy bombers, a number of low-level precision attacks against high value German targets were carried out by Mosquitoes and Typhoons. These included the bombing of a German army headquarters building in Dordrecht on 24 October by Typhoons of 193, 197, 257, 263 and 266 Squadrons. Five days later, and despite poor weather, 24 Mosquitoes from 21, 464 and 487 Squadrons, escorted by eight Mustangs from 315 (Polish) Squadron successfully attacked the Gestapo headquarters building at Aarhus, Denmark. Unfortunately, an attempt by 12 Mosquitoes from 627 Squadron to bomb the Gestapo headquarters in Oslo on 31 December was not a success.

At her new mooring near Tromsø, the *Tirpitz* was now within range of Lancasters operating from the UK. On 12 November 1944, a force of Lancasters from 9 and 617 Squadrons, all carrying 12,000lb 'Tallboys' took off from Lossiemouth to bomb the ship. This attack was a complete success and after sustaining two direct hits, the *Tirpitz* capsized.

BURMA

On 2 January 1945, aerial reconnaissance indicated that the Japanese had pulled back from Akyab Island and the island was recaptured the following day. Nine days later an amphibious assault was launched from Akyab against Myebon on the mainland. A force of 28 Japanese Nakajima Ki-43 (Oscar) and seven Nakajima Ki-84 (Frank) fighter-bombers attempted to intervene, but they were beaten off by Spitfires of 67 Squadron, which shot down five 'Oscars.' Hurricanes laid smoke screens to shield the landings, which were also supported by Republic P-47 Thunderbolts of 134 Squadron and USAAF B-25 Mitchell bombers. As the troops of 3 Commando Brigade pushed towards Kangaw, the Thunderbolts of 5, 123, 135 and 258 Squadrons flew 'cab rank' close air support missions. On 21 January, the island of Ramree was also captured, with support from Liberators and Thunderbolts.

Meanwhile, the 14th Army advanced into central Burma; the army was reliant on air supply for the

A very rare image of a Republic P-47 Thunderbolt II of 60 Squadron over Burma. A total of 830 Thunderbolts saw service with the RAF in Burma, where the aircraft were used for the close air support of ground forces. (Flintham)

operation by the Combat Cargo Task Force and when USAAF C-47 Skytrains were re-allocated to move Chinese troops back to China, two more RAF Dakota squadrons, 238 and 267 Squadrons, were dispatched to Burma. The army advance was two-pronged: the main thrust by 33 Corps was to Mandalay while 4 Corps carried out an outflanking manoeuvre to the west towards the River Irrawaddy at Bagan and thence to Meiktila. Throughout the campaign, Thunderbolts provided close air support. Beaufighters continued to interdict railways and waterways and Liberators attacked supply dumps, including one near Rangoon on 11 February. All of these aircraft were also available for 'earthquake' missions to lay down a barrage or to attack bunkers and strongpoints. Spitfires ensured that Japanese aircraft stayed clear of the battlefield and that Japanese reconnaissance aircraft were unable to detect 4 Corps' movement.

The Irrawaddy was crossed at Singu near Bagan on 13 February 1945 after an 'earthquake' bombing attack on 8 February which included the Thunderbolts of 79, 146 and 261 Squadrons. Thabuktan airfield near Meiktila was taken on 16 February, enabling Dakotas to fly in reinforcements directly from Imphal. The main airfield at Meiktila

was also recaptured shortly afterwards. During February 60,000 tons of supplies were also flown into Meiktila by Dakotas. The Japanese counterattacked and the RAF Regt units on the airfield, 2708 Field Squadron RAF Regt supplemented by flights from 2941 and 2968 Field Squadrons and 2963 Light Anti-Aircraft Squadron RAF Regt, fought an aggressive action to defend it.

Further to the east, Japanese aircraft based at Pyinmana, 150 miles south of Mandalay, began to attack 33 Corps positions and on 12 February the Thunderbolts of 123, 134, 258 and 261 Squadrons carried out strafing attacks against the airfields. The following day British and Indian troops started to cross the Irrawaddy at Myinmu, about 30 miles west of Mandalay. A week later Hurricanes from 20 Squadron were patrolling the jungle near Myinmu, when they found some suspicious buildings. It transpired that these were 12 camouflaged Japanese tanks, which were attacked and destroyed. The battles raged around Meiktila and Mandalay over the next month. Mandalay fell on 20 March, after Thunderbolts of 79 and 261 Squadrons and Hurricanes of 42 Squadron bombed the walls of Fort Dufferin, the old Burmese royal palace, which had walls 45ft thick.

While 4 Corps advanced along the road from Meiktila towards Rangoon from the north, a combined airborne and amphibious assault was prepared to take Rangoon from the south. On 1 May 1945 the Thunderbolts of 5, 30 and 258 Squadrons softened up Japanese gun positions, while airborne troops were delivered to Elephant Point by USAAF C-47 Skytrains. The landing the following day was supported by Thunderbolts of 30, 134, 146 and 258 Squadrons, but it proved to be unopposed as the Japanese had withdrawn to Moulmein. Rangoon was recaptured on 3 May.

BOMBING ITALY & GERMANY

With operations in northwest Europe understandably taking priority for resources, Allied armies in northern Italy were unable to launch an offensive against the Gustav line over the winter. Instead Allied aircraft conducted an interdiction campaign against the lines of communication to the north of the Gustav Line with the intention of cutting off the German army from its supply network. Links to the Brenner Pass were frequently cut, the marshalling yards at Verona were bombed and the entire rail network in north-east Italy was subject to intense attacks. Coastal shipping was also targeted and on 21 March 1945 a force of over 100 fighter bombers, comprising the Kittyhawks of 250 and 450 (RAAF) Squadrons with the Mustangs of 3 (RAAF), 5 (SAAF), 112, and 260 Squadrons carried out a very accurate and highly destructive bombing raid on the docks and railway facilities at Venice. Much damage was caused to the target area, but the cultural centre of the old city remained unscathed.

On 9 April, after an intense bombardment by a force of nearly 1,000 heavy and medium bombers in the vicinity of Lugo, the army pushed forward with support from tactical aircraft and crossed the River Senio. That night the Liberators of 37,

Personnel of 2963 Light Anti-Aircraft (LAA) Squadron RAF Regiment man a 20mm Hispano anti-aircraft gun at Meiktila. Apart from providing air defence to the airstrip, the squadron gunners joined the other RAF Regiment personnel to defend the airfield against aggressive attacks by Japanese infantry. (Pitchfork)

40, 70 and 104 Squadrons continued to bomb German positions, which were marked from the ground by coloured artillery shells, and Lugo was captured the following day. The advance then continued, reaching Verona, Spezia and Parma on 25 April and Turin on 30 April. The German forces surrendered on 24 April and a ceasefire was enforced from 2 May.

The strategic bombing campaign against German oil production and lines of communication continued into early 1945, but in mid-February it was thought that a series of powerfully destructive raids might be enough to paralyse the German administration and bring about early capitulation. The target chosen for the first raid was the city of Dresden, a cultural centre with little industry. The initial raid, which was to have been carried out by the USAAF on 13 February 1945, was cancelled because of the weather in the target area. However, the weather improved that evening and two waves, comprising 244 Lancasters and 9 Mosquitoes in the first and 529 Lancasters in the second, bombed Dresden that night. The following day USAAF bombers attacked the railway marshalling yards. Although the attack on Dresden was indeed powerfully destructive, the raid on Chemnitz the next night, during which most aircraft completely missed the city, was an indication of the inherent inconsistency of large-scale bomber attacks against even relatively large-sized targets.

However, smaller, well-equipped specialist forces could achieve spectacularly accurate results. On 14 March, 28 Lancasters from 9 and 617 Squadrons attacked the Schildescher Viaduct, an important railway bridge near Bielefeld. Most aircraft carried 12,000lb 'Tallboy' bombs, but one of the 617 Squadron aircraft was armed with a much larger 22,000lb 'Grand Slam' bomb. The concentration of heavy bombs successfully dropped a number of spans of the viaduct. Seven days later 18 Mosquitoes from 21, 464 and 487 Squadrons, accompanied by an escort of 28 Mustangs from 64, 126 and 234 Squadrons carried out a successful low-level attack on the Gestapo headquarters in the Shellhuis in Copenhagen. Six Mosquitoes drawn from the same units carried out another attack on a Gestapo headquarters in Denmark, this time in Odense, on 17 April. On this mission, the Mosquitoes were escorted by eight Mustangs from 129 Squadron.

On 18 April 1945 Bomber Command revisited Heligoland, nearly five years after the disastrous raids of the first days of the war. On this occasion 943 Lancaster, Halifax and Mosquito bombers dropped nearly 5,000 tons on the island, for the loss of just three Halifaxes.

THE END IN EUROPE

After the abortive attempt to cross the River Rhine at Arnhem in September 1944, another crossing was forced at Wesel on 23 March 1945. In the days leading up to the operation Typhoons carried out armed reconnaissance sorties in the area, attacking military targets including the destruction of a German airborne forces supply depot on 21 March. Spitfires and Tempests also flew fighter sweeps to draw *Luftwaffe* fighters into battle and on 22 March a formation of 32 Tempests shot down five of 12 FW190 fighters which attempted to intervene. On the day of the crossing, Wesel was bombarded by a force of 77 Lancasters, while a further 212 Lancasters carried out a second attack on Wesel that night. The crossing of the river was also preceded by airborne landings to establish a bridgehead on the eastern side of the river: Albermarles, Halifaxes and Stirlings delivered 440 gliders to the landing zone. All the army operations were supported by Typhoons flying 'cab rank' close air support sorties. Over the next few days the bridgehead was consolidated and expanded under the air cover of the Spitfire and Tempest squadrons, which shot down 12 FW190 aircraft on 24 March.

On the night of 7 April, 47 Stirlings dropped two French battalions of the Special Air Service (SAS) near Groningen. In the battle to capture Groningen, these forces were supported by Typhoons, which also

Curtiss P-40 Kittyhawk IV fighter-bombers of 450 Squadron RAAF armed with 250lb bombs. These aircraft carried out a precision bombing raid on the dock facilities near Venice on 21 March 1945. (Pitchfork)

dropped ammunition and supplies to the troops on 8 and 12 April.

Allied forces advanced steadily across northern Germany, closely supported by the tactical air force; the British army's line of advance was towards Bremen, Hamburg and Lübeck, reaching the River Elbe in late April. At this point *Luftwaffe* aircraft, operating at short range from their remaining bases, attempted to fight back, but they were overwhelmed by Allied fighters.

During March and April, Liberators of 206 and 547 Squadrons had attempted to intercept U-boats working up in the Baltic Sea, but they had no success. However, in order to reach the operational bases in

Norway, the U-boats had to negotiate the narrows of the Kattegat and Skagerrak. The Banff strike wing sank four U-boats in the Skagerrak in April and between 2 and 7 May, a further 14 U-boats were sunk in the Kattegat including five by the North Coates strike Wing, and seven by Liberators of 86, 206, 224, 311 (Czech) and 547 Squadrons.

In one of the last attacks by Bomber Command, 359 Lancasters and 16 Mosquitos attacked *Wolfschanze*, Hitler's mountain retreat at Berchtesgaden, on 25 April. Soon afterwards, Bomber Command suspended offensive operations. Instead, between 29 April and 8 May, Lancasters and Mosquitoes dropped 6,685 tons of food and

In late 1944, 501 Squadron, equipped with the Hawker Tempest V, was deployed to RAF Manston for 'Anti-Diver' patrols to intercept German V-1 'Doodlebug' flying bombs. The fastest of the RAF front-line fighters of the day, Tempests accounted for over 600 V1s. (Charles E. Brown/ RAFM/Getty)

A Liberator B VI of 354 Squadron over the Bay of Bengal. The last bombing mission of the war was carried out by Liberators of 99 and 356 Squadrons operating from the Cocos Islands on 7 August 1945. (Pitchfork)

supplies to Dutch civilians suffering from food shortages in the German-occupied parts of the Netherlands. In a similar timeframe, heavy bombers and transport aircraft commenced Operation *Exodus*, the repatriation of Allied prisoners of war. In May alone, some 72,000 were flown from Europe to the UK.

Germany surrendered on 8 May 1945. The RAF units in Germany remained there, forming the British Air Forces of Occupation (BAFO) to ensure peace and to oversee the dismantling of the *Luftwaffe*.

THE END IN BURMA

The Liberator squadrons in the Far East carried out strategic operations at extremely long ranges: it was not unusual for aircraft to fly over one thousand miles to their targets. One of the longest such missions was mounted on 5 June 1945 when seven Liberators attacked the railway yards at Surasdhani

on the Bangkok–Singapore railway in the far south of Thailand. The flight of 2,400 miles through monsoon weather lasted 17 hours. In another long-range mission ten days later, Liberators from 99, 159 and 356 attacked and sank a large oil tanker which had been located by a Sunderland in the Bay of Siam.

After the fall of Mandalay and Rangoon a sizeable Japanese army was trapped in the Pegu Yomas mountain range in eastern Burma, between the Irrawaddy and Sittang rivers. On 3 July 1945, the Japanese attempted to break out across the Sittang River, but their plans had been compromised and British forces were ready for them. Despite a cloud base of only 1,000ft, Thunderbolts and Spitfires carried out 'cab rank' close support for the army, attacking enemy troop concentrations and rivercraft. On 4 July Thunderbolts from 42 Squadron neutralized three Japanese field guns. Further to the south near Moulmein, Spitfires of 273 and 607 Squadrons, as well as Mosquitoes, operated in concert with Force 136, a Special Forces unit working with local resistance fighters. They killed around 500 Japanese troops near Hpa-An on 1 July and repeated the success a 14 days later. The battle of the Sittang Bend lasted until 29 July, during which time the Thunderbolts and Spitfires attacked the enemy almost continuously. The Japanese lost more than 10,000 men killed. Although the Japanese surrendered on 14 August, operations continued in Burma until 20 July when Thunderbolts of 42 Squadron attacked Japanese troops who had not surrendered.

IMMEDIATELY POST WAR

With the end of the war in Japan, operations commenced to rescue and repatriate Allied prisoners of war and internees. The Dakotas of 31 Squadron operated initially from Seletar, but soon moved to Kemajoran (Jakarta) in Java, where they joined the Thunderbolts of 60 and 81 Squadrons as well as Spitfires of 28 Squadron and Mosquitoes of 110 Squadron. Having rid themselves of the Japanese, the Indonesians were loath to restore the colonial Dutch government and an independent state was declared, which was hostile to both British and Dutch interests. The Thunderbolts, Spitfires and Mosquitoes attempted to maintain the safety of the Dakotas and also covered the evacuation of Dutch civilians. In Vietnam, there was a similar reluctance to welcome the old colonial master and the Spitfires of 273 Squadron were required to carry out large-formation 'shows of force' to deter aggression by the Viet Minh forces until the French retook control of the country.

In six years of war the RAF had expanded to a peak of 500 operational squadrons and had fought simultaneous campaigns over three continents and two oceans. The service had overcome its shortcomings in the early years of the war and it had evolved into an extremely effective fighting force.

A Spitfire FR XIV of 273 Squadron. At the end of World War II, the unit was based at Tan Son Nhut, Vietnam in support of efforts to maintain law and order during the transition from Japanese occupation to the resumption of French colonial rule. (Flintham)

CHAPTER 5

LAST DAYS OF EMPIRE

1946-1959

From its peak strength of over one million personnel at the end of World War II, the RAF was reduced to one-third of that size by the end of the following year. At the beginning of 1946, the operations in Southeast Asia were winding down and for much of the service there was little activity as personnel numbers were drawn down by the 'de-mob' process and as squadrons were reduced in strength or disbanded completely.

In continental Europe in January 1946, the some 60 squadrons on the strength of the Second Tactical Air Force, six months earlier, had been reduced to the still-sizeable force of 30 combat squadrons making up the British Air Forces of Occupation (BAFO). These units included RCAF and RAAF squadrons, as well as Belgian and Polish squadrons. The Canadian and Australian squadrons disbanded in early 1946, swiftly followed by the return of the Polish units to the UK and the transfer of the Belgian squadrons to the new Belgian Air Force. By mid-1946 BAFO comprised just 12 squadrons, which operated from five former *Luftwaffe* bases: there were three light bomber units at Wahn (14, 69, and 98 Squadrons equipped with the Mosquito B16) and three more at Gütersloh (4, 21 and 107 Squadrons equipped with the Mosquito FB6), a photo-reconnaissance unit at Celle (2 Squadron flying the Spitfire PR19) and five fighter squadrons flying Hawker Tempest 5s (3 and 80 Squadrons at Wunsdorf and 16, 26 and 33 Squadrons at Fassberg). Although it was ostensibly a force of occupation, BAFO was also at the frontline of the approaching Cold War and its squadrons were kept busy by routine exercises

Short Sunderland MR 5 flying boats of 230 Squadron being unloaded on the River Havel during the Berlin Airlift. After wartime service in the Far East, the squadron was moved to Calshot, near Southampton before the aircraft were detached to Finkenwerde, near Hamburg on the River Elbe, for the operation. (Ullstein Bild/Getty)

as well as the occasional show-of-force flypast for the benefit of the German civilians. BAFO was also responsible for supporting British interests in Austria and Trieste and during 1947 there were frequent detachments of BAFO aircraft to Zeltweg in Austria.

The home commands had suffered similar reductions in front-line squadrons as the RAF contracted after the war. However, at least the introduction of jet aircraft into Fighter Command's inventory brought an improvement in capability. The year 1946 saw the formation of wings equipped with jet-powered fighters: the Bentwaters (56, 74 and 245 Squadrons) and Boxted (222, 234, 263 Squadrons) Wings were both equipped with the Gloster Meteor F3, while the Odiham Wing (comprising 54, 72 and 247 Squadrons) flew the new de Havilland Vampire F1.

An Avro York of 242 Squadron during the Berlin Airlift. Built utilizing the same wings, undercarriage and engines as the Lancaster bomber, the York could carry a payload of 20,000lb or 24 passengers. (RAFM)

THE BERLIN AIRLIFT

At the end of World War II, Berlin, like the rest of Germany, was administered by the four Allied Powers; UK, USA, France and the USSR. However,

the city lay in the middle of the Soviet-occupied zone of Germany, so three land routes and three air corridors were established to give the Western Allies access to the city. In the spring of 1948, the Soviets started to restrict travel to and from West Berlin, culminating in a total blockade of surface routes on 24 June. Over the next three days the RAF prepared Operation *Knicker*, a contingency plan to supply the Berlin garrison by air. A force of 13 Dakotas from 53 and 77 Squadrons, which were normally based at RAF Waterbeach near Cambridge, were re-positioned to Wunsdorf, near Hanover. The Dakotas started operations early in the morning of 28 July and over the next 24 hours they carried 44 tons of food into Gatow in the British Sector of Berlin. The USAF also started resupply operations to their sector of Berlin on that day. However, it was soon apparent that the scope of the airlift would have to be expanded beyond the needs of the respective garrisons and Operation *Carter Paterson*, later renamed Operation *Plainfare*, began. Six further Dakota-equipped squadrons (18, 24, 27, 30, 46, and 62 Squadrons) joined the force

at Wunsdorf and the nine Avro York squadrons (24, 40, 51, 59, 99, 206, 242, 246 and 511 Squadrons) also started flying to Berlin on 3 July. The airlift was augmented by the Sunderlands of 201 and 230 Squadrons, which flew from Finkenwerder on the River Elbe near Hamburg to the River Havel in Berlin; since the flying boats were protected from salt water corrosion, they could be used to supply the city with salt.

In mid-July, it was calculated that the daily needs of food and coal in Berlin amounted to 3,234 tons per day, but at that stage the airlift could provide only 1,950 tons, leaving a daily shortfall of over 1,000 tons. Civil air contractors were also called in and the operation was consolidated with the larger

aircraft, such as the Avro York and USAF Douglas C-54 Skymaster, operating from Wunsdorf into Gatow, and the smaller Dakotas from Fassberg into Tempelhof, in the US Sector of Berlin. The Dakotas soon moved again to Lübeck to make space at Fassberg for more USAF Skymasters.

RAF transport crews flew an intensive four-day schedule, typically comprising three days of flying three or four round-trips to Berlin each day, followed by one day off. Routing to and from Berlin was via the three air corridors which had been established at the end of the war. USAF aircraft operating from Wiesbaden and Rhein/Main used the southern corridor to fly to Berlin, while the RAF aircraft (and USAF C-54s operating from

Douglas C-47 (DC-3) Dakota transports at RAF Gatow during the Berlin Airlift. The eight Dakota-equipped squadrons flew an almost continuous shuttle service, initially between Wuntsdorf and Gatow, then later between Celle and Tegel. (Getty/Keystone)

Fassberg) used the northern corridor. All aircraft then used the central corridor to return to West Germany. The aircraft – all of which had widely differing performance – were de-conflicted from each other within the corridors by altitude and by timing. For crews flying from Wunsdorf and Celle, the flight time to Berlin was approximately one hour, and they were given a time to be over the radio beacon at Frohnau. If an aircraft did not reach the beacon within 30 seconds of its allotted time, it had to return to its base without landing; similarly, if for some reason the aircraft could not land from its approach, it also had to return immediately to its base of origin. Once on the ground in Berlin, each crew was allowed 15min to unload their cargo and take off for the return flight.

From November 1948, a third airfield became available at Tegel, in the French sector, which was used initially by RAF Dakotas. By this time, the whole RAF, USAF and civil efforts were integrated into the Combined Airlift Task Force. The availability of a third runway, plus the arrival in service of larger aircraft, such as the Handley Page Hastings which had just entered service with 47 and 297 Squadrons, enabled the daily delivery to Berlin to rise to 4,000 tons. Even that figure was doubled by the following April as the operation became more efficient. The airlift continued through the winter and spring, and beyond. Although the Soviet surface blockade of Berlin was lifted in May 1949, the airlift continued through

A Handley Page Hastings C1 is unloaded in Berlin. The Hastings, which entered service with 47 Squadron in October 1948, benefitted from a much improved performance over the York. (Keystone/Getty)

A Spitfire FR18 of 32 Squadron in the Middle East. The type was powered by a 2,050hp Rolls-Royce Griffon 65 engine and despite being designed for the reconnaissance role, it was also armed with two 20mm Hispano cannon and two 0.50in M2 Browning machine guns. (Flintham)

the summer in order to build a surplus of supplies in the city in case of future problems. The Berlin Airlift officially ceased on 30 September 1949.

ISRAEL

As the crisis developed in Berlin, so, too, did another in the Middle East. Israel's declaration of independence on 14 May 1948 precipitated attacks from all of its Arab neighbours two days later. Unfortunately, British forces which were still in the process of leaving Israeli territory were caught up in some of the fighting. On the morning of 22 May 1948, four low-flying Spitfires attacked the RAF airfield at Ramat David, which was the temporary home to the Spitfire FR18 fighters of 32 and 208 Squadrons. A number of aircraft on the ground were destroyed or damaged. Caught by surprise, the RAF responded immediately by mounting standing patrols over the airfield and were thus able to intercept two more sections of Spitfires that carried out further raids during the

course of the day. Four of the attacking aircraft were shot down by RAF Spitfires and another was forced down by ground fire from RAF Regiment gunners. It transpired that the attackers were Spitfires of the Royal Egyptian Air Force (REAF): they had been tasked against the nearby Israeli Air Force (IAF) airfield at Megiddo, but had mistaken Ramat David for their target.

The RAF Spitfire squadrons withdrew from Ramat David to Cyprus in July, but in November 208 Squadron moved to Fayid in the Canal Zone. Meanwhile the de Havilland Mosquito PR34 reconnaissance aircraft of 13 Squadron had been flying regular flights over Israel to monitor events, but on 2 November a routine reconnaissance flight was intercepted and the Mosquito was shot down by the IAF. Two months later, an incident brought home the difficulties of identification when the combatants of three nations were all operating the same aircraft type. On 2 January 1949, a flight of four RAF Spitfires from 208 Squadron were flying a border patrol over the Sinai desert when they came across an Israeli column which (unknown to the RAF pilots) had just been attacked by REAF Spitfires.

Two RAF Spitfires descended to inspect the column, leaving the other pair as top cover. All four RAF aircraft were then engaged almost simultaneously: the lower pair by ground fire (which downed one Spitfire) and the higher pair by two IAF Spitfires. Within a few minutes, all four RAF Spitfires had been shot down, thanks in part to confusion about the identity of the IAF Spitfires. That afternoon another formation of four Spitfires from 208 Squadron, escorted by 15 Hawker Tempests from 6 and 213 Squadrons, set out to search for the missing formation. As they neared the border, the RAF aircraft were attacked by four IAF Spitfires which swiftly shot down one Tempest. There were no further casualties in the ensuing mêlée, but the RAF pilots had great difficulty in identifying which of the Spitfires were friendly and which ones were the enemy. Subsequently, both sides avoided combat and there were no further engagements between the RAF and IAF.

OPERATION *FIREDOG*

During World War II, the British had recruited and trained a sizeable guerrilla force to fight the Japanese in the Malay jungle. At the end of the war, most of the guerrillas gave up their arms and returned to normal life; however, a small but well-organized core of fighters retained their weapons and started an insurrection against British colonial rule. These were mainly ethnic Chinese members of the Malay Communist Party and became known to the British authorities as Communist Terrorists (CTs). At first the CTs only managed to cause minor disruption, but the scope of their operations increased, culminating in a State of Emergency being declared in Malaya on 16 July 1948. Spitfires from 28 and 60 Squadrons were swiftly deployed to Kuala Lumpur, along with Dakotas from 110 Squadron; these were augmented in August by a flight of 45 Squadron Bristol Beaufighter TF10 strike aircraft. One of the first tasks of the aircraft was photographic reconnaissance, not only to try to detect terrorist camps, but also to provide the basis for accurate and up-to-date maps of the region. This was not an easy task because of the weather: cloud cover built up during the course of a day, so any photographic work had to be done in the early daylight while skies were still clear. The photographic survey proved to be a major commitment for the photographic reconnaissance squadrons in the theatre over the next few years.

Above: A Hawker Tempest F6 of 6 Squadron, based at Shallufa. The Tempest became the standard post-war fighter in the Middle East until the de Havilland Vampire entered service. (Flintham)

Opposite: Two Bristol Brigand B1 light bombers of 84 Squadron over the Malayan jungle. Originally intended as a torpedo bomber, the type equipped three RAF squadrons, and operated over Malaya from 1950 to 1954, but it was not a successful aircraft. (Pitchfork)

An Avro Lincoln B2 of 148 Squadron takes off from Tengah for a sortie over the Malayan jungle. The Lincoln B2, which was originally designated as the Lancaster B V, entered service in 1945. Normally based at Upwood, near Cambridge, the squadron was one of a number of units providing bombers for Operation *Firedog*. (Flintham)

The campaign fought in the Malayan jungle was essentially an army operation, in which RAF aircraft were called to support the requirements of ground troops. As the CT camps that were close to towns were systematically attacked, the CTs moved further into the jungle and so, too, did the army units hunting them. One of the prime roles of RAF aircraft was to supply troops from the air, a task carried out by the Dakotas of 48, 52 and 110 Squadrons. The challenge was in dropping supplies accurately into small jungle clearings, a task made more difficult by the clouds and rainstorms typical of tropical afternoons. The aircraft would frequently be flown at low level over the tree tops in order to get beneath the cloud to find the Drop Zone (DZ). In the first few months of 1949, the Dakotas dropped some 67 tons of supplies to troops in the jungle; in September that year the task had reached nearly 84 tons in a single month of supplying troops in the Selangor, Pahang, Kelantan, Perak and Negri Sembilan areas. The Dakotas of

48 Squadron were also used for dropping leaflets in several languages encouraging CTs to surrender.

By 1949 the aircraft responsible for carrying out airstrikes were the Beaufighters (and later Bristol Brigands) of 45 Squadron as well as the Hawker Tempest II fighters of 33 Squadron and Spitfire FR18 fighter-reconnaissance aircraft of 60 Squadron operating from Tengah and Butterworth. These aircraft were augmented in early 1950 by the arrival of the Avro Lincolns of 57 Squadron, which deployed from their home base at RAF Waddington on 15 March and 1 Squadron RAAF, equipped with Lincoln B30 bombers, which was based at RAF Tengah from 1950. The following month there was a major air action against a force of CTs in the jungle hills near Broga, a town to the southeast of Kuala Lumpur. Between 15 and 18 April, 97 sorties were flown by a composite force of Lincolns, Brigands, Tempests and Spitfires. Short Sunderland flying boats were also involved on the second day, joining Spitfires and Tempests which attacked another CT position in the Negri Sembilan region. In that month, 580 sorties were flown to mount 40 airstrikes. Many airstrikes were co-ordinated by Austers from the Army AOP squadron, which could mark the target area with coloured smoke. Another variation was for ground troops to mark their own position with smoke and give the strike aircraft a heading and time to release weapons after they had overflown that position. At night, a similar procedure could be adopted, using searchlights provided by 1st (Singapore) Regiment Royal Artillery shining vertically upwards to indicate the position of friendly forces. Using these techniques, the CTs could be harassed by both day and night.

Five RAF Regiment squadrons had been created in Malaya, with British officers and Malayan troops. These units were primarily intended for the protection of airfields, but each squadron also did its turn working as infantry units in the jungle. In April 1950 both 94 and 95 Squadrons RAF Regt had been in contact with CTs and apart from inflicting casualties they

had also captured a number of terrorists and seized important documents. Another initiative in early 1950 was the establishment of the RAF Casualty Evacuation Flight (later to become 194 Squadron) at Kuala Lumpur, equipped with Westland Dragonfly HC2 helicopters. The helicopters were kept on a nominal 2-hour standby, but they could often be airborne in much less time. After being scrambled they flew to the nearest AOP landing strip and would then carry out a reconnaissance of the casualty's position in the Auster to determine where best to land the helicopter. The Dragonflies were routinely flown into small clearings with only a few feet of clearance from the rotor tips. With a vertical climb-out capability of only 130ft when fully loaded, departing from clearings amongst 200ft trees was a major feat of airmanship.

Air supply and airstrikes continued apace through 1951. By now each Bomber Command Lincoln squadron was taking its turn to send detachments of aircraft to Tengah for *Firedog* sorties. In early March 1951, a Lincoln was called in to support a Dragonfly

A Spitfire PR19 of 81 Squadron in the Far East. The squadron fulfilled a vital function in surveying the Malayan jungle for the production of accurate maps and also locating the camps of communist terrorists (CTs). The last ever operational flight by an RAF Spitfire was flown by a PR19 from 81 Squadron on 1 April 1954.

A Westland Dragonfly HC 2 helicopter evacuating a casualty from a jungle clearing in Malaya. Powered by an Alvis Leonides air-cooled radial engine, the Dragonfly could lift three passengers or two stretcher cases.

which was attempting to pick up a casualty at an isolated police post in east Jahore, which was under attack by CTs. The Lincoln strafed the area until the bandits withdrew, allowing the helicopter to proceed safely. In 1950, 60 Squadron had received its first de Havilland Vampire FB5 jet fighters. These were first used in action on 26 April when Sqn Ldr W.G. Duncan-Smith and Flt Lt W. James attacked a bungalow on an abandoned rubber estate in east Jahore, which was being used as a CT base. The two Vampires fired 60lb rocket projectiles and 20mm cannon to destroy the target completely.

KOREA

The RAF in the Far East was already heavily committed to Operation *Firedog* when North Korean forces invaded South Korea on 25 June 1950. The only forces immediately available were the Short Sunderland flying boats of 88 Squadron and five of these aircraft were dispatched to US Naval Base Sasebo in Japan, near Nagasaki, for operations in Japanese waters in support of the Far East Fleet. However, they were soon bolstered by one more aircraft and redeployed to Iwakuni on Honshu Island. The Sunderlands commenced operational missions on 9 September, initially flying long-range anti-submarine patrols at night over the Yellow Sea and Korea Bay. These sorties usually lasted around 12 hours and a shortage of qualified air gunners soon meant that gunners were flying 160 hours each month. From 17 September, the daily task included day and night patrols of the approaches to Inchon. By this time 88 Squadron's crews and aircraft had been reinforced by a further three Sunderlands from

209 Squadron. The scope of Sunderland missions was enlarged the following month to include mine searches and long-range patrols of the eastern coast, extending as far north as Vladivostock. By November 1950 the RAF Far East Flying Boat Wing's operational commitment had stabilized at six aircraft, operated by 205 and 209 Squadron crews at Iwakuni; these could be supported if required by four aircraft at Hong Kong and five more of 88 Squadron's aircraft at Seletar.

The war changed dramatically in November 1950 when the Chinese entered hostilities on the side of the North Koreans. The Chinese brought with them the MiG-15 – a jet fighter which outclassed most of the United Nations' aircraft in the theatre. Although there were not any RAF fighter or ground attack aircraft in Korea, volunteers were called for and a number of pilots flew combat missions with the USAF and RAAF from 1951 onwards. Four pilots were sent to Japan to help 77 Squadron RAAF convert from the North American P-51D Mustang to the Gloster Meteor F8 in mid-

1951 and subsequently the unit's combat pilots at any time included a handful of RAF pilots who had volunteered to fly an operational tour. After proving to be no match for the MiG-15 in the air-to-air role, the Meteors were used for interdiction sorties against ground targets in North Korea such as trains, convoys and storage depots. In all, some 32 RAF pilots flew with 77 Squadron during the Korean War.

A further 26 RAF pilots flew operational tours over Korea with the USAF: five of them flew the Republic F-84E Thunderjet in the ground-attack role and the others flew F-86E Sabres with the 4th and 51st Fighter Interceptor Wings. Many of these pilots were very experienced veterans of combat during World War II and a number of RAF pilots scored MiG-15 kills over Korea. These included Sqn Ldr G.S. Hulse, who was credited with the destruction of two MiG-15s before he was shot down and killed in March 1953.

Hostilities over Korea continued through 1952 until July 1953. Four RAF pilots were killed in

Flt Lt Keith Williamson (RAF) climbs into the cockpit of a Gloster Meteor F8 from 77 Squadron RAAF at Kimpo Air Base, Korea. One of the 32 RAF pilots who flew operational missions with the RAAF during the Korean War, Williamson later became Chief of the Air Staff between 1982 and 1985. (Pitchfork)

A formation of de Havilland Venom FB1 fighter bombers from 14 Squadron, which was based at Fassberg. A development of the Vampire, the Venom equipped the day fighter/ground-attack squadrons of 2nd Tactical Air Force (2TAF) in West Germany in the mid-1950s. (14 Squadron Association)

action while they were seconded to the USAF in Korea: a further six were killed while serving in the theatre with the RAAF, and one more, Flt Lt O.M. Bergh, was taken PoW in North Korea after he was shot down.

RAF IN GERMANY & THE UK

In 1950, the outbreak of the Korean War served as something of a 'wake-up call' to the membership of the newly-formed North Atlantic Treaty Organization (NATO). Following an American lead, members of the alliance undertook to increase their military commitments in Germany by 1954. In the RAF, the strength of Fighter Command was to be doubled and the run-down of Transport Command was halted. In the short term, reservists were recalled for service and the 20 squadrons of the RAuxAF were

mobilized for three months' training. With expansion came re-equipment with more modern types, but in the short term US-built aircraft were supplied to fill in gaps in the RAF's capabilities: Boeing Washington B1 bombers and Lockheed Neptune P2V-5 MR1 maritime patrol aircraft. Also a number Canadair Sabre F2 and F4 day fighters were loaned to the RAF in the early 1950s.

There was an extensive re-equipment and expansion of BAFO. In 1950, the strength of BAFO had dwindled to just eight front-line squadrons, based at RAF Gütersloh and RAF Wahn. Four years later, the command, which by then had become the Second Tactical Air Force (2TAF), consisted of 36 Squadrons, equipped with de Havilland Venom FB1 ground-attack aircraft, Hunter F4 day fighter, Gloster Meteor NF11 night fighter, English Electric Canberra B2 light bomber and Canberra PR3 and PR7 photo-reconnaissance aircraft. A massive infrastructure programme had also resulted in new airfields being built for the RAF at Geilenkirchen, Wildenrath, Brüggen and Laarbruch and the re-instatement of former *Luftwaffe* airfields at Ahlhorn, Oldenburg and Jever.

STRATEGIC RECONNAISSANCE

In the early 1950s radar photographs of Russian bomber airfields were needed to enable pre-emptive strikes to be planned against them. At that time, the US military was reluctant to overfly the territory of the USSR to acquire such imagery and although the British government was prepared to do so, the RAF did not have aircraft capable of flying such a mission. An agreement was therefore reached in which the USAF would train British crews to fly the North American RB-45C Tornado reconnaissance aircraft and would then loan three aircraft to the RAF for them to carry out the task. A small number of RAF crews led by Sqn Ldr J. Crampton were selected for training in the USA in late 1951 and three RB-45Cs were made available to the RAF in April 1952. On the night

A Sunderland GR5 of 88 Squadron taxis on the Iwakuni Roads, Japan, in October 1950. Throughout the Korean conflict, the Sunderlands of the Far East Flying Boat Wing carried out long distance anti-submarine patrols over the Yellow Sea and the Sea of Japan, often in appalling weather conditions. (Pitchfork)

A total of 88 Boeing B-29 Superfortress bombers were loaned to the RAF between 1950 and 1958 as a temporary measure until the arrival of the jet-powered Vickers Valiant B1. In RAF service the type was known as the Washington B1. This formation is from 115 Squadron, one of the eight units which operated the type.

of 17/18 April, the three aircraft took off from RAF Sculthorpe for Operation *Jiu-Jitsu*. After air-to-air refuelling over the Skagerrak, they proceeded on simultaneous missions over the Orsha (Belarus) and Poltava (Ukraine) regions of Russia. Flying at 36,000ft the Tornados photographed 20 of the 35 known or suspected airfields, without interference from the Soviet defences.

Unfortunately, the results for nine of the airfields covered by Operation *Jiu-Jitsu* were deemed to be 'indifferent' and two years later the Prime Minister authorized a second set of Operation *Jiu-Jitsu* sorties to complete the job. Once again, these were led by Sqn Ldr Crampton, whose second pilot for the mission was Flt Lt R.McA. Furze. Crampton and his team took off on 28 April 1954. After refuelling over Denmark again, Crampton's own route took him over Kiev, where, unlike his previous sortie, the Soviet defences were prepared. 'My reverie was rudely interrupted,' recalled Crampton later, 'by the

sudden heart-stopping appearance of a veritable flare path of exploding golden anti-aircraft fire. There was no doubt about it; it was very well predicted flak – dead ahead and at the same height as we were. My reaction was instinctive – throttles wide open and haul the aircraft round on its starboard wing tip until the gyro compass pointed west. I began a gentle 100ft per minute descent because that made us seem to go a bit faster, although it didn't because we started juddering in the limiting Mach number buffet. So I eased the power off a bit, but kept up the descent on the "it seems faster" principle and since we had been predicted I thought it best to change height as well as speed and direction, thus giving the gunners down below three new problems.' Although Crampton had cut short his own sortie, the other two aircraft had completed their missions successfully, unhindered by the Soviet air defences.

In March 1954, a Canberra B2 of 58 Squadron was modified to mount a 240-in focal length Long

Range Oblique Photography (LOROP) camera. Flying at high level along the Inner German Border (IGB), the aircraft was able to 'look' over the border and photograph details well inside East Germany. During the nine Operation *Robin* sorties, flown over the course of 1954 and 1955, a second Canberra accompanied the LOROP aircraft to ensure that the reconnaissance aircraft kept clear of the contrail levels and could thus remain undetected from the ground. The operation was later expanded to include the border with the Czech Republic and the Soviet-controlled zone of Austria. Other LOROP reconnaissance sorties were able to glean useful intelligence during flights over Eastern Mediterranean.

Two Canberra B2 aircraft had also been issued to 192 Squadron in February 1953 (followed by two Canberra B6s in the following year) to supplement the Boeing Washington which the unit was using for gathering Electronic Intelligence (Elint). In the mid-1950s the squadron flew 'Radio Proving Flights,' or more accurately Elint reconnaissance sorties, around the western periphery of Central European countries and the USSR, including flights into the Baltic and Black Seas. The two different aircraft types operated together on co-ordinated missions: the Canberra would fly aggressively towards the frontier to provoke the air-defence systems into action and the Washington would then record the resulting electronic emissions. All flights had to be approved at ministerial level and the squadron might fly around ten or 20 such operational sorties each month. The Boeing Washington was replaced by the de Havilland Comet in 1958, at which time the unit was re-numbered 51 Squadron. With their superior performance, the Comets were able to sample a wider footprint of emitters by flying at 40,000ft. The Comets also flew lower-level sorties, known as Operation *Claret*, in which Soviet naval vessels were overflown to gather Elint about their radar equipment.

A section of Canadair F-86E Sabre F4 fighters from 112 Squadron, based at Brüggen, West Germany. From 1953, the type equipped two fighter squadrons in the UK and a further ten in Germany, providing the RAF a swept-wing fighter pending the introduction of the Hawker Hunter in 1955. (Pitchfork)

A wintry scene at Binbrook in 1951. A Lincoln from 101 Squadron is parked beyond the English Electric Canberra B2 bombers which replaced it in squadron service. The first RAF jet bomber squadron, 101 Squadron was one of 25 Bomber Command units which operated the Canberra in the 1950s. (Popperfoto/Getty)

One of the most important but least known duties undertaken by the RAF was long-range weather reconnaissance over the Atlantic Ocean. These sorties provided the Meteorological (Met) Office with the information it needed to make accurate weather forecasts. Post-war weather reconnaissance, known as Operation *Bismuth*, was carried out by the Handley Page Halifax GR6 (which were replaced by the Handley Page Hastings Met1 in 1950) of 202 Squadron based at RAF Aldergrove. The nine-hour sorties covered an 800-mile arc ranging from the Bay of Biscay to Icelandic waters. The mission profile involved flying an exact track, determined by the Met Office, into the ocean for some 800 miles at 1,500ft, often directly into approaching storms. Readings of data including temperature, humidity, atmospheric pressure and observations of weather phenomena were reported every 50 miles and every 200 miles the aircraft descended so that readings were taken from 100ft above the sea. At the end of the outbound leg the aircraft would carry out a spiral climb, levelling off every 50 millibars (Mb) so that readings and observations could be recorded, up to an altitude of 18,000ft. After flying to another position, the aircraft would then descend to 1,500ft continue its route, once again recording data every 50 miles on the homebound leg. After more than 4,000 weather sorties, the last Operation *Bismuth* sortie was flown on 31 July 1964.

MAU MAU

Anti-colonial insurrection was not limited to the Far East: in Kenya, an anti-British movement known as Mau Mau started a campaign of intimidation and violence amongst the Kikuyu people in the first years of the 1950s. The level of violence increased dramatically in late 1952 and a State of Emergency was declared in Kenya on 21 October 1952. The only RAF presence in Kenya at that time was a small communications flight, so the RAF's initial contribution was limited to the use of Transport Command's Hastings and Valettas to fly the 1st Battalion Lancashire Fusiliers to Nairobi. Air support to the army and police units was provided by the Kenya Police Reserve (KPR) Air Wing, which comprised about 13 Cessna and Piper light aircraft. By early 1953, police and army activities had pushed the Mau Mau into two large areas, one around Mount Kenya and the other around the Aberdare Range Mountains. The terrain in these areas comprised jungle-covered hills and mountains - ranging from 7,000ft above sea level to peaks of over 17,000ft. Just as in Malaya, aircraft would be needed to supply ground forces deployed into the jungle, and there was also an immediate operational need for aerial

A rare photograph of a North American RB-45C Tornado in RAF markings. Three of these aircraft were loaned by the USAF to the RAF for Operation *Jiu-Jitsu*, which involved clandestine reconnaissance flights over the Soviet Union in 1952 and again in 1954. (Lashmar)

The world's first commercial jet-powered airliner, the de Havilland Comet also became the world's first jet-powered military transport. The Comet C2 entered service with 216 Squadron, based at Lyneham, Wiltshire in 1956. Another three of the type, designated Comet C2(R), equipped to monitor electronic emissions from Soviet and Warsaw Pact air defence systems, were delivered to 51 and 192 Squadrons. The eight Comet C2 transports delivered to 216 Squadron were named and this aircraft, XK697, is 'Cygnus'. It was later transferred to 51 Squadron. (RAFM)

A Handley Page Hastings C1 of 70 Squadron. The type formed the backbone of RAF Transport Command equipping eleven squadrons in the UK and Europe, and a further two overseas. A small number of aircraft designated Hastings Met1 were operated by 202 Squadron for meteorological reconnaissance flights. (© IWM 27470)

reconnaissance and an airstrike capability. The solution was provided by the Rhodesia Air Training Group, which was in the process of disbandment. Four Harvard training aircraft were fitted with a 0.303in Browning machine gun and bomb racks for 20lb anti-personnel bombs and formed into 1340 Flight, and it arrived at Eastleigh in Kenya on 23 March 1953.

The Harvards moved to join the KPR Wing at the airstrip at Mwjeija, about halfway between – and only a few minutes' flying time from – the two operational areas. Here they worked closely with the KPR Wing's light aircraft: the KPR pilots flew

reconnaissance sorties over the jungle and called in the Harvards to attack if they found rebel positions. Sorties were also flown at night, because campfires often gave away the position of rebel encampments in the darkness. These tactics worked well and by the end of July 1953, 1340 Flight was flying over 50 airstrikes per week. As a result of this success, the number of the Flight's Harvards was doubled to eight aircraft and then increased further, up to ten aircraft.

However, greater firepower was needed and from January 1954 a detachment of six Lincoln B1 bombers was based at Eastleigh. The aircraft and crews were provided from Bomber Command squadrons which had deployed to the Middle East for short routine training detachments, known as Operation *Sun Ray*. Instead of dropping practice bombs on a training range, the crews found themselves flying operational sorties against the Mau Mau. Each Lincoln squadron stood its turn to provide aircraft, starting with 49 Squadron in January and followed by 100 Squadron then 61 Squadron. A permanent detachment of two Meteor PR10 reconnaissance aircraft from 13 Squadron was also established at Eastleigh in March. These aircraft did a valuable job in taking photographs for both reconnaissance and map-making over the next year.

Each Lincoln operation was tasked against a specific area of jungle, which was often quite large in size. Friendly troops were withdrawn from that sector, which the Lincolns then bombed with 500lb bombs. The bombers were often followed by a 'sky shouter' aircraft, a Percival Pembroke C1 equipped with a loudspeaker, urging the rebels to surrender to the troops who were sweeping back through

that part of the jungle. When 214 Squadron took its turn at Eastleigh in September 1954, the unit dropped over 2,000 bombs on 176 sorties by both day and night. Like Malaya, the campaign against the Mau Mau was predominantly a joint Army and police counter-terrorist operation, but the RAF's support undoubtedly played a vital role in the operation's overall success. The Mau Mau was largely broken by early 1955, and although the Emergency continued for another four years, the RAF's contribution was greatly scaled back after the summer of 1955. The last sortie by Lincolns was flown in July and 1340 Flight was disbanded on 30 September.

RE-EQUIPMENT

The Lincoln was the last British piston-engined heavy bomber. In the late 1940s, the Air Staff had recognized the need to procure high-performance jet bombers and the first of these, the English

An Avro Lincoln of 61 Squadron over Kenya during Mau Mau operations in early 1954. Based at Wittering, 61 Squadron was re-equipped with the English Electric Canberra B2 later in the same year. (RAFM)

Two English Electric Canberra B2 bombers on either side of a Canberra B6; all are from 12 Squadron based at Binbrook in 1955. The B6 was fitted with the more powerful Rolls-Royce Avon 109 engines and had increased fuel capacity, which gave the variant an improved range over the B2. (RAFM)

Electric Canberra B2, entered service with 101 Squadron at RAF Binbrook in 1951. However, the Canberra did not completely replace the Lincoln, since its bomb bay was not large enough to carry the Blue Danube nuclear weapon that was then under development. It was not until after the next generation of jet 'V-bombers,' the Vickers Valiant, Handley Page Victor and Avro Vulcan, came into service that the Lincoln was finally retired from the front-line service. The first of the V-bombers, the Vickers Valiant B1, was issued to 138 Squadron at RAF Gaydon in 1955. The new aircraft, able

to operate at high subsonic Mach numbers at over 50,000ft, represented a quantum leap in terms of performance and capability over the Lincoln. The first Vulcans and Victors became operational in 1957 and 1958 respectively, replacing both the Lincoln and some Canberras in Bomber Command.

In July 1954, the first of the new Hawker Hunter F1 day fighters were delivered to 43 Squadron, starting Fighter Command's replacement of its obsolescent Vampires and Meteors with a more modern and capable type; the following year, the night fighter force began to be equipped with the RAF's first true all-weather fighter, the delta-winged Gloster Javelin, which entered service with 46 Squadron.

OPERATION *FIREDOG* CONTINUES

Meanwhile, the State of Emergency continued in Malaya throughout the 1950s. Air operations followed the pattern that had been established earlier in the campaign, but with more modern equipment as new aircraft entered service. The efforts of the RAF were also supplemented by the RAAF, RNZAF and the FAA. In October 1953, the Lincolns of 1 Squadron RAAF and 83 Squadron RAF, the Hornet F3 ground-attack fighters of

33 and 45 Squadrons, as well as the Vampire FB9 jet fighter-bombers of 60 Squadron and Sunderlands of the Far East Flying Boat Wing were all heavily involved in airstrikes against CT positions in northern Malaya. The Lincolns also dropped over 14,000,000 leaflets during the month. Perhaps the major achievement for the month was the dropping by the Valettas of 48, 52 and 110 Squadrons of over 18 tons of supplies to ground troops in the jungle in just one day, on 28 October 1953. However even this impressive total was exceeded in July 1954 when a Transport Command Hastings aircraft was attached to the Far East Command and a daily supply drop total of nearly 24 tons was achieved by 21 Valettas and one Hastings. Helicopters also began to prove their worth: apart from the Dragonflies (and later Sycamore HR14) of 194 Squadron,

A Gloster Javelin FAW1 of 46 Squadron. The delta-winged aircraft provided both Fighter Command and RAF Germany with a night/all-weather capability from the late 1950s until the early 1960s.

Above: A Scottish Aviation Pioneer CC1 required a run of only 225ft for take-off, making it ideal for counter-insurgency work in Malaya where it was flown by 267 Squadron (re-numbered 209 Squadron) and later by 78 Squadron in Aden. (© IWM RAF-T1710)

Right: An RAF Douglas C-47 (DC-3) Dakota equipped with loudspeakers fitted to the underside of the fuselage. 'Sky shouter' aircraft, including the Auster AOP and the Hunting Percival Pembroke, were used over rebel areas in Malaya, Kenya and Oman to broadcast messages encouraging insurgents to surrender. (© IWM MAL 80)

which continued the casualty evacuation work, the Westland Whirlwind HAR21 helicopters of 848 Squadron FAA and Whirlwind HAR4 helicopters of 155 Squadron proved invaluable in transporting troops into and out of the jungle. The Whirlwinds were also used for inserting SAS teams into the jungle by parachute. Another aeroplane which was proving particularly versatile was the Scottish Aviation Pioneer, which could carry loads into small airstrips beyond the range of the helicopters. The Pioneers were operated by 267 Squadron, an unusual unit which also operated four more types: Dakotas and Austers were fitted

as 'sky shouter' aircraft, while Pembrokes and Harvards were used for communications duties.

The first jet bombers to become involved in Operation *Firedog* were four Canberra B6s of 101 Squadron, which first deployed to Tengah (via Idris, Habbaniyah, Mauripur and Negembo) for three months in February 1955. Amongst other operations, the aircraft bombed CT encampments on the border between Kedah (in northern Malaya) and Thailand in May during Operation *Unity*, a hunt for the secretary-general of the Malay Communist Party who was reported to be in the area. A semi-permanent detachment of Canberras

A Westland Whirlwind HAR2 of 225 Squadron carrying an underslung load. Some 60 of the type were supplied to the RAF and used in both the transport and Search And Rescue (SAR) roles. (RAFM)

Above: A Vickers Valetta C1 transport on a mission to drop supplies drop to troops deployed in the Malayan jungle. After entering service with the Far East Transport Wing in 1950, the type remained in front-line service with 52 Squadron at Changi, Hong Kong until 1966. (Flintham)

Right: The de Havilland Hornet F3 entered service in 1946 and was the fastest piston-engined fighter in RAF service. In 1952 the type replaced the Bristol Brigand in service with 45 Squadron at Tengah, for operations over Malaya. (Flintham)

was subsequently established at Tengah, with aircraft and crews provided by Bomber Command units for three-month tours: in 1955, 101 Squadron was followed in turn by 617 and 12 Squadrons. Operation *Firedog* continued until the end of the State of Emergency in 1960.

SUEZ CRISIS

Egyptian resentment of British military presence in the Suez Canal Zone built up in the immediate post-war years and in the early 1950s it degenerated into violence. The military coup in Egypt that toppled the monarchy in 1952 did little to improve Anglo-Egyptian relations. In 1954 Britain and Egypt agreed that UK forces would withdraw from the Canal Zone within two years and the last British forces were evacuated from the Zone in April 1956. Three months later the Egyptian government unilaterally nationalized the Suez Canal, which in turn provoked a crisis with both Britain and France. Britain started to build up its forces in the region in preparation for

military action (nicknamed Operation *Musketeer*) and eight Canberra B2 bombers from each of the squadrons at RAF Honington (10, 15 and 44 Squadrons) deployed to Nicosia in the first week of August. These were followed over the following months by eight more Canberra B2 aircraft from each of 18 and 61 Squadrons from RAF Upwood and 27 Squadron from RAF Marham. A further 11 Canberra B6 bombers were provided by 139 Squadron from RAF Binbrook. The rest of the Binbrook Wing, comprising the Canberra B6 units 9, 12, 101 and 109 Squadrons, sent seven aircraft from each squadron to Hal Far, Malta. Also at Hal Far were eight Valiants of 138 Squadron, six Valiants from each of 148 and 207 Squadrons and a further four from 214 Squadrons. In addition to the larger bombers, a Wing of Venom FB4 fighter bombers was assembled at Akrotiri, made up of 6, 8 and 249 Squadrons.

Transport aircraft were also assembled at Nicosia, including Valettas from 30, 84 and 114 Squadrons and Hastings of 70, 99 and 511 Squadrons. These aircraft were busy moving troops and supplies into theatre, but once hostilities started, they would

RAF Nicosia during the Suez Crisis. The airfield is packed with Valetta transport aircraft and Canberra bombers, as well as the resident Armstrong Whitworth Meteor NF13 night fighters of 39 Squadron. The yellow and black identification stripes used by Allied aircraft are visible on all three types. (Flintham)

be used to transport paratroopers into action. As attempts to find a diplomatic solution to the crisis failed, photo-reconnaissance aircraft, Canberra PR7s from 13 Squadron and Valiant B(PR)1s from 543 Squadron, carried out sorties over the region.

The deadline to resolve the crisis by diplomacy expired on 31 October 1956 and the Anglo-French air attack against Egypt commenced that night. The first wave, comprising six Valiants from 138 Squadron and 14 Canberras from 10, 12, 15, 44 and 109 Squadrons led by four target-marking Canberras of 139 Squadron, was tasked against Cairo West airfield at 16:15hrs GMT. However, when intelligence sources reported that US citizens were being evacuated along an adjoining road, the mission was re-tasked at very short notice to Almaza airfield. The second wave, following 2¼ hours later, was made up of six more Valiants, from 148 and 214 Squadrons, and another 14 Canberras from 10, 12, 15, 44 and 109 Squadrons, once more preceded by four target marking aircraft from 139 Squadron. All the bombs were visually aimed on the Target Indicator (TI) flares dropped by the 139 Squadron aircraft. Operations continued through the night with two more combined Valiant and Canberra waves, which bombed the airfields at Kabrit and Abu Seir (both of which were target-marked by 18 Squadron) and a raid by 15 Cyprus-based Canberras from 139, 27 and 61 Squadrons on Inchas. During the night, one Valiant was intercepted by an Egyptian Meteor NF13, but the aircraft was not hit.

At first light the following morning the Venoms from Akrotiri joined French Air Force F-84s and FAA aircraft from the carrier task group in a dawn attack on Abu Seir and Fayid airfields using rockets and guns. The Venom sorties continued throughout the day, with subsequent waves attacking Kabrit and Kasfareet. Although a number of Egyptian aircraft, including MiG-15s were destroyed on the ground during these raids, the majority of the Egyptian Air Force had already escaped to Saudi Arabia. However, some of the Egyptian Air Force aircraft remained operational: two Canberra PR7

reconnaissance aircraft were intercepted over Egypt during the day, but neither was engaged. Unfortunately, another Canberra was shot down over Syria on 6 November by a MiG-15 during a photo-reconnaissance sortie.

The bombing continued on the night of 1/2 November. This time Cairo West was attacked by six Valiants from 138 Squadron and 18 Canberras from 10, 15, 12, 44, 109 and 139 Squadrons, with the latter providing target marking. An hour later a force of 24 Canberras bombed Luxor and then four Canberras from 18 Squadron dropped TIs on Fayid for six Valiants of 148 Squadron and ten more Canberras from 12, 44, 61 and 109 Squadrons. The night's final raid on Kasfareet was carried out by six Valiants from 207 and 214 Squadrons and eight Canberras from 9 and 101 Squadrons, marked by four Canberras of 18 Squadron.

On the morning of 2 November, the work of the Venom Wing continued, starting with a dawn attack against Shallufah and Kabrit. A second morning strike against Huckstep barracks was followed by missions against Abu Seir and Kabrit airfields. The day also saw the first daylight raid by the medium bombers: a total of 20 Canberras from 10, 15, 18, 27, 44 and 61 Squadrons, escorted by 12 French AF F-84Fs, bombed the transmitter masts of Cairo Radio. In the afternoon 22 Canberras from 10, 15, 27, 44, 61 and 139 Squadrons attacked Luxor airfield once more. That night, two raids were planned against the ammunition storage areas and vehicle park at Huckstep barracks. The first wave comprised seven Valiants from 138 Squadron, seven Canberras from 9 Squadron, four Canberras from 18 Squadron and a further eight from 139 Squadron, of which four acted as target markers. Poor weather prevented eight Valiants and 12 Canberras from taking off from Malta, leaving only eight Canberras from Cyprus-based 18 Squadron to carry out the second attack.

The following day, 3 November, Hunter F5 fighters from 1 and 34 Squadrons at Nicosia escorted a force of 22 Cyprus-based Canberras bombing Almaza barracks. However, the Hunters were operating at

A Canberra B6 takes off from Hal Far during the Suez Crisis. The airfield was the base for bombing operations by 9, 12, 101 and 109 Squadrons equipped with the Canberra B6, as well as 138, 148, 207 and 214 Squadrons equipped with the Valiant B1. (Flintham)

their maximum range and could not remain on station for long. An hour later, four Venoms carried out an attack on anti-aircraft guns near Nfisha, just before a second wave of 22 Canberras from Nicosia attacked the railway marshalling yards there; the Canberra crews reported problems seeing the TIs over the target because of thick smoke from burning oil. Two more raids on El Agami and Huckstep barracks were cancelled because of the weather over Malta. Meanwhile, the Venoms carried out armed reconnaissance of roads, military installations and transport infrastructure, engaging any targets that they found with rockets and bombs. One aircraft was lost to ground fire during these operations.

The Venoms attacked radar stations and gun emplacements during daylight on 4 November. There was also a Wing strike against a concentration of tanks and military vehicles some four miles southwest of the Giza pyramids. Additionally, the Venoms of 249 Squadron attacked Egyptian tanks near Huckstep barracks. The last Valiant bombing

attacks took place on the night of 4 November, with Valiant raids against coastal guns and radar installations on El Agami Island near Alexandria and Huckstep Barracks. Four Canberras from 18 Squadron dropped TIs on the first target at 16:45hrs GMT, but the raid did not go well. Of the seven Valiants from 207 and 214 Squadrons, one had to abort because it could not retract its nose-gear and two more did not drop because the crews could not see the markers. Another Valiant dropped on a Navigation Bombing System (NBS) position, but this led to a two-mile overshoot of the target. The nine Canberras from 12 and 109 Squadrons also had difficulty finding the target markers and five aircraft did not drop their bombs. However, the second raid, carried out by six Valiants from 148 and 214 Squadrons and 12 Canberras from 9, 12, 101 and 109 Squadrons, marked by four Canberras from 139 Squadron, fared better.

The airborne assault took place on 5 November when 18 Valettas and 18 Hastings were used to carry the paratroopers and their equipment. Unfortunately, this part of the campaign showed up the unsuitability of the RAF transport fleet for parachute operations: both the Valetta and Hastings had small side-opening cargo doors, so they could not carry equipment internally like aircraft with rear clamshell-type doors, such as the French Noratlas. The RAF aircraft therefore had to carry their loads externally, suspended beneath the aircraft, thus incurring a great drag penalty, which in turn reduced the amount of equipment or troops that could be carried. For example, the full load of a Hastings comprised just 16 troops plus a jeep and trailer. However, despite these practical drawbacks, the transport fleet successfully found the DZ at Gamil airfield, which had been marked by Canberra target markers, and delivered their troops accurately. The assault was supported by tactical aircraft, including the Akrotiri Venom Wing, which provided fighter patrols to ensure that any remaining aircraft of the Egyptian Air Force could not interfere and then carried out rocket

and gun attacks on military vehicles and positions. Flying successive waves, the Venoms remained on station all day. FAA aircraft were also on station, flying 'cab rank' patrols to provide close air support to the paratroopers. One RAF Regt unit, 48 Squadron, deployed to secure Gamil airfield, so that it could be used for aerial resupply. An hour after the first parachute landings a force of 14 Canberras from Cyprus bombed a concentration of tanks, followed 2 hours later by another attack by 21 Canberras. There was a second air drop at Gamil by five Hastings and two Valettas in the afternoon, timed to coincide with a second French parachute assault at Port Fouad.

At dawn on 6 November, 30 aircraft of the Venom Wing flew through a thunderstorm in order to make a mass attack on the heavy gun emplacements at Port Said, prior to the landings which took place that day. At the end of the day during which British and French troops landed at Port Said, a ceasefire was agreed and combat operations were halted. No further RAF missions

HMS *Theseus* with Westland Whirlwind and Bristol Sycamore helicopters of the Joint Experimental Helicopter Unit (JEHU), which operated alongside Royal Navy helicopters.

A stick of paratroops jump from a Hastings during the Suez Crisis. The airborne assault which took place on 5 November 1956 showed the shortcomings of the RAF transport fleet: the lack of a cargo ramp opening on both Hastings and Valetta meant that neither type could carry vehicles or artillery pieces internally. (Flintham)

were flown during Operation *Musketeer* and over the next few months, the various components of the RAF's force in the Eastern Mediterranean were returned to their home bases.

TRUCIAL OMAN

A long-running border dispute between Saudi Arabia and Trucial Oman had come to a head in 1952 when armed Saudi insurgents took over the Buraimi Oasis. The situation was contained for the next three years, without resorting to force, thanks to an aerial blockade of the oasis, firstly by Lancasters of 683 Squadron and then, from late 1953, the Ansons of 1417 Flight. Eventually, in October 1955 the Trucial Oman Levies, reinforced

by two Lincolns from 7 Squadron, which were temporarily detached to Bahrain, were able to re-enter the Oasis and eject the insurgents. However, during 1957 the Sultan of Oman lost control of much of central Oman to Saudi-backed rebels. When the Sultan requested British military assistance in putting down the revolt, the RAF was tasked with providing airlift (in the form of Valettas and Blackburn Beverley C1 transports from 84 Squadron) and airstrikes (by Venom FB4 ground-attack fighters of 8 and 249 Squadrons and Avro Shackleton MR2 maritime patrol aircraft of 37 Squadron). Initial reconnaissance by the Pembroke C1 communications aircraft of 1417 Flight in July identified a number of villages hostile to the Sultan. These settlements were defended by large fortified towers and in the traditions of Air

Control, these were each targeted by a force of up to 12 Venoms using rockets, after due warning leaflets had been dropped by the Shackletons 48 hours earlier. The forts at Izki, Nizwa, Tanuf, Birkat al Mauz, Bakhla and Firq were all destroyed by the Venoms during July 1957. Meanwhile, the Shackletons also dropped leaflets promulgating a curfew in proscribed areas. The curfew was enforced by both Venoms and Shackletons, which patrolled the areas and bombed and strafed any targets they found. The Venoms also used provided close support to the Sultan's ground forces as they moved on Firq, which was captured on 11 August. Although the rebels had been defeated and the Sultan's authority was re-established in the area, it was not the end of the insurrection, for the ring-leaders and some of the rebels had escaped into the high plain of the Jebel Akhdar.

An aerial blockade was established around the Jebel Akhdar, but it proved difficult to enforce because the high terrain and deep valleys provided plentiful cover from patrolling aircraft. Two attempts were made by ground forces, in September and November, to climb onto the Jebel, but they were fought off, despite the efforts of supporting Shackletons and Venoms. A stalemate ensued and in early 1958, the Venoms and Shackletons started a campaign to undermine support for the rebels by systematically destroying the irrigation systems which made agriculture possible on the Jebel. These efforts were augmented by two 'sky shouting' Pembrokes from 1417 Flight. From early December, troops from 22 Regt SAS started patrolling into the Jebel area, supported when necessary by Venoms and Shackletons. The insurrection was eventually

The Avro Shackleton maritime patrol aircraft proved to be one of the most flexible types operated by the RAF in the 1950s and 1960s. Apart from its main duty of anti-submarine warfare, the type was used as an occasional transport aircraft and also, in the Middle East, as a medium bomber. The aircraft is a Shackleton MR2 of 228 Squadron. (BAe Heritage)

Right: A replacement for the Avro Anson in the communications role, the Percival Pembroke C1 entered RAF service in 1953. The type saw service in the UK, Germany, the Middle East and Far East and it was also used as a 'sky shouter' and for reconnaissance duties.

Below: A Blackburn Beverley of 84 Squadron lands on a desert strip 'up country' in Aden. The fuselage had a capacity of some 22 tons and a compartment in the tail boom could accommodate up to 94 passengers. The Beverley could also operate from rough airstrips as short as 2,550ft. (Flintham)

Two Vickers Valiants of 49 Squadron on the apron at Kiritimati, ready for the nuclear test drop on 8 November 1957 which had been postponed because of strong upper winds. (Tuthill)

brought to a close on the night of 26/27 January 1959 when the SAS led a successful assault onto the Jebel.

THE NUCLEAR AGE

Throughout the early 1950s much development work had been carried out to produce an independent British nuclear weapon. By 1955 a weapon casing, known as Blue Danube and roughly the same size as a wartime 'Tallboy' bomb, had entered RAF service. Blue Danube, which could be dropped from a Lincoln, could be fitted with a number of different – and at that stage largely experimental – warheads. In mid-1956, Operation *Mosaic* was a test of nuclear weapons using warheads mounted on test towers in the Montebello Islands off Western Australia. This was followed by Operation *Buffalo* in the Maralinga range (part of the Woomera complex) in South Australia. After the initial tower-based test detonations, Operation *Buffalo* culminated on 11 October 1956 in an air drop of a low-yield Blue Danube weapon. To minimize the dangers of nuclear fallout, the weapon was dropped as an 'airburst' (ie the nuclear fireball would not touch the ground) from a 49 Squadron Valiant B1 captained by Sqn Ldr E.J.G. Flavell. The

tests were supported by Canberras of 76 Squadron, which were equipped for air sampling and flew through the nuclear cloud to monitor and record the radiation levels.

The following year, a more ambitious test programme, Operation *Grapple*, took place at Kiritimati (Christmas Island) in the Pacific Ocean. Once again, the Valiants of 49 Squadron were used to drop the weapons and the Canberras of 76 Squadron and 100 Squadron were on hand to record radiation levels. The operation was a major undertaking, with, at its peak, over 1,300 RAF personnel on Kiritimati. In addition to Dakota aircraft for transport and resupply, the force included the Whirlwind helicopters of 206 Squadron and the Shackleton MR3 maritime patrol aircraft from 240 Squadron.

The first drop took place on 15 May 1957, when Wg Cdr K.G. Hubbard and his crew dropped a Blue Danube weapon armed with a Short Granite warhead at Malden Island, about 400 miles south of Kiritimati. A second weapon dropped by Sqn Ldr D. Roberts on 31 May carried an Orange Herald warhead and this was followed, on 19 June, by a third drop by Sqn Ldr L.A.G. Steel with a Purple Granite warhead. Finally that year, Sqn Ldr B.T. Millet dropped a 1.8-megaton weapon over Kiritimati itself on 8 November. Operation *Grapple*

Right: A Hastings of 24 Squadron at Kiritimati during Operation *Grapple*. The task force for the nuclear tests included Shackleton, Canberra and helicopter squadrons as well as a significant naval force and a large army contingent – the population of the island peaked at about 1,300 RAF personnel. The Hastings transport fleet played a vital role in the logistic back-up for the task force.

Opposite: The Bristol Bloodhound Mk1 surface-to-air missile (SAM) equipped ten air defence missile squadrons within Fighter Command for defending V-bomber and Thor bases. The system, which entered service in 1958, could engage targets at altitudes up to 50,000ft. (© IWM RAF-T-2703)

continued into the next year, with three more drops of different warheads over Kiritimati on 28 April, 2 and 11 September 1958.

1957 DEFENCE WHITE PAPER

The Defence White Paper published in April 1957 represented a major review of Britain's defensive needs and commitments. It heralded sweeping change through all three services, as well as ending National Service and consolidating the British aircraft industry into a small number of viable companies. For the RAF, the main results of the White Paper were the cancellation of most of the manned-aircraft projects under development in favour of missile systems, the disbandment of the RAuxAF, the loss of 75 percent of the RAF Regiment and the halving of the RAF presence in Germany. From its strength of 33 squadrons in 1955, 2TAF was to be reduced to 18 squadrons: the White Paper envisaged that by the end of 1958 there were to be, in Germany, four Day Fighter/Ground Attack (DFGA) squadrons, four strike/night interdiction squadrons, four all-weather fighter squadrons and

six reconnaissance squadrons. In the UK, the force of 160 Canberra light bombers would be reduced to just 80 aircraft, but these were to be endowed with a nuclear capability. However, the White Paper also noted the importance of establishing a core of modern transport aircraft within the RAF for the swift deployment of ground troops if needed. Finally, it was stated that 'all three services will be provided with the newest weapons,' which would include a British megaton-size nuclear weapon.

One of the missile systems referred to in the White Paper was the Douglas SM-75 Thor Intermediate Range Ballistic Missile (IRBM), which was first deployed at RAF Feltwell in September 1958. The first Thor unit was 77 Squadron: eventually 20 Thor squadrons, each equipped with three missiles, supplemented the V-force as Britain's nuclear deterrent. The year also saw the introduction of the Bristol Bloodhound 1 Surface-to-Air Missile (SAM), which equipped ten squadrons. Many of the Bloodhound squadrons took the 'number-plates' of the former Javelin units which had been disbanded during the implementation of the new government policy of replacing aircraft with missiles. However, the surviving Javelin squadrons were to get missiles

The de Havilland Firestreak infra-red homing air-to-air missile (AAM) was the first guided AAM to be used by the RAF. It equipped the Javelin (as seen here) and later the English Electric Lightning. (© IWM RAF-T-2151)

of their own: the RAF's first Air-to-Air Missiles (AAM), the de Havilland Firestreak came into service with Javelin squadrons in late 1959.

AIR-TO-AIR REFUELLING

A cliché often used when referring to air-to-air refuelling (AAR) is 'force multiplier', but the phrase does illustrate how fortunate it was, at a time when the RAF was beginning to shrink in size once again, that an AAR capability was already being developed for the V-force. Experimental work in 1951 using Lincolns and Canberras as tankers had come to nothing operationally, but it did become the basis of the trials by Flight Refuelling Ltd on behalf of the Ministry of Supply (MoS) with Valiants during 1957. This work resulted in a clearance the following

year for the Valiant to operate both as a tanker and receiver. Based at RAF Marham, 214 Squadron was the Valiant squadron chosen to undertake the in-service proving trials for the technique and the unit carried out a number of successful long-range flights. On 16 April 1959, Wg Cdr M.J. Beetham DFC took off from RAF Marham and rendezvoused with another 214 Squadron Valiant, a tanker aircraft, over Libya. After refuelling at 40,000ft, Beetham continued to Salisbury, Rhodesia, achieving, in just over 10 hours, the first non-stop flight between the UK and Rhodesia. Three months later Beetham flew a further record-breaking non-stop flight, this time from Marham to Cape Town. Reflecting the new capabilities of the aircraft, Bomber Command's Valiants were re-designated as Valiant BK1 or BK(PR)1 – the 'K' denoting a tanker aircraft – and both 214 and 90 Squadron converted to the tanker role. The other V-force aircraft were also equipped as AAR receivers.

CHANGING ROLES

Just as it had done after World War I, the RAF had shrunk dramatically at the end of World War II; it also found itself once more enforcing British rule in regions where the old status quo had been overturned by the conflict. By the end of the 1950s the colonial conflicts in the Far East, Africa and the Middle East had largely been resolved. However, political tensions in Europe had increased and a new world order had emerged, dominated by the USSR and the USA. Although it was clear by the end of that decade that the British Empire was a declining power, British military force still played an important role in global security. By the beginning of the 1960s, the RAF had adapted itself to meet the new challenges of the Cold War.

A Douglas SM-75 Thor Intermediate-Range Ballistic Missile (IRBM) is prepared for a practice launch. A total of 20 squadrons equipped with the IRBM augmented the V-Bomber force to form the UK's independent nuclear deterrent of the late 1950s and early 1960s.

CHAPTER 6

COLD WAR

1960-1974

By 1960 the world had settled into the uneasy stalemate of the 'Cold War' between the USA and the USSR, each supported by their respective allies. As an independent nuclear power, the UK played a leading role in the NATO alliance and the RAF maintained the British nuclear deterrent force comprising 18 squadrons of Valiant, Victor and Vulcan bombers, known as the 'V-Force'. These were supplemented by the 20 squadrons of Thor IRBMs. The RAF also maintained a substantial force in continental Europe: now designated RAF Germany (RAFG) the force included nuclear-capable Canberra B(I)6 and B(I)8 bombers, which could be armed with the US-supplied Mk7 nuclear weapon.

Although the focus of the Cold War was in Europe, where NATO and the Warsaw Pact faced each other across the Inner German Border (IGB), the RAF was also deployed across the world in support of the UK's global interests. In Cyprus, four squadrons of Canberra B2 bombers made up the Middle East Air Force (MEAF) Strike Wing, which was the UK's contribution to the Central Treaty Organization (CENTO). Cyprus was also home to 13 Squadron (Canberra PR7), 70 Squadron (Hastings) and 284 Squadron (Whirlwinds), while further photo-reconnaissance Canberras (of 39 Squadron) and Shackleton MR2s (of 38 Squadron) were based in Malta; another Shackleton unit (224 Squadron) was based in Gibraltar. Further to the east, Britain maintained a sizeable presence in Aden, where the RAF contingent at RAF Khormaksar comprised squadrons of Hunter FGA9s (8 Squadron), Shackleton MR2s

An Avro Lancaster, built in World War II flies over Avro Vulcan B2s on the Operational Readiness Platform (ORP) at RAF Waddington in the early 1970s. (Hulton-Deutsch/ Corbis/Getty)

An English Electric Lightning F6 of 23 Squadron intercepts a Soviet Naval Aviation (AV-MF) Tupolev Tu-95RTS (NATO reporting name Bear-D) Elint reconnaissance bomber. During the late 1960s, incursions into the UK Air Defence Region (UKADR) by Soviet long-range aircraft became increasingly common and intercepts by RAF Lightnings launched from Quick Reaction Alert (QRA) were frequent. (Crown Copyright)

(37 Squadron), Beverleys (84 Squadron) and Twin Pioneers (78 Squadron).

The Far East Air Force (FEAF), based in Singapore, was winding down from Operation *Firedog*, but it still boasted an impressive order of battle, including squadrons of Hunter FGA9s (20 Squadron), Canberra B2s (45 Squadron), Canberra PR7s (81 Squadron), Shackleton MR2s (205 Squadron), Beverleys (34 Squadron), Valettas (52 Squadron) and Sycamore HR14s (110 Squadron).

In the UK, Fighter Command started the new decade in spectacular style: the first English Electric Lightning F1 interceptors were delivered to 74 Squadron in 1960, bringing with them a Mach 2 performance that represented a massive improvement in capability over the previous generation of Hunters and Javelins. Over the next four years, Fighter Command operated a mixture of aircraft as Lightnings replaced its Hunters and Javelins. The fighters were supplemented by ten squadrons of Bloodhound 1 Surface-to-Air Missiles, which

protected the strategically important V-Bomber bases and the Thor sites.

LONG-RANGE DEPLOYMENTS

In parallel with the developing AAR capability within the V-Force, two Javelin FAW9 all-weather fighter squadrons also started practising AAR from Valiant tankers in 1960. The first Javelin unit to qualify its crews in AAR was 23 Squadron, which was followed later in the year by 64 Squadron. In late September, two pairs of Javelins from 23 Squadron flew to Mauripur (Karachi) staging in eight legs via Orange, Luqa, El Adem, Nicosia, Diyabakir, Mehrabad and Sharjah. On 29 September 1960 two more Javelins set off from RAF Coltishall for Exercise *Dyke*, an AAR-supported deployment to Singapore. Accompanied by Valiants of 214 Squadron, the Javelins routed via Akrotiri to Mauripur (Karachi), achieving the journey in just in two legs. Four Javelins (operating in two pairs and accompanied by Valiant tankers) then flew via Gan to Changi, arriving on 4 and 7 October. Exercise *Dyke* was the first long-range deployment of RAF tactical aircraft supported by AAR.

Having proved that a long-range deployment was possible and having proved the route, the next step was to move a squadron-sized force. This exercise would be more complex because of the need to manage multiple refuelling brackets with a relatively small number of tankers for a relatively large number of receivers. Exercise *Pounce*, which started on 8 June 1961, was the deployment of eight Javelin FAW9s (five from 23 Squadron and three from 64 Squadron) to Mauripur. All the Javelins reached Mauripur on 14 June, with stopovers at Akrotiri and Bahrain. Through Exercise *Dyke* and Exercise *Pounce* the RAF had demonstrated the capability to deploy swiftly a fighting strength of tactical aircraft globally.

HUMANITARIAN RELIEF

The new decade brought with it a new role for the RAF, that of providing humanitarian aid in the wake of natural disasters. The first of these was an earthquake on 1 March 1960, which destroyed the Moroccan city of Agadir. In the aftermath of the earthquake, the Shackletons of 224 Squadron flew in food, blankets and medical supplies; they were also used to evacuate survivors, ferrying them to Marseilles, Rabat, Casablanca and Gibraltar. A Blackburn Beverley C1 also transported 5 tons of disease-control chemicals into Agadir. Two months later, on 22 May, the most powerful earthquake ever recorded struck the city of Valdivia in Chile. Once again, the RAF provided assistance; this time supplies were flown to Chile by Bristol Britannia C1 transports of 99 Squadron.

In early 1961, the northern provinces of Kenya were affected by a severe drought, which led to famine across the region. During March and April, the Beverleys of 30, 47 and 53 Squadrons dropped over 140 tons of maize and 9 tons of biltong to people living in inaccessible areas. Later in the year, severe flooding in the region brought further problems. In an operation which commenced at the beginning of October, the Scottish Aviation Twin Pioneers of 21 Squadron delivered 120 tons of food to people stranded by flood waters. Meanwhile, operating from Mogadishu, Valettas from 233 Squadron dropped food into areas of Somalia which were also affected by the flooding.

May 1960 saw the start of the process to qualify the Gloster Javelin FAW9 crews of 23 Squadron in air-to-air refuelling (AAR). A Javelin of 23 Squadron refuels from a Vickers Valiant B(K)1 of 214 Squadron. Both units were involved in Exercise *Dyke* in October 1960 when four Javelins were deployed to Singapore.

The short take-off and landing (STOL) performance of the Scottish Aviation Twin Pioneer CC1 gave the aircraft a unique capability to operate in areas impossible to other types. Known by its crews as the 'Twin Pin,' the type saw service in Aden, Borneo and Bahrain, as well as Kenya. During the emergency of October 1961 four aircraft from 21 Squadron flew 146 sorties to deliver food to villages which were cut off by floodwater. (RAFM)

Shackletons from 42, 204 and 219 Squadron, Hastings from 24 Squadron and Britannias from 99 and 511 Squadrons were also heavily involved in airlifting supplies into Belize in the wake of Hurricane Hattie, which had caused devastation in British Honduras in October 1961.

KUWAIT CRISIS

The agreement by Britain in June 1961 to continue to guarantee the security of the independent state of Kuwait was countered a few days later by a claim by Iraq that Kuwait was in fact part of Iraq. When Iraqi troops and armour were subsequently reported to be heading towards the Kuwaiti border, the British initiated Operation *Vantage*, a contingency plan to reinforce the region. The first forces to arrive were the Hunters of 8 Squadron (based at Khormaksar) and 208 Squadron (based at Nairobi), which deployed to Bahrain on 30 June. They were joined by two Shackletons from 37 Squadron. Four Canberra B(I)8 interdictors of 88 Squadron arrived at Sharjah from Wildenrath, Germany, on 1 July and they were followed by four Canberra B(I)6 interdictors from 213 Squadron the next day. HMS *Bulwark* arrived with 42 Commando Royal Marines (42 Cdo RM) a day later. Meanwhile, transport aircraft were re-tasked to meet the challenge of transporting troops and equipment to the Gulf; this task was complicated by being unable to overfly most of the states in the Middle East and by a temporary ban on overflights by Sudan and Turkey. Nevertheless, by 4 July the air transport fleet serving the Kuwait deployment comprised 14 Britannias, 24 Beverleys, 27 Hastings and six Valettas. The long-range aircraft flew their loads into Bahrain where the Valettas and half of the Beverleys (those based in the Middle East) flew a shuttle service to Kuwait. Meanwhile the Hunters had moved to Kuwait. The build-up of forces was completed by 9 July and the swift show of strength was sufficient to deter any aggression by Iraq. Most of the force was withdrawn by the end of the month, but a force of Hunters (provided in turns by 8 and 208

Squadrons) remained in Kuwait for the next three months and 12 Beverleys from 30 and 84 Squadrons remained in Bahrain ready to return the 2nd Battalion Parachute Regiment (2 Para) to Kuwait if needed.

BERLIN

The closure of the border between East and West Berlin on 13 August 1961 and the subsequent building of the Berlin Wall triggered an international crisis. For NATO forces in Germany the immediate issue was to ensure the integrity of air corridors into Berlin. At RAF Gütersloh, the Battle Flight was increased to six armed aircraft comprising a pair on the Operational Readiness Platform (ORP) by the runway at 2min readiness, another pair at 5min and a third pair at 30min. Battle Flight was maintained by the Hunter F6 day fighters of 14 Squadron during daylight hours and through the night by missile-armed Javelin FAW8 all-weather fighters of 41 and 85 Squadrons, which had been hastily deployed from the UK. As a reflection of the heightened tension, Battle Flight was launched 26 times in the month of August – about three times the normal number. Four-month detachments by UK-based Javelin squadrons continued to bolster RAFG's air defence capability for the next year.

INDONESIAN CONFRONTATION

The proposal to incorporate the states of Sabah and Sarawak in northern Borneo into the Federation of Malaysia in 1963 was strongly opposed by Indonesia, which also laid claim to the entire island of Borneo. On 8 December 1962 Indonesian-backed dissidents started a rebellion in Brunei. Troops of the Gurkha Rifles, swiftly deployed that afternoon from Singapore to Brunei in three Beverleys of 34 Squadron and a Bristol Britannia from 99 Squadron, were able to regain control of Brunei town the following morning. However, rebels still held the oilfield area at Seria.

A Westland Whirlwind HAR10 of 110 Squadron in Borneo, where the campaign proved the true value of the helicopter in RAF service. Unlike earlier piston-engined types, the HAR10 was powered by a Bristol Siddeley (Rolls-Royce) Gnome gas turbine engine. (RAFM)

The following morning a Beverley of 34 Squadron flown by Flt Lt M.G. Fenn delivered the Queen's Own Highlanders onto the waterlogged and rebel-held airfield at Anduki, near Seria. Simultaneously, five Twin Pioneers of 209 Squadron landed Gurkhas on an airstrip ten miles to the west. Both forces converged on Seria and two days later the rebels had been cleared from the area.

For the next few months, British troops remained in the Brunei jungle to mop up remaining rebels. Tactics similar to those used in Malaya worked well, using helicopters to ferry troops and supplies around the jungle. Initially, the helicopters were provided by the Royal Navy, but these were augmented by Sycamore and later Whirlwind HAR10 helicopters

of 110 Squadron and four Bristol Belvedere HC1s from 66 Squadron, which were based at Labuan. Also at Labuan, four Hawker Hunters from 20 Squadron were available for airstrikes if necessary. President Sukarno of Indonesia announced a policy of 'Confrontation' in April 1963 and sporadic low-level violence continued over the next few months. However, when the Malaysian Federation was formalized in September 1963, armed incursions into Sabah and Sarawak by Indonesian troops became widespread.

In Singapore, a Quick Reaction Alert (QRA) nicknamed Operation *Tramp* had been established at Tengah in early 1963, comprising two live-armed Javelin FAW9 fighters from 60 Squadron.

In October, the *Tramp* state was increased to six aircraft at Tengah and a further two at Butterworth and the following month FEAF was reinforced by four Javelin FAW9R aircraft from 64 Squadron, which had been participating in Exercise *Shiksha* in India. There were a number of scrambles to intercept Indonesian aircraft which approached Malaysian airspace. Four more Javelin FAW9R aircraft from 23 Squadron were dispatched to FEAF in January 1964 during Operation *Merino*. Despite an official ceasefire in early 1964, the Indonesians declared the intention of resupplying rebel groups in Borneo by air and it was clear that Javelins would also be needed to fulfil air-defence requirements over Borneo. Detachments of two aircraft each were therefore established at Labuan and Kuching, joining the four Hunters from 20 Squadron already at each of these locations. Apart from maintaining QRA readiness, the Hunters and Javelins were used for low-level standing patrols and also as escorts for transport aircraft carrying out supply drops. By the end of February 1964, the Javelins of 60 Squadron were responsible for the air defence of a 1,000-mile frontage from Butterworth in the northwest to Labuan. At this time, the Operation *Tramp* task

increased to carry out low-level coastal patrols at dawn and dusk.

Coastal patrols were also conducted by Shackletons of 205 Squadron (which was reinforced by 203 Squadron in late 1964). Operating from Labuan, the Shackletons carried out night patrols to prevent weapons being smuggled along the coast. In Borneo, the air transport operation had become an impressively efficient organization: by mid-1964 it was estimated that the transport fleet, comprising Beverleys of 34 Squadron, Hastings of 48 Squadron and Armstrong-Whitworth Argosy C1 transports of 215 Squadron, had carried over 52,000 personnel and 2,700 tons of freight between Singapore and Borneo. The same aircraft, augmented by Valettas of 52 Squadron, Bristol freighters of 41 Squadron RNZAF and Twin Pioneers of 209 Squadron were used to airdrop supplies to ground forces stationed in remote jungle sites. Helicopters from all three services were also proving invaluable for moving troops and equipment. The RAF component of the helicopter force in Borneo comprised the Belvederes of 66 Squadron and Whirlwinds of 103 and 110 Squadrons and later also the Whirlwinds of 230 Squadron.

A Gloster Javelin FAW9 of 60 Squadron flying a low-level patrol along the coast of Malaya (Malaysia). The squadron was responsible for the defence of a 1,000-mile long area from northern Malaya to Borneo. (Pitchfork)

The crisis deepened in September 1964 when Indonesian troops landed on the west coast of Malaya and a force of paratroops was dropped into Jahore province, although they were rounded up swiftly. Another landing was made on the southwestern tip of Jahore on 23 December and the Hunters of 20 Squadron and Canberra B15 bombers of 45 Squadron carried out rocket and strafing attacks against these insurgents, directed by a Forward Air Controller (FAC). As part of a reinforcement programme, RAFG was tasked to dispatch eight Canberra B(I)8 aircraft to Malaysia to operate in the interdictor role. After 48 hours' notice, four Canberras each from 3 Squadron (based at Geilenkirchen) and 14 Squadron (based at Wildenrath) deployed to Kuantan, arriving on 30 October. A further eight Canberras from 73 Squadron at Akrotiri and the Javelin of 'A' Flight 64 Squadron also deployed to Tengah as reinforcements. In fact, the RAFG and Near East Air Force (NEAF) Canberras were not needed operationally and they returned to Germany the following month. A longer deployment to Kuantan by RAFG aircraft started in February 1965 for eight Canberras from 16 Squadron, which was normally based at Laarbruch. These aircraft remained at Kuantan for four months and on one occasion were called to strafe a suspected insurgent position in the jungle of northeast Malaya. Thereafter a continuous detachment of Canberras was maintained at Kuantan by aircraft and crews from NEAF, with each squadron (6, 32, 73 and 249 Squadrons) standing a two- or three-month tour.

The Javelins in FEAF were further reinforced in April 1965 by the re-formation as a complete squadron of 64 Squadron. During the year, Operation *Tramp* launches intercepted Indonesian Tupolev Tu-16 aircraft on numerous occasions. The Indonesian offensive action in Borneo began to falter after a coup in Jakarta in late 1965, but the RAF's air operations, particularly by helicopters and transport aircraft, continued apace in support of the army's campaign in the jungle. After four years of intensive operations, the Confrontation ended in August 1966.

NUCLEAR DETERRENCE

Britain's nuclear deterrent at the beginning of the decade consisted of the 20 Thor IRBM squadrons and the 18 V-Force squadrons armed with the Yellow Sun free-fall nuclear weapon. The withdrawal of the Thor in 1962 coincided with the entry into service of the Avro Blue Steel W100 missile. Launched from a Vulcan B2A or Victor B2BS, the rocket-powered Blue Steel could carry a megaton-range warhead some 150 miles after launch, giving the bomber a 'stand-off' capability and enabling it to stay clear of the target defences. The weapon was introduced into service by 617 Squadron at Scampton in October 1962 and the remaining two

A Bristol/Westland Belvedere HC1 of 66 Squadron delivers supplies to a Gurkha detachment in Borneo. The Belvedere was powered by two Napier Gazelle NGa2 gas turbines and could carry 18 fully armed troops or an underslung load of up to 5,250lbs. (RAFM)

Vulcan units at Scampton, 27 and 83 Squadrons, were similarly equipped in early 1963. The Victors of the Wittering Wing, comprising 100 and 139 Squadrons, were also armed with Blue Steel. For the next six years, the UK's first line of deterrence was maintained by a small number of Blue Steel-armed V-Bombers standing nuclear Quick Reaction Alert (QRA[N]). The QRA aircraft were held at a nominal 15min readiness, but on exercise scrambles they could usually be airborne in under 4min.

The shooting down of a USAF Lockheed U-2 aircraft over Russia in 1960 showed that Soviet surface-to-air missile (SAM) technology would soon close off the high-level airspace to bombers and that year 207 Squadron's Valiants started operating at low level. They were followed by the Valiants of 148 and 49 Squadrons, and the Vulcan and Victor

squadrons followed suit in 1963. Although Blue Steel had originally been designed to be dropped from medium level. modification to the W200 standard gave it a low-level launch capability. By late 1963, the Valiants had been converted to the AAR tanker role, but the type was hastily withdrawn from service in early 1965 after cracks were found in the wing spars of a number of aircraft. As a result of this unforeseen development, six Victors were converted to the tanker role in 1965 and over the next three years the Victor was phased out of the bombing role completely as the rest were converted to be exclusively a tanker aircraft.

From 1966, the Yellow Sun weapon was replaced by the WE177, which was capable of being dropped from a low-level laydown attack; however, the RAF was soon to hand over responsibility for maintaining

A Shackleton MR2C of 205 Squadron at low level over the Borneo jungle. Unique to 205 Squadron, the aircraft were MR2 airframes updated with the navigation and attack systems of the Shackleton MR3. (RAFM)

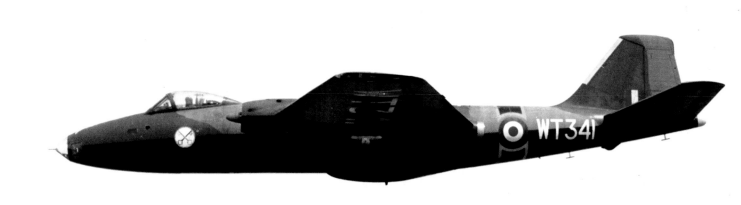

the UK nuclear deterrent to the RN submarine force. At midnight on 30 June 1969, the Polaris A-3 Submarine-Launched Ballistic Missile (SLBM) took over from Blue Steel, which was withdrawn from service at the end of the year.

During the 1960s, the Victors and Vulcans of Bomber Command carried out frequent detachments abroad, including Exercise *Moonflower* and Exercise *Sunflower* to Singapore, *Western Ranger* to Offut AFB, Nebraska and Exercise *Goose Ranger* to Goose Bay in Labrador and also Exercise *Sunspots* to Cyprus. The latter detachments included exercises as part of CENTO, flying sorties from forward operating bases in Iran. In early 1969, there was a more permanent Vulcan presence in the Middle East when 9 and 35 Squadrons moved to Akrotiri to replace the Canberras of the NEAF Strike Wing.

CYPRUS

Over the course of 1963 the constitution of the recently independent Cyprus started to unravel. Violence broke out between Greek and Turkish Cypriots in mid-December, and British forces on the island found themselves in the midst of warring factions. Turkish

fighters flew at low level over Nicosia city, as armed gangs from both sides threatened the security of RAF personnel. The crisis came to a head just before Christmas and Transport Command started a major airlift of reinforcements into the island. Between 26 December and 4 January, nearly 3,000 armed troops were flown into Cyprus along with 120 tons of cargo, 36 Landrovers and three Westland Scout helicopters. On 28 December five Beverleys from 47 Squadron transported the armoured cars of the 14/20 Hussars from Libya to Akrotiri. On 13 February 1964, eight Britannias ferried the 1st Battalion Duke of Edinburgh's Regiment from Malta to Cyprus and a week later a fleet of ten Britannias from 99 and 511 Squadrons, assisted by three Argosies from 114 Squadron and two Beverleys from 47 Squadron transported the entire Divisional HQ of 3 Division into Cyprus.

The Javelins of 29 Squadron had been moved overnight at short notice from Nicosia to the more secure base at Akrotiri. The squadron flew 62 operational sorties, mainly standing patrols designed to deter the low-level incursions by Turkish aircraft. After a brief return to Nicosia, the Squadron was back at Akrotiri in mid-January 1964 and flying was limited to operational tasks. The standby commitment was for one aircraft at 2min readiness during daylight hours

A Canberra B(I)8 of 16 Squadron, one of the RAF Germany units which deployed to Kuantan in response to the Indonesian Confrontation. (RAFM)

An Avro Vulcan B2A of 617 Squadron armed with an Avro Blue Steel stand-off missile. Between 1962 and 1966 the Vulcan and Victor aircraft of Bomber Command were equipped with the Blue Steel missile to provided Britain's independent nuclear deterrent. (RAFM)

and for one aircraft at 10 min at night; for both day and night another back-up aircraft was maintained at 30min readiness. Scrambles by the Battle Flight to intercept Turkish Republic F-84F Thunderstreak fighter-bombers became regular events over the next three months. The political tension had dissipated a little by early April and the last 'live' interception was by Flt. Lt. J Sneddon and Flt. Lt. Bullock, who intercepted a single F-84F some 60 miles northwest of Akrotiri; however, the target was already heading back towards Turkey at 18,000ft.

RADFAN OPERATIONS

Following the revolution in Yemen in 1962, Egypt began to stir up insurrection amongst dissident tribes in Yemen and the Radfan against the British presence in Aden. A State of Emergency was declared in Aden after the attempted assassination of the British High Commissioner in December 1963. The following month Operation *Nutcracker* was mounted as a show of force in the Radfan.

On 4 January 1964, Arab Federal Regular Army (FRA) troops were inserted into the hills above the Wadi Rabwa by Bristol Belvedere helicopters of 26 Squadron. The landings were opposed by snipers and the second Belvedere was hit by rifle rounds as it landed. When snipers could be located, airstrikes by the Hunters of 8 Squadron were called in to neutralize them. The Belvederes were also used to lift 105mm howitzers from the Royal Horse Artillery (RHA) into firing positions on the high ground. Hunters from 8 and 43 Squadrons mounted intensive operations over the next few days in support of the ground forces.

However, the FRA then found itself overstretched across the protectorate and had to withdraw from the Radfan in early March. This move was interpreted as a sign of weakness by the Yemenis, who then mounted cross-border raids into the Aden hinterland. In response to these incursions, a force of 16 Hunters from 8 and 43 Squadrons mounted a rocket attack on the Yemeni fort at Harib on 28 March. The raid was successful, leaving the fort in ruins.

A second operation was mounted in Radfan, starting in April 1964, this time the ground force, known as 'Radforce,' was made up of troops from 45 Cdo RM and 3 Para. In preparation for an airborne assault drop by 3 Para, a SAS patrol was inserted into the area by helicopter on the night of 29 April in order to secure and mark the DZ. Unfortunately, the SAS patrol was discovered by rebels the following morning, still short of its objective and it was pinned down by a well-armed force of 40 to 50 rebels. During the day, the patrol was supported by Hunters of 43 and 208 Squadrons, which kept up almost continuous strafing attacks on rebel positions until the patrol was able to extract itself after nightfall.

The Hunters were in action again on 1 May, providing close air support for 3 Para as it advanced into the Wadi Taym. At times the Hunters were called in to attack rebel positions only 150 yards away from friendly troops, and some injuries were caused amongst the paratroopers by empty cannon cartridges ejected from the Hunters as they flew low overhead. At Khormaksar two armed Hunters were now kept at cockpit readiness, able to take off within 10min if they were needed in the Radfan area. On 7 May, the Hunters were again called in to clear the way when the advance on the Jebel Huriyah met heavy fire from well-defended positions along the ridge.

The Hunters also supported the Belvederes which were lifting 105mm howitzers into forward positions.

A Hawker Hunter FGA9 of the Khormaksar Wing makes a low pass over troops of 45 Commando Royal Marines (RM) deployed in the Radfan. (Terry Fincher/Daily Express/Hulton Archive/ Getty)

Throughout the Radfan campaign, the Belvedere crews distinguished themselves by manoeuvring the howitzers precisely onto precipitous firing positions amongst the mountains, often operating above the published ceiling of the aircraft. The operation in the Radfan was kept supplied by airlift into the 1,000yd airstrip at Thumier, which was just long enough to be used by Beverleys of 84 Squadron from Khormaksar. The Scottish Aviation Twin Pioneers of 78 Squadron also played a vital role in the resupply operation.

On 23 and 24 May, Hunter airstrikes were called in by 3 Para, whose advance on the Bakri Ridge was held up by rebel positions comprising a complex of caves and tunnels at the top of the ridge. Hunter airstrikes were also called for on 26 May against rebels in the Wadi Dhubsan, which lay at the bottom of a steep-sided ravine, presenting challenging flying conditions.

Flying in support of operations in the Radfan was intense and during May and June each of the Hunter squadrons at Khormaksar flew in the region of 150 sorties each month. The army had established control over most of the area by the end of June and for the next

three months RAF aircraft were used for 'air control' operations. Most of the rebel villages had conceded to the government by October and the last settlement was brought to heel after Hunters destroyed the rebel hideouts there in early November 1964.

BERLIN CONTINUES

The air corridors to Berlin were threatened once more in April 1965, when the Soviets attempted to prevent the Bundestag from meeting in Berlin on 7 April. The Soviets claimed that they were holding an air exercise between 5 and 10 April and that they could not guarantee the safety of aircraft in the Berlin air corridors. Operation *Gopherwood* was initiated on 6 April and five Javelin FAW9 fighters from 5 Squadron deployed forward from Geilenkirchen to Celle. They were joined by two Argosy C1 aircraft from Transport Command, which flew ten probing sorties over the next few days along the air corridors into Gatow. The Bundestag

The Bristol Britannia entered service with 99 and 511 Squadrons at RAF Lyneham in 1959. Capable of carrying 113 passengers or 37,400lb of freight, the type served as the strategic transport aircraft suppling British military interests across the globe. (RAFM)

Above: The Armstrong Whitworth Argosy saw service in the UK, Cyprus, Aden and the Far East. The cockpit was above the spacious cargo hold and loads could be air-dropped through the 'crocodile jaw' doors at the rear of the aircraft. (RAFM)

Left: A Blackburn Beverley of 84 Squadron on a desert landing area in the Radfan. During the campaign the aircraft operated into the 3,000ft airstrip at Thumier to resupply the ground forces. (RAFM)

Above: A Hawker Hunter FGA9 of 8 Squadron over the Radfan. The aircraft of the Khormaksar Wing provided close air support to ground forces throughout the campaign. (RAFM)

Right: A Bristol Belvedere twin-rotor helicopter of 26 Squadron carrying a 105mm howitzer. During the Radfan campaign 26 Squadron drew admiration for the ability to carry guns over difficult terrain and place them accurately into firing positions. (RAFM)

meeting took place as planned and the crisis did not escalate any further; the Javelins were stood down on 10 April. However, the Javelins were fast becoming obsolescent and they were replaced by the Lightning F2 fighters of 19 and 92 Squadrons, which arrived at Gütersloh and Geilenkirchen respectively in late 1965.

STRATEGIC RECONNAISSANCE

The strategic reconnaissance work started in the 1950s continued into the next decade. Equipped with Comet C2(RC) and Canberra B6(RC) aircraft, 51 Squadron continued clandestine operations to gather Elint from the periphery of the Soviet Union and the Warsaw Pact countries. The Comets also worked closely with the Victor B(SR)2 which had replaced the Valiant B(PR)K1 in 543 Squadron in late 1964. These aircraft were tasked with obtaining imagery of the routes that might be taken by V-Bombers on their way to targets in the Soviet Union. The Victors were also used for long-range maritime radar reconnaissance, tracking the movements of naval forces, which became an increasingly important role as the Soviet Fleet grew in strength through the 1960s. Strategic reconnaissance was carried out in close co-operation with the US military, including the participation of RAF pilots in

An Avro Shackleton MR 3 parked next to its replacement in the role of maritime patrol, a Hawker Siddeley Nimrod MR1. Three Nimrod R1 variants were also built to replace the Comet C2(RC) Elint aircraft. (RAFM)

Project *Aquatone*, the Lockheed U-2 programme. Four RAF pilots, who were trained to fly the U-2 in 1958, carried out missions from Incirlik in the early 1960s and a small cadre of RAF personnel remained part of *Aquatone* through the rest of the decade.

ZAMBIA

The political tension that had been growing in southern Africa through the early 1960s came to a head with Rhodesia's Unilateral Declaration of Independence (UDI) on 11 November 1965. The UK response included economic sanctions – and also preparations to move military forces into Zambia, a political gesture ostensibly to deter the Rhodesians from attacking the Kariba Dam. On 28 November, ten Javelins of 29 Squadron took off from Cyprus, routing over the next five days via Diyabakir (Turkey), Dezful/Vahdati (Iran), Masirah, and Khormaksar to Nairobi. After a three-day stay in Nairobi, nine Javelins deployed to Ndola in Zambia's Copperbelt to take up a defensive readiness state. Three Hastings from 70 Squadron provided transport for the ground crew and support staff.

At Ndola, the Javelin detachment was able to use Zambian Air Force facilities on the airfield for its operational needs, but the personnel were accommodated at the premises of the Zambia Trade Fair, where the domestic arrangements were basic. However, the main problem facing the squadron was a lack of fuel: the normal route for oil imports to Zambia was through Rhodesia, so the economic sanctions impacted directly on the activities of 29 Squadron in the country. A major airlift operation organized from Aden brought fuel and oil into Zambia by Britannias and Argosys via Aden, but even so in the early days of the detachment there was only enough fuel for three Javelin sorties per day. The fuel situation improved as the airlift gathered strength, but throughout the detachment the flying programme was severely hampered by a shortage of fuel.

On 9 December 1965, four aircraft were deployed forward to Lusaka, where a mobile Ground Control Intercept (GCI) site had been set up. Here the conditions were even more challenging and the squadron operations centre was set up in tents. Operationally, the short runway, some 4,000ft above sea level, was close to the limits for Javelin operations so flying was limited to daylight only. Initially, flying from Lusaka was limited to operational scrambles only. Two fully armed aircraft were kept at readiness, one at 10min and one at 30min. Over the next eight months of the detachment, the QRA aircraft were typically scrambled about twice a month, but any tracks from Rhodesia had usually turned south well before they reached Zambian airspace.

A Victor B(SR)2 strategic reconnaissance aircraft of 543 Squadron banks away to display the reconnaissance equipment. Fitted inside the bomb bay in three sections, the equipment could be varied to suit the task and could include a F49 vertical, F96 oblique or night-capable F89 camera, photo-flash flares, air sampling equipment and/or extra fuel tanks. (RAFM)

Above: Gloster Javelin FAW9Rs of 29 Squadron, armed with Firestreak missiles maintain QRA readiness at dusk from Lusaka during the Rhodesian UDI crisis. (RAFM)

Right: A Bristol Britannia on the apron at Majunga Airport, Madagascar during the Rhodesian crisis. Apart from flying aviation fuel into Zambia for use by the Javelins of 29 Squadron, they provided logistic support to the detachment of Shackletons operating from Madagascar to enforce the oil embargo on Rhodesia. (Flintham)

Aircraft were routinely exchanged between Zambia and Cyprus so that servicing could be carried out at Akrotiri and this in turn gave opportunities for some personnel to return home, even if only temporarily. In general, the Javelin held up well in the arduous conditions, although two aircraft were damaged beyond repair in landing accidents in June. The last operational scramble from Lusaka was made on 11 August 1966 by Fg Offs M.B. Langham and R.J.P. MacRae to investigate an unidentified contact coming from the south, but once again the target turned away without violating Zambian airspace. The 29 Squadron detachment to Zambia was eventually withdrawn at the end of August 1966.

Meanwhile from March 1966, Shackletons of 37 Squadron had been detached to Majunga in Malagasy (Madagascar) in support of the naval blockade of the Mozambique port of Beira. The aircraft patrolled the sea areas and identifying shipping and passing details of name, port of registration, position

and course on to the RN ships enforcing the blockade. The Beira blockade continued until February 1972, covered by sequential detachments of Shackletons from 37, 38, 42, 204 and 210 Squadrons.

WITHDRAWAL FROM ADEN

Although the Federal Government of South Arabia had re-established its authority in the Radfan in 1964, there was increasing terrorist activity throughout South Arabia in the following years. The British statement in 1966 that South Arabia would become independent 'no later than 1968' had started a race for post-colonial power by competing nationalist movements, of which the National Liberation Front (NLF) regarded terrorism and criminal violence as being acceptable political methods. The main role of the RAF in counter-terrorism was to support ground troops, mainly by providing airlift and air supply.

A Lockheed C-130 Hercules of 36 Squadron, based at RAF Lyneham. The first unit to receive the type was 48 Squadron at RAF Changi and it also equipped 24, 30, 36 and 47 Squadrons in the UK and 70 Squadron at RAF Akrotiri, Cyprus.

A flypast over the Joint Headquarters (JHQ) at Rheindahlen shows the aircraft types operated by RAF Germany in the early 1970s. Three McDonnell Douglas F-4M Phantom FGR2 aircraft from the Brüggen Wing lead a Lightning F2A from 19 Squadron (based at RAF Gütersloh), two Buccaneer S2Bs from the Laarbruch Wing and a Harrier GR1 from 20 Squadron based at RAF Wildenrath.

However, the Hunters were sometimes called upon to intervene during operations 'up country'. In 1966, it was decided that all such operations would be covered by Hunters and landing by tactical transport aircraft would be preceded by a low-level 'beat up' of the airstrip by a pair of Hunters to advertise their presence. All the dependents of servicemen, amounting to some 6,600 women and children, were evacuated in a major airlift operation between May and June 1967 by Vickers VC10s, Britannias and Comets of Air Support Command. This was followed in November by another, larger operation, to evacuate all service personnel. Many of the flying

units had either been disbanded or re-deployed elsewhere, but there were still 3,700 personnel to be withdrawn in just seven days. Once again, the VC10s of 10 Squadron and Britannias of 99 and 511 Squadrons were used, operating from Bahrain; they were supplemented by two new types – the Short Belfast from 53 Squadron and the Lockheed Hercules of 36 Squadron. Each day there were around four Britannia flights into Khormaksar, each aircraft picking up 110 passengers, seven Hercules flights picking up both freight and passengers and two Belfast flights, carrying freight only. Aircraft spent just 40min on the ground before departing to

Bahrain, from where passengers were flown back to the UK by VC10 or Britannia. The last aircraft left Khormaksar on 28 November 1967.

CYPRUS CONTINUES

Inter-communal tensions rose again in Cyprus after disturbances on 15 and 16 November 1967. The Turkish Air Force started reconnaissance flights over Cyprus on the morning of 18 November, including some violations of the Sovereign Base Areas (SBAs). Seven F-84Fs were involved on the first day and all were intercepted by the Lightnings of 56 Squadron. Turkish overflights continued over the next days as the crisis deepened. Turkish F-100 Super Sabres were also used over Cyprus for the first time. Every 'raid' was intercepted by the 56 Squadron QRA pilots, but the Lightnings kept their distance in order not to provoke any further action from the Turks. Some Turkish naval

vessels were detected to the north of the island, so a detachment of Shackletons which had been due to leave Cyprus was retained. Meanwhile plans were laid to evacuate British nationals from the island by mass airlift, if necessary. The Turkish overflights peaked at 14 aircraft on 1 December, but by 4 December the crisis had been defused. The Lightnings had carried out over 50 QRA launches and claimed a 100 percent record in intercepting the Turkish aircraft.

RE-STRUCTURING & RE-EQUIPMENT

Sweeping changes to the RAF resulted from the Defence Review of 1968, in particular the withdrawal of forces in the Far East and Persian Gulf in the early 1970s. The small forces in Bahrain, comprising the Hunters of 8 and 208 Squadron and in Sharjah, comprising Andovers of 84 Squadron and Shackletons

The Vickers VC10 C1 entered service with 10 Squadron at RAF Fairford in 1966. The military version of the aircraft was based on the fuselage of the civilian airliner, but was fitted with the more powerful Rolls-Royce Conway 301 engines and the improved fuel capacity of the Super VC10. (RAFM)

Lightning F3 fighters (the second aircraft is a Lightning T5) of 56 Squadron at readiness on the line at RAF Akrotiri. During the tension in late 1967, the squadron's aircraft intercepted a number of Turkish Air Force aircraft including the Republic F-84F Thunderstreak, RF-84G Thunderflash and North American F-100 Super Sabre.

of 210 Squadron, would be withdrawn in 1971. FEAF and its constituent units in Singapore, comprising the Lightning F6 fighters of 74 Squadron, Hunters of 20 Squadron, Canberra B2 bombers of 45 Squadron, Canberra PR3 photo-reconnaissance aircraft of 81 Squadron and Whirlwinds of 103 Squadron would be disbanded in 1971, leaving the Whirlwind HR10 helicopters of 28 Squadron at Hong Kong as the only flying unit permanently based east of Suez. The last flying unit based at Gibraltar, 203 Squadron equipped with Shackletons, had already returned to the UK, but NEAF remained intact with aircraft based in Cyprus and Malta.

The command structure in the UK was also streamlined, with the merging of Fighter, Bomber and Coastal Commands into a single Strike Command. Each of the former Commands became, instead, a Group within Strike Command: 1 Group had responsibility for the Strike/Attack role within the UK, 11 Group for Air Defence and 18 Group for Maritime Operations. Transport Command had already been redesignated as Air Support Command and now included two Hunter FGA9 Squadrons (1 and 54 Squadrons) as part of the UK Mobile Force (UKMF).

The V-Force, which had peaked at a strength of 18 squadrons in its heyday of the early 1960s, closed the decade with just two Vulcan Wings at Scampton (comprising 27, 83 and 617 Squadrons) and Waddington (comprising 44, 50 and 101 Squadrons). The Victor B(SR)2 remained in service with 543 Squadron and the Victor K1A tankers with 55, 57 and 214 Squadrons at Marham. The AAR tanker role had become a critical part of the UK air defence system, as the Lightning F6 which now equipped 5, 11, 23, 29 and 111 Squadrons, was essentially a short-range aeroplane and long-range interceptions of Soviet aircraft depended on tankers accompanying the fighters. During the 1960s an increasing number of Soviet long-range aircraft were intercepted in the UK Air Defence Region (UKADR) by fighters launched from QRA.

However, for all its reductions in squadron numbers, the Defence Review did usher in some high-quality improvements in equipment. The

Hawker-Siddeley Nimrod MR1, which was the long-overdue replacement for the Shackleton in the maritime patrol role, marked a massive increase in capability. In the early 1960s the Soviet Navy had completed the transition from its origins as a coastal force at the end of World War II, into a truly global blue-water force. NATO needed effective long-range Maritime Patrol Aircraft (MPA) to counter the huge Soviet submarine force, a capability that Nimrod provided to the RAF. Obsolescent Canberra strike/attack aircraft were also to be replaced by the Hawker-Siddeley Buccaneer S2 and the McDonnell-Douglas Phantom FGR2, two aircraft which represented significant improvements in performance over their predecessors. Furthermore, the introduction of the Hawker-Siddeley Harrier GR1 with its unique Vertical/Short Take-Off and Landing (V/STOL) capability gave the RAF new dimensions of flexibility for its Close Air Support (CAS) aircraft. The Harrier entered service with 1 Squadron at Wittering in 1969 and subsequently equipped three more units, 3, 4 and 20 Squadrons at Wildenrath in Germany. From January 1971, RAFG also boasted two Buccaneer strike/attack squadrons (15 and 16 Squadrons) at Laarbruch and three Phantom squadrons (14, 17 and 31 Squadrons) at Bruggen. Three more Phantom units, 6, 41 and 54 Squadrons, were part of 38 Group, a mobile tactical force intended to reinforce 'hotspots' when required.

OPERATION *SHEEPSKIN*

The population of the small Caribbean island of Anguilla staged a commensurately small revolution in early 1969 to highlight their objection to being amalgamated with St Kitts. The rather heavy-handed response from London was Operation *Sheepskin*, an invasion of Anguilla on 19 March 1969 by RM commandos from two frigates as well as two companies of 2 Para, which were delivered by aircraft. Four VC10s, one Britannia and one Comet transported the troops and 40 officers from the Metropolitan Police to Antigua, from where

A Hawker Siddeley Andover C1 of 46 Squadron touches down in Anguilla during Operation *Sheepskin* in 1969. The type had an impressive short take-off and landing (STOL), being able to operate from unprepared strips less than 3,000ft long. The type was fitted with a rear ramp and 'kneeling' main undercarriage to facilitate cargo operations.

they were flown to Anguilla in the seven Hercules and three Andovers which had transported their equipment via Keflavik, Gander and Bermuda. Unsurprisingly, the landings were unopposed and 'peace' was quickly restored.

NORTHERN IRELAND

A rather more serious operation started on 14 June 1969 when a detachment of four Wessex HC2 helicopters from 72 Squadron were sent to Ballykelly, Northern Ireland, to support the authorities in the deteriorating situation. In August, the annual march in Londonderry degenerated into wide-scale rioting across the Province and when the police lost control, the army was hastily called in to assist the civil power. The duty 'Spearhead Battalion' deployed to the Province by air on 14 August. This was the start of the 'Troubles' and also the start of Operation *Banner*, which was to become the British army's longest ever operation. From the start the RAF was heavily involved, providing air transport at both a strategic level, flying troops from their bases into and from the airhead at Aldergrove, and at tactical level by support helicopters. Additionally, the RAF Regiment was responsible for the security of RAF Aldergrove and its surrounding areas, a tactical Area of Responsibility (AOR) of some 100sq km. In November 1969, 33 Wing RAF Regiment (comprising 16, 37 and 48 Regt Squadrons) also deployed at short notice in the infantry role, as a replacement for a RM Commando responsible for an AOR covering Omagh, Enniskillen, Dungannon and Armagh. Four years later 26 Regt Squadron was also deployed to Ireland in the infantry role when it joined 22 Regt Royal Artillery to make up a battalion-sized unit.

The 72 Squadron aircraft and crews were relieved by 18 Squadron in March 1970, but 72 Squadron took responsibility for the detachment again later in the year. From 1972, as the Troubles escalated, there were semi-permanent detachments in Northern Ireland of both Wessex from 72 Squadron and Westland-Aerospatiale Pumas of 33 Squadron. Typically, crews rotated through the detachment on a six-week roulement. Helicopter operations in Northern Ireland were carried out in conjunction

A Hawker Siddeley Nimrod MR1 at low level over the sea. From 1970, the type equipped five squadrons of Strike Command in the maritime patrol and anti-submarine roles. (Coleman)

with the Army Air Corps (AAC) and FAA and included insertion and extraction of infantry patrols, particularly in rural areas, and logistic movement to and from remote sites. A Wessex could carry a load of 16 troops and the aircraft proved invaluable in moving troops around the Province swiftly. Although the helicopters were based at Aldergrove, a forward operating base was established at Bessbrook Barracks, where rotors-running refuelling could take place between sorties.

The RAF air transport fleet was heavily committed to Operation *Banner*. During the Troubles, battalion-sized units carried out four-month tours of duty in the Province and at the peak of the deployment for Operation *Motorman*, at the end of July 1972, there were 25 battalions in Northern Ireland. With the larger part of the army based in Germany, in the British Army of the Rhine (BAOR), the task of regularly moving troop battalions between Germany and Northern Ireland was therefore a significant one.

FURTHER HUMANITARIAN RELIEF

In early 1973, the RAF mounted what some claimed to be the biggest airlift since Berlin, known as Operation *Khana Cascade*. Two years of poor harvest had brought famine to remote areas in Nepal and four Hercules were dispatched to the small airstrip at Bhairawa, close to the Indian border, at the beginning of March 1973 to deliver food and supplies to the affected areas. Over the next month, the Hercules dropped nearly 2,000 tons of maize and rice into inaccessible villages in the west of the country. The airlift was complicated by the mountainous terrain, with peaks up to 20,000ft and villages at altitudes of 9,400ft as well as heavy rain and hail storms and unpredictable mountain winds. There was little margin for error during the flying operations. Supplies were either dropped directly from 50ft without a parachute, or in some cases where such a low-level delivery was not possible, by parachute from 700ft. Small-scale detachments to Biratnagar, in eastern Nepal and Serkhet in the west also delivered 200 and 650 tons respectively.

Later in the year, two more Hercules took part in famine relief operations in western Africa from 4 to 31 August 1973. Operation *Sahel Cascade* was part of a multi-national relief effort. Operating from Daka in Senegal the Hercules flew nearly 2,500 tons of grain into remote areas of Mali, Mauritania, Senegal, Upper Volta, Niger and Chad.

SECOND COD WAR

Long-running disagreement about British trawlers fishing in the waters around Iceland had first reached a crisis in 1958 after Iceland unilaterally extended its Exclusive Economic Zone (EEZ) to include the sea area within 12 miles of its coast. This crisis, known as the First Cod War, led to confrontation between Icelandic Coast Guard vessels and RN ships that had been sent to protect British trawlers. It was resolved (in Iceland's favour) in 1961, but a second extension of the EEZ to 50 miles declared in September 1972 led to the Second Cod War. Once again, RN ships were deployed into the area and Icelandic gunboats attempted to thwart the efforts of any trawlers fishing within the new EEZ by cutting their nets. RAF Nimrods from 120, 201 and 206 Squadrons at Kinloss kept up a continuous patrol of the area to gather information about the positions of trawlers, gunboats and frigates. Much of the 9hr sorties was flown at low level so that the Nimrod crews could visually identify the various fishing vessels. The UK operation was known as Operation *Dewey*.

From 17 July 1973, some of the sorties were flown by Britannias in order to preserve Nimrod fatigue life. For the 9½hr Operation *Dewey* missions a single Britannia was flown from Brize Norton to Kinloss with a double crew – one from 99 Squadron and one from 511 Squadron. The crews then flew alternate sorties from Kinloss, each of which was also reinforced by half a Nimrod crew to assist with the operational

A Shorts Belfast of 53 Squadron, the only RAF unit to operate the type. The aircraft could carry large loads including, for example a Chieftain main-battle tank or three Whirlwind helicopters; alternatively it could carry 150 troops. Unfortunately, however, it suffered from poor performance and the relatively short service life from 1966 to 1976. (RAFM)

duties. On a typical sortie, about 6 hours would be spent at low level in the operational area. Operation *Dewey* drew to a close in October 1973.

OMAN

Although British forces had withdrawn from permanent deployment 'east of Suez,' the UK continued to provide military assistance to the Sultan of Oman with his campaign against insurgents in Dhofar. SAS troops fought on the ground and most of the aircrew of the Sultan of Oman's Air Force (SOAF) were RAF pilots on secondment. The Sultan requested additional helicopter support in 1974 and four Wessex HC2s of 72 Squadron were deployed to Salalah on 4 April. The aircraft were repainted in SOAF markings for the duration of the eight-month detachment. Their main task was to help construction of the Hornbeam Line defensive positions, but apart from carrying building materials to the outposts, the helicopters were also used for troop lifts, casualty evacuation and resupply operations. Additionally, the aircraft participated in six major offensive operations, taking patrols into forward areas, moving artillery pieces and even providing improvised artillery direction. The Wessex worked closely with other SOAF aircraft including Bell 205 helicopters and BAC Strikemasters. During one operation, rebels were hiding in caves and the Wessex were flown along the wadis at night with their lights on, in order to attract rebel fire; when the rebels gave themselves away by opening fire, Strikemasters orbiting overhead attacked the positions. In daylight, Wessex pilots also acted as Forward Air Controllers (FACs) for the Strikemasters. The Wessex detachment returned to the UK in November 1974.

INVASION OF CYPRUS

A *coup d'état* which ousted Archbishop Makarios from power on Cyprus on 15 July 1974 plunged the island into yet another crisis. Four days later a Malta-based Nimrod located a force of 40 Turkish naval vessels heading towards Cyprus. While shadowing this force, the Nimrod was intercepted by a Turkish North American F-100 and later an F-84F, although both of these aircraft had, in turn, been intercepted by Cyprus-based Lightnings. At dawn on 20 July 1974, Turkish amphibious forces and paratroops landed on Cyprus. Although British forces on the SBAs were not directly threatened, the Vulcans of the NEAF Strike Wing were moved to Malta as a precaution. However, the Vulcans were used for Maritime Radar Reconnaissance (MRR) from high level to the south of the island when the Turkish declared a war zone in sea areas to the north of the island and thus denied that area to the Nimrods operating at low level. Over the next week, RAF transport aircraft also evacuated 132 service dependents that were living outside the SBAs.

Two Phantoms from 41 Squadron arrived at Akrotiri on 23 July to provide reconnaissance for UK troops on the island and a further 12 Phantoms from 6 Squadron were deployed to Cyprus two days later. Six of these aircraft were kept ready in the ground-attack role and the other six were immediately re-tasked into the Air Defence role. The two Victors which had accompanied the Phantoms were also pressed into the air defence organization, flying tanker tow-lines to the south of the island. The Phantoms, with their better loiter capability, maintained Combat Air Patrols (CAPs) on the western end of the island, whereas the shorter-range Lightnings mounted QRA from Akrotiri, covering the eastern end. There were a number of incursions into the SBAs and although they were probably accidental, each was vigorously intercepted so that Turkish pilots would become more circumspect.

Reconnaissance flights over the region were also flown from Malta by the Canberras of 13 Squadron and the Nimrods of 203 Squadron. The latter gave search and rescue support to the crew of the Turkish destroyer *Kocatepe* which was mistakenly sunk off Paphos by Turkish aircraft on 23 July. Whirlwinds of 84 Squadron and RAF Air Sea Rescue (ASR) boats from 1153 Marine Craft Unit (MCU) also assisted in this operation.

A detachment of Puma helicopters from 33 and 230 Squadrons was transported to Akrotiri by Belfasts

of 53 Squadron on 25 July and these aircraft were used to police the Greco-Turkish ceasefire line from the end of the month. Airfield defence reinforcements in the shape of 15 Squadron RAF Regt were flown into Akrotiri the following day; they were replaced by 26 Squadron RAF Regt in September. During August the conflict flared up once again and more Turkish landings took place. Contingency plans for the evacuation of civilians on Cyprus were put into action and a joint operation by the RN helicopters from HMS *Bulwark* and RAF transport aircraft evacuated nearly 10,000 civilians from the island, including service dependents, British subjects and tourists of other nationalities. Since the road between the western SBA at Dhekalia had been blocked, Hercules aircraft flew a shuttle from Kingsfield airstrip at Dhekelia to the western SBA at Akrotiri, where the passengers were transferred onto VC10s, Comets and Britannias for the flight back to UK.

NATO CENTRAL REGION

In the aftermath of the invasion, the RAF's continued presence in Cyprus was re-evaluated and NEAF's fixed-wing squadrons, comprising the Vulcan squadrons of the NEAF Strike Wing, the Lightnings of 56 Squadron and the Hercules of 70 Squadron, were all repatriated to the UK in January 1975. This left the Whirlwinds of 84 Squadron as the only RAF unit in Cyprus, although the Canberras of 13 Squadron and Nimrods of 203 Squadron continued to be based in Malta.

Thus, by the end of 1974, the RAF had contracted dramatically from its position in 1960 as a force with permanent world-wide deployments and a responsibility for the UK's nuclear deterrent. Over the 15 years from 1960, changing world geo-politics, including the loss of many of Britain's colonial responsibilities as well as challenging financial constraints had all affected the strategic role of the armed forces. The resources of RAF were now concentrated on its important commitments to NATO, including maintaining the security of the UKADR, the forward deployment of a tactical air force in Germany and the provision of anti-submarine forces in the Atlantic Ocean and the Mediterranean Sea.

A McDonnell Douglas F-4M Phantom FGR2 of 41 Squadron at low level over the sea. Based at RAF Coningsby, 6, 54 and 41 Squadrons were assigned to the UK Mobile Force, which was intended to reinforce 'hot spots' around the world. The Phantoms of 6 and 41 Squadrons were deployed to Cyprus during the crisis of 1974. (Felger)

CHAPTER 7

THE TEMPERATURE RISES

1975-1989

One of the many paradoxes of the Cold War was that the traditional 'front-line' aircraft tended to be more involved with QRA duties or exercises than with flying on active operations. By the mid-1970s the NATO system of Tactical Evaluation (Taceval) dominated the calendars of the fast jet and maritime squadrons. An annual Taceval tested each unit's preparedness for war and their ability to continue to operate effectively in Nuclear Biological and Chemical (NBC) conditions and under enemy attack. As a result, the RAF stations of the late Cold War were exceptionally well prepared to fight a war that never came. The Taceval system included the Air Transport (AT) and Support Helicopter (SH) forces, but they were also involved in operational flying beyond the NATO Central Region, either in support of the other services or in humanitarian relief operations. In particular, the SH squadrons had become an integral part of army operations in Northern Ireland. SH squadrons were the only units based permanently in Cyprus (84 Squadron) and Hong Kong (28 Squadron), where they also supported routine army operations. The only fixed-wing assets based outside the Central Region were Nimrods of 203 Squadron and Canberra PR7 and PR9 reconnaissance aircraft in Malta.

1975 DEFENCE WHITE PAPER

The Defence White Paper published in spring 1975 reaffirmed the policy of the 1968 White Paper to concentrate the armed

Two McDonnell Douglas F-4M Phantom FGR2s from 56 Squadron based at RAF Wattisham carrying their operational weapon load. Each aircraft is each armed with four AIM-9L Sidewinder infra-red seeking AAMs and four BAe Dynamics Skyflash semi-active radar homing AAMs. In the late 1970s five Phantom squadrons (23, 29, 43, 56 and 111) were responsible for the air defence of the UK and a further two units (19 and 92 Squadrons) were based in RAF Germany. (Richard Cooke)

forces in Central Europe and the Eastern Atlantic. However, it went further than the previous document by announcing the removal of the RAF squadrons based in Malta by 1979 and the halving of the RAF's air-transport fleet. Four transport squadrons were to be disbanded: 46 Squadron equipped with Andovers, 99 and 511 Squadrons both equipped with Britannias and 216 Squadron equipped with Comets. The numbers of Hercules and VC10s would also be reduced. This left the Belfasts of 53 Squadron as the only AT force to be untouched, although in fact they did not survive the following year's review. However, the White Paper confirmed that the Harriers of 1 Squadron and four Wessexes of 72 Squadron would continue to be committed to the Allied Command Europe (ACE) Mobile Force and that the UK Mobile Force would continue to include the Phantoms (shortly to be replaced by the SEPECAT Jaguar GR1s) of 6, 41 and 54 Squadrons, the Wessexes of 72 Squadron and Pumas of 33 and 230 Squadrons. The Nimrod force would be reduced by 25 percent (to be achieved by the disbandment of 203 Squadron), but the rest of Strike Command's forces would remain extant. The Vulcan Wings at RAF Waddington and RAF Scampton remained, as did the Victor Tanker Wing at RAF Marham; however, 543 Squadron had already been disbanded and the strategic-reconnaissance role taken over by Vulcan B2(SR) aircraft of 27 Squadron. At RAF Honington two squadrons of Buccaneer S2Bs (12 and 208 Squadrons) provided a maritime strike capability.

At that time, most of the Lightnings were in the process of being replaced by Phantoms as those aircraft were released from the ground-attack role by the introduction of the Jaguar. The first Phantom FGR2 Air Defence (AD) unit was 111 Squadron, at RAF Leuchars, in October 1974, although 43 Squadron had operated the Phantom FG1 in the AD role since 1969. By summer 1976, the UK's AD force comprised the Phantoms of 23, 29, 43, 56 and 111 Squadrons, the Lightnings of 5 and 11 Squadrons and the Bloodhound 2 SAMs of 85 Squadron. Aircraft and missile systems were part of an integrated warning and control organization, which received data from the Linesman air-defence radars at Burrington, Neatishead, Saxton Wold, Boulmer, Buchan, Saxa Vord, Benbecula and Bishop's Court (as well as the Ballistic Missile Early Warning System (BMEWS)at RAF Fylingdales). These ground-based radars were augmented by the Shackleton AEW2 early warning aircraft of 8 Squadron. Incursions into the UK Air Defence Region (UKADR) by Soviet aircraft were relatively common occurrences, about four per week in 1978 rising to six per week by 1980; they would be intercepted by Phantoms or Lightnings, accompanied by Victor tankers.

At the focal point of the government's 'Central Europe policy,' RAFG remained undiminished by the White Paper; indeed, it was in the process of another major upgrade. The Strike/Attack Wing at RAF Brüggen, comprising the Phantom FGR2 aircraft of 14, 17 and 31 Squadrons, was in the process of re-equipping with Jaguars. The Lightning F2A fighters of 19 and 92 Squadrons at RAF Gütersloh would soon be re-equipped with Phantoms which would then be redeployed to RAF Wildenrath; this would free Gütersloh for the Harrier GR3 Wing (comprising 3, 4 and 20 Squadrons at Wildenrath) to join the Wessexes of 18 Squadron there, putting them much closer to the army units they would support in wartime. At RAF Laarbruch, which was also home to Buccaneers of 15 and 16 Squadrons, 2 Squadron would replace its Phantoms with Jaguars in the tactical reconnaissance role. The Bloodhounds of 25 Squadron provided another layer of defence to the 'Clutch' stations of RAF Brüggen, Wildenrath and Laarbruch, and an in-theatre AT facility was provided by the Pembrokes of 60 Squadron.

BELIZE

Guatemala began to re-assert its long-standing claim to the territory of Belize in the summer of 1975. When Guatemalan troops were reported to be massing close to the border, the army garrison was reinforced and three Puma helicopters from

A BAe Harrier GR3 of 1 Squadron operating from a rough strip in Belize. After a temporary detachment in late 1975 and early 1976, the Harriers were redeployed to Belize in 1977 for what became a permanent detachment. (Richard Cooke)

33 Squadron, were transported to Belize by Belfasts of 53 Squadron on 11 October. On 8 November, six Harriers from 1 Squadron also arrived at Belize City airport. A programme of 'flag waving' sorties appeared to defuse the situation and the Harriers were withdrawn in April 1976, leaving the Pumas and a detachment of RAF Regiment Bofors anti-aircraft guns to support the army garrison. The contingency plan for any future reinforcement of Belize was to send four Hunter FGA9 aircraft from the Tactical Weapons Unit (TWU) at Brawdy, as had been done successfully at Gibraltar.

However, this idea proved impractical firstly because of the difficulty in deploying the aircraft with no AAR facility over such a distance and secondly because of a shortage of TWU instructors, so when the crisis reignited in June 1977, six Harriers from 1 Squadron were again sent to Belize. This time the Harrier detachment remained in the country and it was formalized in 1980 as 1417 Flight; the Puma detachment became 1563 Flight. Both units were manned by personnel, both aircrew and ground crew, on roulement from the UK and RAFG squadrons. The responsibility for the RAF Regiment Bofors detachment was also shared between 58, 48 and 66 Squadrons RAF Regt. The RAF retained the force of Harriers and Pumas in Belize until July 1993.

MARITIME OPERATIONS

A third 'Cod War' dispute with Iceland over fishing in the North Atlantic was triggered in November 1975 by the unilateral declaration by Iceland that its EEZ now extended to a distance of 200 miles – rather than 50 miles – from the coastline. Once again, the RN sent ships into the disputed area to ensure the safety of British fishing vessels and RAF maritime patrol aircraft supported their efforts. These activities were known as Operation *Heliotrope*. The bulk of this task was flown by the Nimrod squadrons, although

some sorties were flown by the Hastings T5 radar training aircraft of 230 Operational Conversion Unit (OCU), which was equipped with the same radar as the Vulcan. Despite the increased sea area to be covered during this iteration of the 'Cod War,' the Nimrod tasking for Exercise *Heliotrope* was not as intense as it had been for Exercise *Dewey*, because of the Nimrod Force's additional tasking to maintain the security of the UK's offshore oil and gas rigs. The third Cod War continued until June 1976.

When the UK introduced its own EEZ on 1 January 1977, patrolling the new fishery area and surveillance of the energy production sites was formalized into Operation *Tapestry*. Initially four extra aircraft (one per squadron) were allocated to the Nimrod force to cover the new task of flying five nine-hour patrols of the EEZ each week. During these sorties the position and identity of all fishing

A Hawker Siddeley Nimrod MR1 of 206 Squadron over Findhorn Bay. Three squadrons (120, 201 and 206) equipped with the type patrolled the Norwegian Sea and the North Atlantic from RAF Kinloss, Scotland. The southwest approaches to the UK were patrolled by 42 Squadron from RAF St Mawgan, Cornwall. (Crown Copyright)

vessels were noted and checked. The Nimrod units also maintained a 24-hour standby for Search And Rescue (SAR) duties; in the SAR role the aircraft was invaluable firstly in locating vessels in distress, using the Searchwater radar fitted to the Nimrod MR2 and secondly in acting as a communications relay for SAR helicopters or lifeboats. Additionally, the aircraft were routinely fitted with dinghies and survival aids that could be dropped if necessary.

The bulk of the work carried out by the Nimrod squadrons was the finding and tracking of Soviet submarines. The submarines were usually detected by the Sound Surveillance System (SOSUS) as they transited through the Iceland–Faroes gap. NATO Maritime Patrol Aircraft (MPA) would then be called in to locate the vessel by dropping a pattern of Sonobuoys and then to track its progress, again using Sonobuoy drops. When one MPA came to the end of its patrol, another would take its place, and in this way the Soviet submarines could be kept under surveillance for most of their time at sea. Detachments to Gibraltar, Sigonella (Sicily) and Cyprus enabled the Nimrod force to keep track of Soviet submarines and surface vessels in the Mediterranean.

EXERCISE *RED FLAG*

A notice at the main gate at RAF Brüggen in the late 1970s encapsulated the ethos of the RAF in the latter days of the Cold War: 'Our task in peace is to train for war – and don't you forget it.' While the regime of Taceval ensured that the command and control of the front-line forces were of the highest standards, it was arguably participation in Exercise *Red Flag* that honed the aircrew's operational skills. The exercise had been born from the USAF's experiences over Vietnam, where the US military found firstly that aircrew were most likely to be shot down in their first eight to ten

A Blackburn (BAe) Buccaneer S2B flying over the Nevada desert. The aircraft is painted in an experimental camouflage for the first RAF participation in Exercise *Red Flag* at Nellis Air Force Base, in 1977. (Rolfe)

combat sorties and secondly that if they could survive those sorties, their chances of surviving the rest of their combat tour were increased dramatically. Not only that, but they became much more operationally effective after those initial sorties. In fact, this finding closely matched their findings after the Korean War as well as the observations of both Adolph Galland in World War II and Manfred von Richthofen in World War I. The concept of this exercise, which was held in the Nevada desert to the north of Las Vegas, was to replicate as closely as possible the experience of the first few sorties in a real war. In the training areas north of Nellis Air Force Base, life-size replicas of Warsaw Pact airfields, as well as industrial targets and troop concentrations were built, defended by a Soviet-style integrated air defence system with Soviet missile and gun systems and an 'Aggressor' squadron of fighters using standard Warsaw Pact tactics. The whole system included video recording and telemetry so that every sortie could be debriefed in great detail and the lessons from each exercise sortie could be fully learnt.

Exercise *Red Flag* was first held in November 1975 and two years later the RAF was invited to be the first foreign participant. Over the four-week period of the exercise in August and September 1977, the RAF contingent comprised two Vulcans and ten Buccaneers. In the first 14 days, the Buccaneers were crewed by personnel from 208 Squadron and in the second 14 days they were flown by crews from RAFG. The aircraft were fitted with Electronic Counter-Measures (ECM) pods and crews were cleared to fly as low as 100ft above ground level (AGL). For the Vulcans the limit was 300ft AGL but the Vulcans also flew night exercise sorties using the aircraft's rudimentary Terrain Following System to fly at 1,000ft AGL. Each exercise mission included numerous other tactical aircraft, including other ground attack aircraft, defence suppression aircraft and fighter escort, so there might be over 100 aircraft in the training areas.

The following year, the Vulcans and Buccaneers returned to Nellis AFB along with Jaguars from

A Westland Aerospatiale Puma HC1 flying snow-covered terrain in Norway. The type equipped 33 and 230 Squadrons at RAF Odiham, and was used to support army operations and exercises from the Arctic to the Caribbean. (Crown Copyright)

A Westland Wessex HC2 of 28 Squadron over Hong Kong. The helicopters were used to support the army in the colony and also for search and rescue (SAR) operations. An additional role was in the fight against smuggling by flying operations to halt the lucrative black market trade between Hong Kong and the People's Republic of China. (RAFM)

both Strike Command and RAFG. Participation by RAF aircraft had become a permanent feature of Exercise *Red Flag* and in the late 1970s and 1980s every RAF strike/attack squadron could expect an exercise 'slot' once every two years.

HELICOPTER OPERATIONS

The first operational squadron to use helicopters in the SAR role was 22 Squadron, which received Whirlwind HAR2 aircraft in 1955; however, this was not an entirely successful venture and it was not until the later advent of the Whirlwind HAR10 that helicopter SAR became truly viable. Through the 1960s the operation matured and by the mid-1970s the SAR force was an efficient and effective organization covering rescue operations both at sea and in mountainous areas. UK SAR operations were controlled by two Rescue Co-ordination Centres (RCC), one in Plymouth and one at

Pitreavie Castle, which co-ordinated the efforts of the RAF, RN, Coast Guard and RNLI. In 1979, the RAF's SAR force comprised two squadrons, 22 Squadron and 202 Squadron, which between them operated detached flights at RAF Lossiemouth, Leuchars, Boulmer, Leconfield, Coltishall, Manston, Culdrose, Chivenor, Brawdy and Valley. Both squadrons had also recently exchanged their Whirlwinds for more capable aircraft: 22 Squadron operated the Wessex HAR2 and 202 Squadron the Sea King HAR3. With great courage and skill, often flying in the most appalling weather conditions, RN and RAF SAR helicopters would typically respond to about 1,300 callouts each year in the late 1970s, resulting in an annual total of around 1,000 lives saved; in 1979, this included the rescue of 139 survivors from 24 yachts which capsized during the year's Fastnet Race. In 1980, the Sea Kings from 202 Squadron were involved in rescue operations after the Alexander Kielland oil rig capsized in the North Sea 'Ecofisk' oilfield.

The overseas-based helicopter units, 84 Squadron in Cyprus and 28 Squadron in Hong Kong, also had SAR responsibilities in their theatres. For 28 Squadron, a major additional task was the support of naval and police counter-smuggling operations. Frequently operating at night, smugglers – often smuggling illegal immigrants into Hong Kong – were equipped with high-performance motor boats, which were much faster than the patrol craft used by the authorities. The helicopters were used to find and chase the smugglers' boats, often using 'Nightsun' searchlights, to make them predictable enough for the naval or police vessels to intercept them.

In late 1979, six Pumas from 230 Squadron were detached to Rhodesia for four months to support the Commonwealth Monitoring Force in disarming the combatants in the civil war and preparing the country for a new future as Zimbabwe. A number of Hercules were also involved in the operation.

In Northern Ireland, the operational helicopter tasking had increased during the late 1970s and 72 Squadron was deployed permanently to Aldergrove on 12 November 1981. Apart from patrol insertion and extraction, sometimes under small-arms fire, the helicopters were also used for transferring internees from police holding areas to the Maze prison. Such missions would be undertaken by a formation of five Wessexes: four carrying internees and one providing 'top cover' with armed troops on board. Another task was to fly 'Eagle Patrols' along the border with Eire. This involved reconnaissance of roads along the border, carrying a section of troops; if a suspicious vehicle was seen, the helicopter would land the troops ahead of it to set up a roadblock. This proved to be an effective tactic in reducing arms smuggling across the border.

THE FALKLANDS WAR

One of the unintentional consequences of the 1981 Defence Review was that the withdrawal of the Antarctic Survey ship HMS *Endurance* was perceived by the Argentinian junta to be a signal that the UK was not prepared to defend its interests in the South Atlantic. On 19 March 1982, a group of Argentine marines landed on the British overseas territory of South Georgia island and claimed the island for Argentina. Then, on 2 April, London was again taken by surprise when a large Argentinian naval assault force landed on the Falkland Islands. In response, a British naval task force, including the aircraft carriers HMS *Invincible* and HMS *Hermes*, began to assemble and ships started the voyage towards the Falklands from 5 April. By this time, the RAF had already established a forward operating base at Wideawake airfield on Ascension Island, which lay just over half way between

When the Falklands Campaign was launched an air-to-air (AAR) capability had to be hastily introduced for the Nimrod MR2 fleet, to enable the aircraft to fly long-range patrols from Ascension Island. Here a Nimrod MR2P refuels over the South Atlantic from a Victor K2 of 57 Squadron. (120 Squadron Archive)

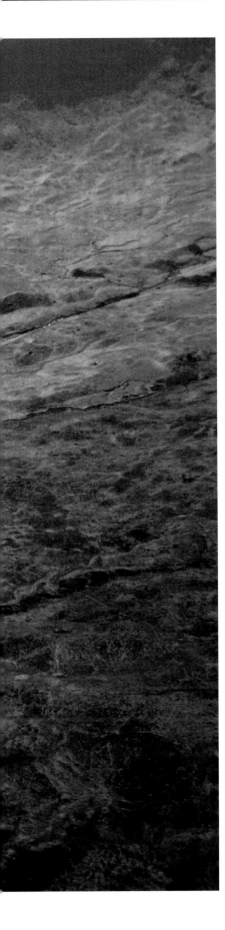

the UK and the Falklands. However, the 4,000-mile distance between the UK and Ascension still presented challenges: the Hercules could not fly that distance directly, so they were routed via Dakar in Senegal. By 5 April 1982, eight flights a day were leaving for Ascension and a week later, after dropping non-essential tasks, Hercules were departing their base at RAF Lyneham for Ascension every 45min through the day. By the end of the conflict the RAF Hercules fleet had flown some 7,000 tons of supplies into Ascension Island.

Two Nimrod MR1 MPAs from 42 Squadron started patrols from Ascension Island from 5 April and a fortnight later they were joined by five Victor K2 tankers from 55 and 57 Squadrons. The Victors were tasked with carrying out Maritime Radar Reconnaissance sorties around South Georgia and on 20 April Sqn Ldr J. Elliott completed the longest distance ever flown on an operational reconnaissance flight when he covered over 7,000 miles in a 14-hour 45min sortie. The radar imagery showed that the area was free from Argentine warships, so the naval task force could start the operation to take back the island. South Georgia was retaken by naval forces and SAS troops on 25 April.

On 29 April, Vulcans from 44, 50 and 101 Squadrons started to arrive at Ascension Island. The next evening, a Vulcan from 101 Squadron captained by Flt Lt M. Withers, accompanied by ten Victors, took off from Ascension for Operation *Black Buck*, a 3,900-mile bombing mission to the Falkland Islands. After five AAR brackets, the Vulcan left the last Victor and descended to low level to remain under the radar horizon from the Falklands. Nearing the target, the Vulcan climbed to 10,000ft and dropped 21 1,000lb bombs, which were radar-aimed at the runway at Port Stanley airfield. The Vulcan returned safely to Ascension after 15 hours and 45min, having hit the runway and having completed the longest ever bombing mission under combat conditions. The raid on Port Stanley airfield was followed up by another bombing attack on the airstrips at Port Stanley and Goose Green just after dawn by the Sea Harriers of 800 Squadron FAA, operating from HMS *Hermes*. Both of the FAA Sea Harrier units in the task force, 800 and 801 Squadrons, included RAF pilots on exchange postings to the FAA and the first air-to-air kill of the campaign was achieved by Flt Lt P. Barton of 801 Squadron, who shot down a Dassault Mirage III on 1 May.

A second *Black Buck* mission was flown on the night of 3/4 May by a Vulcan from 50 Squadron, again tasked against the airfield with free-fall bombs. Once again, the raid was followed up by a Sea Harrier strike against the airfield. Air operations were limited over the next two weeks because of poor weather in the South Atlantic. However, a steady stream of equipment and supplies was arriving at Ascension Island, thanks to the large-scale airlift by RAF Hercules and VC10s. More aircraft began to gather there, too, including the first Nimrod MR2P aircraft from 120, 201 and 206

Two Harrier GR3s from 1 Squadron armed with 68mm SNEB rockets carry out a training sortie over Scotland: scenery very similar to that of the Falkland Islands. The squadron deployed to the South Atlantic, with ten aircraft based on Ascension Island and a further six aircraft embarked on HMS *Hermes*. Combat operations over the Falklands started on 20 May 1982. (Richard Cooke)

Right: A Harrier GR3 from 1 Squadron prepares for a sortie aboard HMS *Hermes*. The aircraft is loaded with a 1,000lb Paveway II Laser Guided Bomb (LGB). These weapons were used briefly at the end of the campaign: for the majority of ground-attack missions the Harriers were armed with 1,000lb high-explosive (HE) bombs or BL755 Cluster Bomb Units (CBUs). (RN Official Photographer/IWM/Getty)

Below: A BAe Harrier GR3 lands on the flight deck of HMS *Hermes* after an operational sortie over the Falkland Islands.

Squadrons. Amongst some hasty modifications which were approved and installed in the early days of the crisis was an AAR capability for the Nimrod MR2, using surplus Vulcan AAR probes. These aircraft were designated Nimrod MR2P, some of which were also modified to carry AIM9-L missiles for self-defence. The first operational patrol by these aircraft was flown by a 201 Squadron crew on 15 May: after completing two AAR brackets, the aircraft flew to approximately 150 miles north of the Falklands then headed west towards Argentina before turning back northbound to parallel the coast on the return leg, scanning the sea with its Searchwater radar. This 19-hour sortie confirmed that there were no Argentinian naval vessels at sea which might threaten the Task Force. Similar Nimrod MRR patrols were repeated over the next week, including a sortie on 21 May by a 206 Squadron crew which covered some 8,453 miles, thus setting another record for the longest distance ever flown on an operational reconnaissance flight.

Ten Harriers of 1 Squadron were flown to Ascension Island in the first week of May. Four of these aircraft were armed with AIM9-L Sidewinder air-to-air missiles to provide air defence for Ascension Island as an interim measure until three Phantoms from 29 Squadron arrived to take over on 25 May. Meanwhile, the remaining six Harriers had been flown onto the container ship *Atlantic Conveyor* on 6 May for transport to the operational area. The ship also carried four Boeing-Vertol Chinook helicopters from 18 Squadron. The Harriers were transferred from the *Atlantic Conveyor* onto HMS *Hermes* on 18 May and flew their first mission two days later, against a fuel dump on the eastern side of West Falkland. They were in action again providing close air support to troops during the landings in San Carlos Water on 21 May. Over the next days, the Harriers of 1 Squadron carried out airstrikes on the airstrip at Pebble Island and the airfield at Port Stanley, as well as CAS missions, sometimes operating in conjunction with Sea Harriers.

A Boeing CH-47C Chinook HC1 lifts stores from an improvised helideck on the RMS *Queen Elizabeth II*. Only one Chinook survived the sinking of the MV *Atlantic Conveyor*, but it played a vital part in the land campaign in East Falkland. (JHDC Archive/Getty)

Three of the Chinooks aboard the *Atlantic Conveyor* were lost when the ship was sunk on 25 May, but the following day the remaining Chinook arrived at Port San Carlos where it was pressed into service. The aircraft, which could carry an impressive load of 10 tons of ammunition or stores or 80 troops, played a vital role in the campaign. On the night of 30 May it was used to lift three 105mm artillery guns into new firing positions on Mount Kent. The following night a Vulcan of 50 Squadron carried out another long-range mission, this time an attack against the Argentinian early warning radars on the islands. The aircraft fired two AGM-45 Shrike anti-radiation missiles but the results were inconclusive. Meanwhile, the Harriers had continued to fly CAS missions in support of the troops advancing inland from San Carlos; however, they had also lost three aircraft to ground fire in that time, so two replacement Harriers were flown directly from Ascension Island to the Task Force on 1 June. Two more reinforcement aircraft arrived a week later.

Another Vulcan Shrike mission on 3 June successfully neutralized a Skyguard gun-control radar near Port Stanley; on the same day 63 Squadron RAF Regt assumed responsibility for the air defence of Port San Carlos with its BAe Dynamics Rapier SAMs. Poor winter weather again intervened to disrupt air operations over the Falklands, but on 5 June it cleared sufficiently for Harriers and Sea Harriers to use a temporary airstrip (known as 'Syd's Strip') at Port San Carlos to reduce their normal transit time from the Task Force to the operational area. By now the Argentinian forces had been pushed back to the easternmost tip of East Falkland, around the capital Port Stanley. Harrier operations continued apace over the next week using BL-755 Cluster Bomb Units (CBUs) and rockets and, for example, on 11 June ten sorties were flown into what was a hotly defended area. Argentine troop positions near Port Stanley airfield were also attacked the next day by a Vulcan from 101 Squadron, which dropped 21 airburst-fused 1,000lb bombs. From 13 June, Harriers armed with 1,000lb Laser-Guided Bombs (LGBs) flew missions co-ordinated by ground-based Forward Air Controllers (FACs) equipped with laser designators, but further use of these weapons was not needed: Argentine forces surrendered the following day.

A Shrike-armed Avro Vulcan frames a busy scene at Wideawake Airfield on Ascension Island during the Falklands War: the Hercules transports and Chinook and Wessex helicopters were a vital part of the logisitcs support for combat operations. (Thomas)

After the ceasefire, the Task Force remained in the South Atlantic until the end of the month. On 4 July, the Harriers of 1 Squadron were transferred from HMS *Hermes* to Port Stanley airfield where they were tasked with the air defence of the islands. Once again this was a stop-gap measure until the airfield could be repaired and lengthened sufficiently for the Phantoms of 29 Squadron to use. At 4,000ft the runway at Port Stanley was far too short for Phantom operations, but the Royal Engineers were able to extend it by another 2,000ft using steel 'matting;' since this represented the very minimum distance required by the Phantom, five arrestor wires were also installed. The first four Phantoms deployed to Port Stanley on 17 October 1982, followed by the rest of the squadron in the following days. Although most of the 1 Squadron personnel had been repatriated by then, the Harrier detachment remained in the ground-attack role and to cover the air defence duties on days when strong crosswinds prevented Phantom operations. The Phantom and Harrier detachments were manned by personnel on four-month roulements, as was the RAF Regiment Rapier detachment.

LEBANON

During attempts to end the civil war in Lebanon, a multi-national peacekeeping force was stationed in Beirut. This included a British army element,

'Britforleb,' which was based in a block of flats in the Hadath district of the city from February 1983. However, by September the situation in Beirut had become critical and Britforleb was considered to be at risk of attack by a number of the many armed factions in the city. Six Buccaneers equipped with Pave Spike laser-designation pods were flown to Akrotiri for Operation *Pulsator* in early September. The aircraft were flown by crews from both 12 and 208 Squadrons who had been selected for their Pave Spike experience. The first task was to fly a Show of Force over Hadath, firstly to demonstrate to the local warring groups that Britforleb was backed up by air power and secondly to provide a morale raiser for the British troops. On the morning of 11 September 1983, two Buccaneers overflew Beirut at ultra-low level, followed two hours later by a second pair. The exercise was repeated by another pair on 13 September.

The original tasking envisaged targeting being provided by a Forward Air Controller (FAC) in the Hadath flats, but it soon became clear that the potential targets were more likely to be artillery pieces firing from some distance outside the city. The tactics changed to self-designation using Pave Spike from medium level, using a 40° dive profile. After practising the unfamiliar delivery profile at Episkopi range, a pair of LGB-armed Buccaneers was kept at 30min readiness throughout daylight hours; crews were stood down at dusk since Pave Spike had no night-time capability. There were regular exercise

An Avro Vulcan armed with an AGM-45 Shrike Anti-Radiation Missile (ARM) mounted under the left wing and a Westinghouse AN-ALQ101 Electronic Countermeasures (ECM) pod under the right wing. This was a typical fit for the later *Black Buck* missions. The mounting points on the Vulcan were originally intended to carry the GAM-87 Skybolt Air-Launched Ballistic Missile (ALBM), which was cancelled in 1962. (Thomas)

Above: Two Blackburn (BAe) Buccaneer S2Bs of 208 Squadron get airborne from RAF Akrotiri for an Operation *Pulsator* sortie over Beirut, Lebanon. (Pitchfork)

Opposite: Sacks of foodstuffs are loaded into a Puma HC1 for distribution to remote villages during humanitarian operations in Africa. (Crown Copyright)

launches to train crews and the tasking organization to ensure that the aircraft could support Britforleb swiftly if required. A Phantom squadron which was holding its Armament Practice Camp (APC) at RAF Akrotiri was also co-opted into Operation *Pulsator* to provide air defence cover for the Buccaneers if necessary. Although neither the Buccaneers nor the Phantoms were required for further operational sorties, both Wessex and Chinook helicopters which had also been earmarked for the operation were used to evacuate wounded US and French servicemen after a bomb attack on their bases on 23 October. The operation ran down and the Buccaneer detachment returned to RAF Lossiemouth on 26 March 1984.

HUMANITARIAN AID

Despite the withdrawal from world-wide defence commitments in the 1970s and 80s, the AT fleet was frequently called upon to secure Britain's global influence and reputation by providing humanitarian aid and disaster relief. In 1980 alone, RAF aircraft had provided assistance in Nicaragua, Dominica and Kampuchea at the request of the Red Cross and a VC10 aircraft from 10 Squadron, supported

by three Hercules, had also evacuated 650 people from Tehran after the Iranian revolution.

The combination of civil war and drought led to a severe famine in Ethiopia in 1984. The first component of the international relief effort was two RAF Hercules, which were deployed to Addis Ababa on 4 November. In the first three months of Operation *Bushel*, the aircraft carried over 6,000 tons of supplies from Addis Ababa and the port of Assab into the remote famine-hit areas. Much of the affected region was in mountainous terrain with rough landing grounds at 7,000ft above sea level. Where landing was considered too hazardous, food supplies were dropped from a low flypast at 30ft. Throughout the following year, the RAF detachment continued to work closely with other relief teams, including those from the German, French and Soviet Air Forces. When the operation finished on 19 December 1985, the Hercules detachment had flown every day for 409 consecutive days and lifted over 30,000 tons of supplies.

After the earthquake in Mexico City on 19 September 1985, two Pumas were despatched from Belize to Mexico, where they were joined by a Hercules from RAF Lyneham to assist with relief operations. The helicopters had not long returned

Above: The end of one era and the beginning of another: a Panavia Tornado GR1 of 9 Squadron refuels from a Vulcan tanker from 50 Squadron. The Vulcan was retired from RAF service in 1984.

Right: A Phantom FGR2 of 23 Squadron at Stanley airstrip in the Falklands. The runway had to be extended with AM2 aluminium matting to allow Phantom operations, but even so the type needed to use the Rotary Hydraulic Arrestor Gear (RHAG) to stop after landing. The lowered arrestor hook is clearly visible. (Peter Butt/Wikimedia/ Public Domain)

to Belize when they were ordered to Colombia to aid rescue efforts after a volcanic eruption destroyed the town of Armero on 13 November 1985. Once again, the Pumas were joined by a Hercules from RAF Lyneham.

OPERATIONAL DETACHMENTS

The most important operational detachments through the 1980s were undoubtedly those in the Falkland Islands and Belize. In early 1983, the Phantom detachment at Port Stanley changed its identity to 23 Squadron, while the Harrier detachment became 1453 Flight and they were joined by 1312 Flight equipped with two Hercules KC1 aircraft converted to be AAR tankers. In early March 1983, two Buccaneers from 12 Squadron deployed to Port Stanley to demonstrate the capability to operate maritime strike aircraft

from the islands. After a ten-day stay, the Buccaneers returned to RAF Lossiemouth. During the year work was also started on building a larger, more suitable airfield at Mount Pleasant, some 25 miles southwest of Port Stanley. The new airfield at Mount Pleasant was formally opened on 12 May 1985. Two new flying detachments joined the force in the Falklands: 1310 Flight operating Chinooks for support of the army and 1564 Flight operating Sea Kings in the SAR role. In 1988, the Phantom detachment was re-named once again, becoming 1435 Flight, while the Chinook and Sea King flights had already been amalgamated into 78 Squadron. RAF Mount Pleasant was served by a twice-weekly Hercules resupply flight, which routed via Ascension Island and required AAR to complete the final leg to the Falklands. This scheduled service was taken over by the Lockheed TriStars of 216 Squadron, which could reach the Falklands from Ascension Island without refuelling, from March 1989. Other occasional visitors to Mount Pleasant included Nimrod aircraft.

A Phantom FGR2 of 23 Squadron and a Hercules of 1312 Flight at low level over the Falkland Islands. (Lewis)

The detachments of 1417 Flight Harriers and 1563 Flight Pumas continued throughout the decade, successfully deterring any Guatemalan designs on the British protecterate. Belize City, like Mount Pleasant, was defended by detachments of RAF Regiment Rapier squadrons.

RE-EQUIPMENT

The Falklands conflict had broken out in the last days of the Vulcan's service life. The Scampton Wing had already disbanded in early 1982 and the Waddington Wing was also winding down. Soon after the Falklands campaign, 44 and 101

Squadrons disbanded at RAF Waddington, leaving only 50 Squadron, which, with its aircraft converted to Vulcan K2 standard, had converted to the AAR tanker role. These aircraft were finally retired in 1984, leaving the Victor K2 tankers of 55 and 57 Squadrons as the last vestiges of the V-Force. In its heyday with 18 squadrons in the early 1960s, the V-Force had held the frontline of Britain's nuclear deterrent; 20 years later it had carried out the world's longest bombing missions and in its final form, as just two AAR tanker squadrons, it continued to play a vital role in the operational effectiveness of the RAF. The AAR force was also augmented after the Falklands war by the acquisition of TriStar KC1s, operated by 216 Squadron at RAF Brize Norton,

The Panavia Tornado GR1, which entered service with 9 Squadron at RAF Honington in 1982, gave the RAF, for the first time, a true night/all-weather strike/attack capability. The heart of the aircraft was a Terrain Following Radar (TFR) system that enabled crews to fly the type at low level at night or in adverse weather. (Richard Cooke)

and the conversion of VC10 transports operated by 10 and 101 Squadron to the tanker role.

Although the Vulcans were being retired, they were being replaced by the Panavia Tornado GR1 which brought with it a formidable day and night all-weather strike/attack capability. The first Tornado squadron, 9 Squadron, was formed on 1 May 1982, followed the following year by 617 and 27 Squadrons. In October 1984, four Tornados from 617 Squadron took part in the USAF Strategic Air Command (SAC) Bombing Competition. The RAF had participated in this annual competition

since 1951, when the competing crews had flown Boeing B-29s. The most successful year to date had been 1974 when Vulcan crews from 230 OCU, 44 and 101 Squadrons had won the Matthis Trophy and the Navigation Trophy. In 1984, the 617 Squadron Tornado team triumphed again, taking the first two places in the Curtis LeMay Bombing Trophy and also winning the John C. Meyer Trophy. The following year both trophies were won again by a team from 27 Squadron.

The introduction of the Tornado GR1 into service continued over the next few years: by early

Members of the elite reconnaissance troop of 45 Commando (RM) jump from a Hercules over Barduffos, Norway. (Richard Cooke)

1990 there were wings of four squadrons each at RAF Brüggen (9, 14, 17 and 31 Squadrons) and RAF Laarbruch (2, 15, 16 and 20 Squadrons). A further three units were based in the UK: 13 Squadron at RAF Honington and 27 with 617 Squadrons at RAF Marham. In Germany, the Tornado took over the RAF's tactical nuclear strike capability from the Buccaneer and Jaguar with the WE177 weapon. Nuclear-armed aircraft were maintained at both stations on 15min readiness QRA until late 1987 when a thawing of the Cold War led to the requirement being relaxed.

Another version of the Tornado, the Tornado F3, began to replace the Lightning and Phantom in the air defence role in the late 1980s. The first units, 29 and 5 Squadrons were based at RAF Coningsby, with wings established later at RAF Leeming (11, 23 and 25 Squadrons) and RAF Leuchars (43 and 111 squadrons). Phantoms remained in service with 19 and 92 Squadrons at Wildenrath and 56 and 74 Squadrons at RAF Wattisham.

END OF THE COLD WAR

In 1989 the façade of Communist rule in Central Europe was cracking. Democratic elections were held in Poland and more were promised in Hungary – and there was a steady stream of people leaving East Germany for the West. On 9 November, the crossing points of the Berlin Wall were opened, signalling the end of the Cold War. Over the previous three decades it was the Cold War that structured the RAF and the late 1980s had been a relatively stable and predictable period for the RAF's frontline. The service ended the decade well able to face the challenges in the new world order that would be established in the next decade: potent new aircraft, the exercise regimes of Taceval and Exercise *Red Flag*, and the recent combat experiences in distant theatres all combined to mould a particularly effective fighting service. The only question that remained was what form would the new world order take?

Opposite: A Lightning F6 of 5 Squadron armed with two BAe Red Top infra-red seeking air-to-air-missiles (AAM). The last units equipped with this British-built fighter were 5 and 11 Squadrons based at RAF Binbrook. In 1988, both were re-equipped with the Panavia Tornado F3. (Crown Copyright)

Below: An AIM-9 Sidewinder AAM is fired from a Panavia Tornado F3 during a training sortie. Like the Phantom which it replaced, the Tornado F3 was armed with four Sidewinder and four Skyflash missiles. By 1989, six front-line air-defence squadrons had been equipped with the type. (Crown Copyright)

CHAPTER 8

RETURN TO THE MIDDLE EAST

1990-1998

Arguably the most significant influence on Britain's armed services since World War II was the 1957 Defence White Paper. Apart from the policy changes it introduced, it was also the watershed between the expansion of the early 1950s and a steady reduction in the size of the armed forces thereafter. This reduction was driven by a number of factors including Britain's declining position as an imperial power and the increased capabilities of modern weapons systems; however, it was also undoubtedly driven by financial pressures. There could be no surprises, then, when the 1990 Defence White Paper, titled 'Options for Change,' seemed to be intent to secure a 'Peace Dividend' generated by savings in defence expenditure now that the Cold War was over. For the RAF, this was to be achieved by the disbandment of five squadrons (three Tornado GR1 and two Phantom FGR2) in RAFG, which would enable the closure of Wildenrath and Gütersloh, and the closure of Wattisham with the disbandment of its resident Phantom squadrons (56 and 74 Squadrons).

Despite the apparently decreased threat from the Warsaw Pact, very real operational tasks continued in seven areas. Firstly, Air Defence QRA continued to be the UK's first line of defence against aerial attack: Northern QRA was mounted by the Tornado F3 squadrons at Leuchars (43 and 111 Squadrons), while Southern QRA was shared between the Tornado F3 units at Coningsby (5 and 29 Squadrons) and the Phantom FGR2

British Aerospace (BAe) Harrier GR7 aircraft at the Italian Air Force base at Gioia del Colle, between Bari and Taranto, during operations over the Balkans in the late 1990s. (Crown Copyright)

A Panavia Tornado F3 interceptor of 25 Squadron based at Leeming, North Yorkshire escorts a Soviet Tupolev Tu-142M (Bear-F) anti-submarine aircraft as it transits through the UK Air Defence Region (UKADR). (Crown Copyright)

and Phantom F-4JUK units from Wattisham. AAR provision for both Northern and Southern QRA was by the Victor K2s of 55 Squadron at Marham. Secondly, the task of the Nimrod MR2 Wing at Kinloss, comprising 120, 201 and 206 Squadrons, to monitor the movement of Soviet submarines remained extant and thirdly the defence forces in the Falklands remained at a high state of alert. These comprised the Phantoms (later replaced by Tornado F3 in July 1992) of 1435 Flight, the Hercules of 1312 Flight, and the Chinooks and Sea Kings of 78 Squadron. Fourthly, in Belize the Harriers of 1417 Flight and the Pumas of 1563 Flight continued to deter aggression by neighbouring Guatemala. Fifthly, the helicopter squadrons in Cyprus (84 Squadron equipped with Wessex HU5C) and Hong Kong (28 Squadron flying Wessex HC2) supported army operations in those respective regions and also provided SAR cover. Sixthly, in Northern Ireland the Wessex HC2 of 72 Squadron, supplemented by a Chinook detachment

provided air mobility to the army for Operation *Banner*. These helicopters frequently came under attack by small arms fire or occasionally Rocket Propelled Grenades (RPGs); in July 1991, a pair of Wessex were also fired upon with a SAM-7, which fortunately passed between the aircraft, missing them both. Finally, the SAR squadrons, 22 Squadron with Wessex HAR2 and 202 Squadron with Sea King HAR3, continued to be on call for rescue operations across the UK and its adjoining waters throughout the year.

GULF WAR

Before the disbandments announced in Options for Change could take place, the diplomatic rumblings in the Persian Gulf region, which had started when Iraq accused Kuwait in 1989 of slant drilling into the Rumaila oil field, exploded into a full international crisis when the Iraqi army invaded Kuwait on 2 August 1990. While the US sent a task force to the Gulf and assembled an international Coalition to liberate Kuwait, British forces were also hastily dispatched to the region. The first RAF aircraft to arrive were 12 Tornado F3 fighters from 5 and 29 Squadrons, which arrived at Dhahran on 11 August. They were followed by 12 Jaguar GR1A ground attack aircraft from 6 Squadron, which landed at the SOAF airbase at Thumrait the next day.

Meanwhile, the first of four Nimrods left Kinloss for Seeb on 12 August. Seeb was very familiar to the Nimrod Force, which had deployed there frequently in the previous years for Exercise *Magic Roundabout*, so the aircraft were flying operationally from Muscat soon after arriving in theatre. The Nimrods were initially tasked with gathering intelligence for UN sanctions against Iraq, which seemed to be inevitable.

Two 6½hr patrols were flown daily over the Gulf and all shipping was identified visually and then contacted by radio to determine the port of departure and its destination. The Nimrods were joined at Seeb in mid-August by VC10 K2/3 tankers from 101 Squadron and Nimrod R1 Elint aircraft from 51 Squadron. With the Tornado F3 squadrons concentrating on the Gulf region, the air defence of Cyprus was allocated to Phantoms of 19 and 92 Squadrons from RAFG.

The RAF presence in the Gulf was further enhanced by the arrival at Bahrain of 12 Tornado GR1 strike/attack aircraft from Brüggen, led by 14 Squadron, on 28 August. These aircraft were augmented a month later by 12 more Tornados, six each from Marham and Laarbruch. The force was then split between Bahrain and a second base at Tabuk in western Saudi Arabia. The Tornado F3 force had also been reinforced in September by the arrival

Two Tornado F3s of 1435 Flight on patrol over the Falkland Islands. The unit was manned by crews detached for a five-week tour from squadrons based in the UK. (Crown Copyright)

A SEPECAT Jaguar GR1A fitted with the self-defence suite carried during the Gulf War: over-wing mounted AIM-9L Sidewinder air-to-air missiles (AAM), a 1,200lt centre-line fuel tank, with an AN/ALQ101-10 electronic countermeasures (ECM) pod and a Phimat chaff and flare dispenser pod on the outboard pylons. This configuration leaves the inboard under-wing pylons free for weapons. (BAe Heritage)

of another six aircraft, bringing the total in theatre to 18. The Tornado F3 and GR1 detachments were supported by a detachment of Victor K2 tankers from 55 Squadron at Bahrain. Over the next few months the Tornado F3 and GR1 crews and the Jaguar pilots carried out work-up exercises to ensure that they were fully prepared for combat. At Tabuk, this included a first look at the BAe Dynamics ALARM anti-radiation missile, which had still not been fully released to service. The Jaguar detachment relocated from Oman to Bahrain in November and in January 1991, a third Tornado GR1 detachment, led by 31 Squadron from Brüggen and incorporating six Tornado GR1A reconnaissance aircraft, was established at Dhahran. The tanker aircraft were also relocated, with nine VC10 K2/3s and a TriStar K1 at Riyadh and the eight Victors at Bahrain.

The airlift of supplies and personnel into the region had started with the initial deployment of the RAF aircraft, but it increased dramatically as preparations

were made for war and once the army units were ready to move. Many troops were ferried by sea with their heavy equipment, but others flew into Saudi Arabia. Hercules from 24, 30, 47 and 70 Squadrons plus VC10s from 10 Squadron and TriStars from 216 Squadron were all heavily committed to the airlift operation. 15 Pumas from 230 Squadron and three of 15 Chinooks from 7 Squadron were also airlifted into Saudi Arabia by Lockheed C-5 Galaxy transports of the USAF. The helicopters then flew to their operating base at Ras Al Khair, on the coast some 150 miles north of Dhahran.

The UN deadline to Iraq to withdraw from Kuwait expired on 15 January 1991 and the air campaign commenced in the early hours of 17 January. All three Tornado GR1 wings launched missions against Iraqi Main Operating Bases (MOBs) at Tallil, Mudaysis, Al Asad and Al Taqaddum in the early hours, armed with JP233 airfield denial weapons. The missions were generally flown as four-ship formations (although the mission flown by the Bahrain Wing against Tallil comprised eight aircraft). Formations flew at medium-level for pre-strike AAR and then descended to low-level using the aircraft's Terrain Following Radar (TFR) to carry out low-level night attacks against the MOBs. The attacks were part of larger Coalition operations and were supported by USAF or USN Suppression of Enemy Air Defences (SEAD) assets including stand-off jammers and Wild Weasel aircraft. In the case of the mission from Tabuk against Al Asad, the SEAD was provided by six ALARM missiles fired by a pair of supporting Tornados. However, despite the SEAD support, all of the missions were met with heavy defensive anti-aircraft fire.

The first Jaguar mission was launched at daylight. Operating at medium level, Jaguars armed with 1,000lb bombs were tasked against a police barracks in Kuwait. Another Tornado GR1 mission launched from Bahrain in the morning to harass the MOB at Shaibah, by lofting 1,000lb free-fall bombs onto the airfield. One Tornado was shot down during this sortie. During the day, the Tornado F3 fighters also maintained a number of Combat Air Patrols (CAPs)

near the Iraqi border and two Nimrod missions worked closely with the USN over the Persian Gulf to the north of Bahrain.

Tornado missions resumed that night, with JP233 attacks against Shaibah, Al Jarra, Al Asad, Mudaysis, Wadi Al Khirr, H3 and Jalibah. Once again, the airfields were heavily defended with barrages of anti-aircraft fire. One of the Bahrain-based aircraft was seen to hit the ground after delivering its weapons over Shaibah. During the day, the Jaguars once again attacked targets in Kuwait, including vehicles and a barracks. The first Tornado GR1A reconnaissance missions took place on the night of 18 January: two aircraft carried out low-level line searches over the western desert of Iraq, looking for SCUD tactical ballistic missile launchers. This pattern would continue throughout the next two months, with two or three Tornado GR1A aircraft flying 'SCUD hunting' missions each night.

In daylight on 19 January, eight Jaguars were tasked against three SAM-2 sites in Kuwait. The weather was poor including thick cloud cover for most of the route, but the Jaguars found breaks in

The Handley Page Victor K2 tankers of 55 Squadron, based at Bahrain, provided much of the air-to-air refuelling (AAR) support for aircraft operating against ground targets. (Glover)

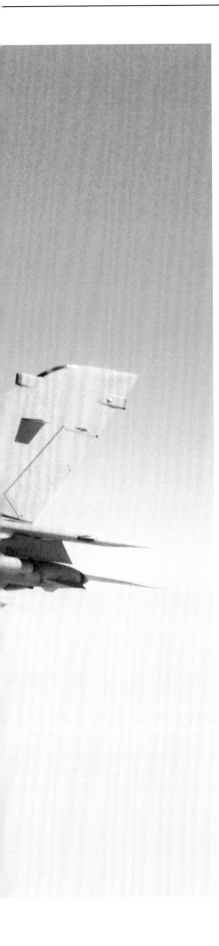

the clouds and despite heavy anti-aircraft fire they carried out steep dive attacks from 15,000ft to drop their bombs accurately onto the missile sites.

That night was the third night of attacks by the Tornado GR1 wings against Iraqi MOBs, with missions flown from Tabuk against H2 and Ruwayshid from Bahrain against Tallil and Al Jarrah and from Dhahran against Jalibah. One Tornado was shot down by a Roland SAM during the attack on Tallil. By now the Tornado crews were questioning the effectiveness of JP233 attacks and in fact the Tabuk and Dhahran Wings had already stopped using the weapon, choosing instead to loft 1,000lb free-fall bombs to give the aircraft some degree of stand-off from the anti-aircraft defences. The missions against Tallil and Al Jarrah were also the last JP233 missions flown by the Bahrain Wing.

Although the Jaguar force mounted two missions into Kuwait during the morning of 20 January, the weather over the next two days precluded any more operations. However, the Tornado F3 crews continued their routine mounting of defensive CAPs. Tornado GR1 missions also continued into their fourth night offensive against the MOBs. The airfields at Al Taqaddum, H3 were attacked from low level, but the Bahrain Wing experimented with an eight-ship medium-level operation against An Najaf. The 1,000lb free-fall bombs were aimed at the centre of the airfield complex, leaving ballistic dispersion to scatter them across the target area.

The Nimrods had been active in Direct Support operations, patrolling the Persian Gulf at medium level each night of the campaign. The aircraft used their Searchwater radar to locate surface contacts and vector aircraft from the Surface Unit CAP (SUCAP), or on occasions RN Lynx helicopters, onto them. In the busy waterway of the Gulf, which was also crowded with oil rigs, wrecks and marker buoys, the detection of small targets such as fast patrol boats was a challenge. On 21 January, the Nimrod identified four targets, which were engaged by the SUCAP. The Nimrods were not the only RAF aircraft involved in maritime operations, as the Jaguar Force was also tasked to provide pairs of aircraft for SUCAP sorties.

On the night of 21/22 January, the Bahrain and Dhahran Wings both attacked Jalibah airfield from medium level. Although operating from medium level put the Tornados above the anti-aircraft defences, weapon aiming from that height provided a major challenge in an aeroplane which had been specifically designed for low-level weapon delivery; thus, the safety of the aircraft was gained at the cost of weapon accuracy. The Tabuk Wing launched two more low-level missions that night against H3 and Ar Rutbah. One Tornado was lost on the second of these sorties, after which the Tabuk Wing also switched to medium-level operations. The night campaign against the Iraqi MOBs continued

Carried in pairs under the fuselage of a Panavia Tornado GR1, the Hunting JP233 runway denial weapon was used against Iraqi airfields in the first three nights of the Gulf War. The weapon is in two sections, one of which contained 30 SG-357 runway cratering sub-munitions, designed to destroy concrete. The other contained 215 HB-876 anti-personnel mines, designed to stop support teams from repairing any damage. (Glover)

A Tornado GR1 from the Tabuk Wing, carrying two BAe Dynamics ALARM anti-radiation missiles under the fuselage, heads into Iraq on an operational mission during the Gulf War. (Bellamy & Roche)

until 24 January, after which the Tornado tasking switched to the oil production and electrical power infrastructures as well as ammunition storage. For example, on 25 January the Tabuk Wing attacked petroleum storage at H3, the Dhahran Wing attacked a power station at An Nasiriyah and an ammunition depot at Khan Al Mahawil and the Bahrain Wing attacked an oil-pumping station at Al Zubayr.

The weather had improved sufficiently for Jaguar operations to recommence on 23 January with missions against well-defended artillery positions. On 25 January, the weather intervened again when eight Jaguars were tasked against further artillery positions and only one aircraft managed to drop. Jaguars armed with Bristol Aerospace CRV-7 rockets also flew SUCAP sorties on that day. The following day Jaguars each armed with four 1,000lb bombs destroyed a Hai Ying (HY-1) Silkworm anti-shipping battery in Kuwait. On 29 January, two Jaguars on SUCAP were sent to visually identify surface contacts which were heading east from the Kuwaiti coast near to the Saudi border. They discovered 13 Fast Patrol Boats (FPB), which greeted the Jaguars with accurate anti-aircraft gunfire. Between them, the Jaguars fired 76 CRV-7 rockets, hitting four of the boats and driving off the

rest. At night, the Nimrods were also busy directing SUCAP sorties, typically US Navy A-6 Intruders, onto surface contacts.

The night of 23 January marked the start of operations behind enemy lines by Special Forces: two Chinook HC2 helicopters of 7 Squadron Special Forces (SF) Flight inserted a patrol from the Special Boat Service (SBS) to the main road to Basra, approximately 35 miles south of Baghdad, to cut the communications cabling which linked to the south of the country. Thereafter, the Chinooks, as well as Hercules C1 aircraft of 47 Squadron SF Flight, carried out numerous flights into Iraq to insert or extract SAS and SBS patrols or to resupply them.

Over the last days of January 1991, the Tornado Force started a concerted effort against Iraqi fuel storage depots. On the night of 27/28 January, the store at H3 was attacked by ten aircraft from Tabuk in the morning and a further 12 aircraft from Tabuk attacked the storage at Haditha that evening. Eight aircraft from Dhahran attacked the storage at Uwayjah and ten from Bahrain attacked An Najaf. Bombs dropped by an eight-ship from Bahrain caused some impressive explosions at the oil refinery at As Samawah and the following day an eight-ship from

Dhahran bombed the Sayyadah petroleum facility, Al Taqaddum airfield was revisited by ten more Tornados from Tabuk and eight aircraft from Bahrain attacked the petroleum facility at Ad Diwaniya.

The pattern continued over the next four days: in that period, the Tornado Force from all three bases attacked airfield facilities at Al Jarrah, Taqaddum, and Q'alat Salih, the SAM supply facility at Shaibah, the EW site at Wadi Al Khir and petroleum storage and pumping stations at Ar Ramadi, Al Hillal and H2. However, while these attacks against large-area targets caused a degree of 'harassment,' radar-aimed bombing at night had reached its limitations and a new tactic was clearly needed for the Tornado GR1 Force. In fact, the first of an eventual 12 Pave Spike-equipped Buccaneer S2 aircraft drawn from 12 and 208 Squadrons and 237 OCU had arrived at Bahrain on 26 January. These aircraft would provide

the capability to drop Laser Guided Bombs (LGBs), enabling precision attacks on point targets.

Jaguars were in action on SUCAP again on 30 January, when two were dispatched to a contact which proved to be a *Polnocny*-Class landing ship. After confirming that the vessel was hostile the Jaguars attacked with CRV-7 and 30mm cannon, leaving the ship completely ablaze. On the same day and despite haze and half cloud cover over Kuwait, eight Jaguars each dropped two CBU-87 cluster weapons on two 2S1 self-propelled artillery batteries. SUCAP activity continued into 31 January. One pair was diverted to a Battlefield Air Interdiction (BAI) task against armoured vehicles on the coastal highway leading north from the Saudi border. It was only during the final stages of the attack on what had been identified as an Armoured Personnel Carrier (APC) that the formation leader realized that he was actually bombing

A Jaguar GR1 armed with Aerojet General/ Honeywell CBU-87 cluster bombs, operating from Bahrain during the Gulf War. Unlike the British-built Hunting BL-755 weapon, the CBU-87 could be dropped from medium-level. (Pitchfork)

Two Tornado GR1s, each armed with eight 1,000lb free-fall bombs, refuel from a Vickers VC10 K2 tanker of 101 Squadron during an operational sortie in 1991. (Glover)

a ZSU 23-4 self-propelled anti-aircraft gun. However, the vehicle was destroyed, along with a nearby truck, by eight BL755 cluster weapons. A second pair of Jaguars also on SUCAP was re-tasked to bomb anti-aircraft positions on Faylaka Island in support of a USN operation. Five aircraft attacked a Silkworm battery on the coast to the south of Kuwait City on 2 February and although the mission was successful, it brought home the problems of co-ordination with a large number of other Coalition aircraft in marginal weather.

Tornado F3 CAP missions had been flown throughout the period and by the end of January the Tornado F3 detachment had flown over 250 sorties. The air-defence Tornados were supported by the TriStar K1 of 216 Squadron, while the Victors of 55 Squadron and the VC10s of 101 Squadron worked with the Tornado GR1 Wings. However, the Victors and VC10s also refuelled USN aircraft, including Grumman A-6 Intruders, Grumman F-14 Tomcats, McDonnell-Douglas F/A-18 Hornets and Grumman EA-6 Prowlers, as well as Canadian McDonnell-Douglas CF-18 Hornets and Royal Saudi Air Force Tornados. Low-level reconnaissance sorties by Tornado GR1A aircraft had also continued every night.

After two more nights of medium-level night bombing, the Tornado Force received its first daylight tasking on 3 February, enabling crews to use a steep dive-attack profile to increase the accuracy of their weapon aiming. Over the next few days four- or eight-ship attacks were launched from

Dhahran against storage warehouses at As Samawah, airfield facilities at Al Jarrah and from Tabuk against ammunition storage at Qubaysah and Karbala, the power station at Al Musayib and later the petroleum production plant at Al Hillah. Meanwhile the Bahrain Wing bombed the ammunition storage facilities at Tall Al Lahm and joined the Dhahran Wing in a mission against the petroleum storage at An Nasiriyah. In some cases the weather precluded visually-aimed dive attacks, leaving crews to rely once more on radar aiming. However, this was not a complete move to daylight operations: night attacks continued, as well, with targets including Shaik Mazhar ammunition depot and As Samawah petroleum storage bombed by the Dhahran wing and Al Iskandariyah ammunition plant attacked by the Tabuk Wing.

The first LGB mission was carried out from Bahrain on 3 February, when four Tornado GR1 bombers supported by three Buccaneer designators dropped the suspension bridge over the River Euphrates at As Samawah. A second four-ship from Bahrain attacked another bridge at As Samawah later that afternoon and the last remaining bridge at As Samawah was destroyed two days later by another formation from Bahrain. On that day, the first LGB

sortie from Dhahran successfully attacked a road bridge across the River Tigris at Al Kut. Tornado GR1 operations on the next two days consisted entirely of daylight raids against oil or petroleum facilities by aircraft dropping free-fall bombs or against bridges by aircraft dropping LGBs. Since Pave Spike was a purely optical system it was limited to daylight only, the LGB missions were all flown in daytime.

On 6 February, there were daylight raids by the Tabuk Wing against the airfield facilities at H3 Southwest and by Dhahran-based aircraft against the Al Jarrah SAM support facility; the Bahrain Wing also attacked Al Jarrah that day, concentrating on the hangar buildings. That evening, eight Tornados, with support from a pair of ALARM aircraft, took off from Tabuk to revisit the power station at Al Musayib.

For the Jaguar Force, the first days of February brought daily tasking against SAM sites and artillery targets in Kuwait. At least two attack waves were launched each day, although operations were hampered by poor weather on 6 and 7 February. The Jaguars also flew daily SUCAP missions, although these were for the most part uneventful. Nimrod operations moved further north on 7 February when the aircraft were cleared to fly into the

A typical interdiction formation as used in the latter half of the Gulf War: two Tornado GR1s armed with laser-guided bombs (LGBs) are accompanied by a BAe Buccaneer S2B equipped with an AN/AVQ-23E Pave Spike, electro-optical laser designator targetting pod. (Glover)

northern reaches of the Gulf. From then onwards, each night would see the Nimrod flying a 'figure of eight' pattern at medium level, some 30 miles off the Kuwaiti coast, opposite Faylaka Island. From here the aircraft were able to detect small resupply boats moving between the mainland and the island and one such contact was made on 7 February. The Jaguar Wing resumed a full flying programme on 8 February with attacks using 1,000lb bombs against artillery positions and entrenched storage areas in Kuwait over the next days. The targets struck by the Jaguars also included a Silkworm missile battery on 10 January.

From 7 to 11 February, mixed formations comprising pairs of LGB-armed Tornado GR1 bombers accompanied by a single Pave Spike-equipped Buccaneer, continued the work of destroying the bridges over the Euphrates and Tigris rivers. Meanwhile, all three Tornado GR1 bases had also been launching four- or eight-ships armed with free-fall bombs against ammunition depots and petroleum storage facilities. The ammunition stores at Al Iskandariyah, Tall Al Lahm, Habbaniyah and H3 as well as the petroleum storage plant at Uwayjah were all attacked. Eight aircraft from Dhahran also bombed the storage tanks at Basra on 10 February. However, the fact that all of these targets had been attacked previously is perhaps an indication of the overall inaccuracy and ineffectiveness of dropping free-fall bombs from medium level.

Two prototype GEC-Ferranti Thermal Imaging Airborne Laser Designator (TIALD) pods had been flown to Tabuk in early February and the first operational TIALD designated sortie was flown on 10 February. The targets were the HASs on H3 Southwest airfield and the tactics mirrored those

Above: A Tornado GR1 flying from Bahrain in the immediate aftermath of the Gulf War. A small force of RAF aircraft remained in the region to ensure the security of Kuwait after the war had ended. (Lumb)

Opposite: The BAe Nimrod MR2 played a vital role during the Gulf War, monitoring the movements of shipping in the Persian Gulf and also directing tactical aircraft onto maritime targets. (Crown Copyright)

already being used successfully by the Bahrain and Dhahran Wings, with one designator working with two bombers. A second operational TIALD sortie on the night of 11 February targeted the HASs on H3 Northwest airfield. The advantage of TIALD over Pave Spike was that its infra-red sensor enabled it to be used at night. More crews were hastily trained to use the equipment to provide ten TIALD-qualified crews, which would allow almost round-the-clock operations. On 12 February, eight Tornados from Bahrain, plus a further eight from Dhahran, bombed the liquid propellant production plant at Latifiya and seven aircraft from Tabuk attacked the EW site at Ar Ruwayshid. These were the last missions in which unguided free-fall weapons were used, and for the rest of the conflict Tornado GR1 aircraft operated in pairs or four-ships dropping LGBs in co-operation with Pave Spike or TIALD designators.

Over 12–16 February the Tornado GR1 Wings switched their attention from bridges to airfields once more. Aircraft from all three Wings were employed in systematically destroying every individual HAS on the Iraqi Air Force MOBs. The airfields at H2, H3, Al Amarah, Al Asad, Al Taqaddum, Al Jarrah, Tallil, Kut Al Hayy, Mudaysis, Jaliba, Q'alat Salih were all attacked over this period. One Tornado was shot down over Al Taqaddum on 14 February. In the same period, the Jaguars from Bahrain continued to target artillery positions in Kuwait, including a four-ship attack on a multiple rocket launcher battery with CBU-87 on 15 February. Once again co-ordination with other Coalition aircraft proved to be problematic and a flight of General Dynamics F-16 aircraft also appeared to have the same Time over Target (ToT) on the same target. That night a Nimrod assisted in the attack on an Iraqi destroyer. One Jaguar mission was forced to abort the following day because of heavy smoke, a problem which had plagued two aircraft which had been switched a few days previously to the tactical reconnaissance role with a Vinten LOROP pod: haze and smoke made it difficult to acquire useful imagery. Because targets were becoming small, mobile and hard to find, the LOROP-equipped Jaguars made up the last aircraft in each strike formation, in order to take some imagery of likely target areas for the following day's tasking.

On 17 and 18 February, poor weather in the region limited flying, but the Tornado Force was able to return to the River Euphrates finish off the bridges at As Samawah, Ramadi and Fallujah. From 18 February the focus for operations moved to the operating surfaces and ancillary services on the MOBs. Placed on critical points of the taxiways and runways, a single LGB could create a large enough crater to render the concrete unusable, far more effectively that could a JP233. Furthermore, other small buildings which had been unscathed by earlier attacks, could also be pinpointed. The Jaguars' missions on these days and over the next five days before the land war started, continued the campaign against Iraqi artillery units, although sometimes they had to attack alternative targets such as revetments and storage areas when clouds, haze and smoke obscured their primary targets.

Most of the Tornado GR1 missions on 20 February against Shaibah, Q'alat Salih, Rumaylah and Kut Al Hayy brought their weapons back because poor weather obscured all of the targets. The cloudy weather continued into the next morning, but the skies had cleared enough on the afternoon of 21 February for successful sorties against Rumaylah by the Dhahran-based aircraft; however, missions against Shaibah (by Tabuk-based aircraft) and against Q'alat Salih and Kut Al Hayy (by Bahrain-based aircraft) were thwarted by the clouds. Two days of relatively good weather then followed, allowing the Tabuk Wing to neutralize Al Jarra and Mudaysis, the Dhahran Wing to complete their work at Rumaylah and the Bahrain Wing to attack Kut Al Hayy and Q'alat Salih.

The ground war started on 23 February and from this day the skies began to fill with thick black smoke after Iraqi forces set light to the Kuwaiti oil wells. Although Jaguar missions were launched after this, the combination of weather, smoke from burning oil wells and the proximity of friendly forces meant that none could deliver their weapons. Nimrod operations had also reduced to just one sortie a day by 26 February, but patrols continued into March. As might be expected, most of the flying done at this stage of the campaign was by the Chinooks and Pumas in support of the army. The Iraqi army surrendered on 28 February. However, Tornado F3 CAPs continued to be flown until 8 March 1991.

HUMANITARIAN RELIEF & SECURITY

Although most of the aircraft in the Gulf theatre returned home between 11 and 15 March, a small RAF contingent of Tornado GR1s, Buccaneers and Nimrods, plus Victor AAR support remained in the region for the next few months. Six Chinooks were also retained, but these were soon redeployed to Diyabakir, Turkey in April. UN Security Council Resolution issued on 6 April 1991 demanded an end to the repression of the Kurds in the north of the country by Iraqi forces and a safe haven was declared for the Kurdish people in northern Iraq. A No-Fly Zone (NFZ) for Iraqi aircraft was also established north of the 36th Parallel, enforced by US and French aircraft. Along with other Coalition partners, RAF aircraft started the work of distributing food and medical supplies to Kurdish refugees from 8 April. Six more Chinooks, bringing the total to 12 aircraft, were also sent to Turkey to support 3 Commando

A Lockheed C-130K Hercules C1 over the Zagros mountains on the border between Iraq and Iran during Operation *Haven* in the spring of 1991. The RAF contribution for this humanitarian operation comprised three Hercules transport aircraft and 12 Chinook helicopters. (Pitchfork)

A Dhahran-based Tornado GR1, equipped with a Ferranti-manufactured Thermal Imaging Airborne Laser Designator (TIALD) pod, on patrol in the No Fly Zone (NFZ) over Southern Iraq in late 1992. The aircraft also carries 2,250-litre under-wing fuel tanks and the BOZ-107 chaff and flare dispenser.

Brigade which deployed forward into northern Iraq to secure the safe haven. Three Hercules were based at Incirlik in Turkey for this operation and by 18 April they had delivered over 240 containers to Kurdish refugees who were sheltering amongst the mountains. In July Operation *Haven* was completed and it was replaced by Operation *Warden* (which was also known by the US designation '*Northern Watch*'). Eight Jaguars, initially crewed by 54 Squadron pilots, deployed to Incirlik to provide reconnaissance support to the operation in September 1991. Thereafter each Jaguar squadron took its turn to run the operation for consecutive two-month periods. Flying in pairs and supported by VC10 tankers from 101 Squadron, which were also based at Incirlik, the Jaguars flew daily sorties into the NFZ using the BAe Reconnaissance pod to photograph areas of interest.

In the early 1990s the former Republic of Yugoslavia was riven by a series of particularly savage civil wars. By mid-1992 the Bosnian capital Sarajevo was besieged by Serbian forces and cut off from supplies. On 2 July 1992, a Hercules C1P from 47 Squadron Special Forces Flight was among NATO aircraft that commenced airlifting food and medical provisions into Sarajevo. The aircraft, which had been modified with armour protection for the flight deck and chaff and flare dispensers, was frequently subject to small arms fire, but was only hit on two occasions. During 1994, it was also illuminated by SAM-2 radar systems. Based initially in Zagreb, but later moving to Ancona, the Hercules flew three or four resupply sorties into Sarajevo every day until 9 January 1996. During that time 26,577 tons of freight were delivered in just under 2,000 sorties.

In Angola, too, a long-running civil war continued to rage. In late 1992, the fighting reached the outskirts of Luanda and it was decided to evacuate UK citizens in the country. Routing via Ascension Island, a TriStar C1 from 216 Squadron flew to Luanda on 1 November 1992 where it picked up 167 evacuees.

Another country pulled apart by civil war was Somalia where continuous conflict between warring factions had destroyed the agriculture, which in turn resulted in a countrywide famine. On 12 December 1992, two RAF Hercules were flown to Mombasa, Kenya, where they joined other aircraft from the USAF, German and Canadian air forces. Over the next three months, relief flights were mounted into Mogadishu and Kismayu as well as smaller rural airstrips, delivering a total of 3,500 tons of supplies.

Meanwhile, in Iraq, another NFZ, this time south of the 32nd Parallel, was established on 27 August 1992 to protect Shia Marsh Arabs from the attentions of the regime. Once again, the RAF undertook to provide the reconnaissance platforms for the operation. In view of the increased threat levels in southern Iraq, aircraft had to operate above 10,000ft within the NFZ and unfortunately the Tornado GR1A reconnaissance system was unsuitable for medium-level operation. Instead, Tornado GR1 aircraft would use the camera and video recording system within TIALD pods to film activity on the ground below the NFZ, thus pre-dating the US concept of Non-Traditional Intelligence Surveillance and Reconnaissance (NTISR) by ten years. British participation in the operation was nicknamed Operation *Jural*, although once again the American term '*Southern Watch*' was also used to describe the operation. Six Tornados led by 17 Squadron, but including a number of TIALD specialists from other units, deployed to Dhahran in August 1992 to commence operations. A Victor tanker from 55 Squadron deployed to Bahrain to provide AAR support for the detachment. Since the operating area was larger than that of Operation *Warden* in

the north, the aircraft flew operational sorties in two pairs to cover the areas of interest. In practice the four Tornados would make up only part of a much larger coalition package operating within the NFZ and there was an almost continuous presence of Coalition air-defence aircraft such as McDonnell-Douglas F15C/D Eagles and Dassault Mirage 2000s. Like the Jaguar Force, each squadron was responsible for providing crews for a three-month period, but rather than the entire squadron deploying for the whole period a system of 'roulement' was introduced, whereby crews were cycled through Dhahran for a six-week tour. Staggered starting dates for each pair of crews meant that there would be a continuous presence of locally experienced crews. In the first changeover, 617 Squadron took over from 17 Squadron who then, in turn, handed over to 14 Squadron in November.

Although the daily task over southern Iraq had become routine by mid-December 1992, there were strong indications that the Iraqis intended to contest the NFZ. SAM systems were deployed below the NFZ and on 27 December when an Iraqi MiG-25 Foxbat aircraft was shot down by a USAF General Dynamics F-16 fighter, tensions rose dramatically. In January 1993 two large airstrikes were carried out by Coalition aircraft against the nodal points of the Iraqi air defence system south of the 32nd Parallel. In each case the RAF contributed four Tornado GR1 aircraft armed with LGBs to these airstrikes: the aircraft (crewed from 14, 31 and 617 Squadrons) successfully attacked the air defence headquarters and radar control bunker at Al Amarah on 13 January and the radar control bunker at An Najaf five days later.

THE BALKANS

In response to the continuing civil war in the Former Yugoslavia, NATO established a NFZ over Bosnia in April 1993. The NATO Operation *Deny Flight*

A Jaguar GR1 in transit over the Adriatic Sea during an Operation *Deny Flight* mission in late 1994. The Jaguars operated in support of the multi-national United Nations Protection Force (UNPROFOR) in Bosnia-Herzegovina. (Kerss)

began at noon GMT on 12 April 1993, enforced by aircraft from the UK, USA, France and the Netherlands. The UK contribution to these forces was six Tornado F3 fighters operating from Gioia del Colle, supported by a Boeing E-3C Sentry Airborne Warning and Control System (AWACS) aircraft flying from Aviano and two VC10 tankers based at Palermo.

The Harrier GR3 detachment in Belize, 1417 Flight, disbanded in July 1993 and the imminent loss of that commitment in turn freed the Harrier Force to take on operational duties over northern Iraq. The Harrier GR7 aircraft of 1 Squadron relieved the Jaguars on Operation *Warden* at Incirlik in March 1993. However, the Jaguar Force's break from operational flying was short-lived: on 12 July 1993, 12 Jaguars from 6 Squadron deployed to Gioia del Colle, to provide CAS and tactical reconnaissance for the

UN Protection Force (UNPROFOR) in Bosnia-Herzogovina. The concept was to keep an armed presence over the UNPROFOR contingents. Launching in pairs throughout the day and loaded with 1,000lb bombs, the Jaguars would be allocated to a Forward Air Controller (FAC) with an UNPROFOR unit. They would then set up a holding pattern overhead and make dummy attacks on various targets chosen by the FAC. Some missions were also supported by a TriStar tanker which was based at Palermo. Once again, the three Jaguar squadrons took turns in manning the detachment for two-month tours.

One particular advantage of the Foxhunter radar equipping the Tornado F3, over the AN/APG-63 fitted to USAF F-15 Eagle and F-16 Fighting Falcon, was that it could detect slow-flying aircraft such as helicopters. Although a number of helicopters from both sides were intercepted, the rules of engagement prevented any further action by the Tornado crews. However, on 13 May 1994 two Tornado F3 fighters forced down a Croatian helicopter which had been delivering ammunition to the Bosnian Croat Army (the HVO). Four more Jaguars deployed to Gioia del Colle on 11 February after the expiry of a UN deadline for Serbian forces to remove heavy weapons around Sarajevo. HMS *Ark Royal* also arrived in the Adriatic Sea in early 1994 and the Sea Harrier FRS1

aircraft of 801 Squadron also joined in operations over Bosnia. One Sea Harrier was shot down on 16 April. Over the summer there were sporadic attacks by NATO aircraft on Serbian targets and on the evening of 22 September two Jaguars flown by 41 Squadron pilots were called in to assist a USAF Fairchild A-10 Thunderbolt II attacking a Serbian T55 tank near Sarajevo. They each dropped 1,000lb bombs on the target.

A Jaguar GR1 banks over Mostar, Bosnia-Herzegovina. Apart from a self-protection suite, the aircraft is armed with a single 1,000lb bomb, in case it might be called in for a 'show of force.' (Kerss)

A Lockheed TriStar from 216 Squadron carrying members of 12 Squadron back to RAF Lossiemouth after their deployment on Operation *Desert Fox*. The aircraft is being escorted by two Tornado GR1s from 617 Squadron. (Crown Copyright)

During early November 1994, Serbian aircraft flying from Udbina airfield carried out three air attacks on civilian targets in the 'Safe Area' around Bihac in northwest Bosnia. In response, NATO carried out an airstrike on the military airfield at Udbina on 21 November. The airstrike by a 'package' of over 40 aircraft was led by the Royal Netherlands Air Force (RNLAF) was the largest combined air operation mounted by NATO at that stage. It included USAF F-15Es and F-16Cs, USMC F/A-18 Hornets, RNLAF F-16s, French AF Jaguars and Mirage 2000s and four RAF Jaguars flown by 54 Squadron pilots. The attack aircraft were protected by RNLAF F-16 escorts and General Dynamics EF-111A jamming aircraft. Two RAF Jaguars bombed the taxiway intersections from medium level, dropping free-fall 1,000lb bombs. Another Jaguar equipped with a LOROP pod and escorted by another bomb-armed aircraft carried out the post-strike reconnaissance.

Throughout the NATO operations over Bosnia, Nimrods carried out periodic patrols of the Adriatic Sea and Canberra PR9 aircraft of 39 Squadron also flew regular high-level photographic reconnaissance over the region. In early 1995, there were eight Tornado F3s and nine Jaguars at Gioia del Colle, with another three Jaguars kept at readiness at Coltishall. These aircraft were supported by two Sentrys at Aviano and two TriStars at Palermo. Operation *Deny Flight* ended on 20 December 1995 and the Tornado F3 aircraft returned to their UK bases, but the Jaguars remained in theatre to support UNPROFOR. As the result of an Urgent Operational Requirement (UOR) established the previous year for LGB capability over the Balkans a number of Jaguars were modified in-house to carry the TIALD pod; these were designated Jaguar GR1B, three of which were deployed to Gioia del Colle during mid-1995.

In April 1995, the Tornado GR1s from 617 Squadron relieved the Harriers at Incirlik. Operation *Warden* then became the responsibility of the UK-based Tornado GR1 units (2, 12, 13 and 617 Squadrons) and Operation *Jural* fell to the Brüggen-based units (9, 14, 17 and 31 Squadrons). Each squadron would now have to complete a four-month tour of duty. In turn 12 Harrier GR7 aircraft of 4 Squadron relieved the Jaguars at Gioia del Colle on 1 August 1995; however, with tension mounting in the Balkans the three Jaguar GR1Bs remained to provide the RAF detachment with a precision attack capability.

At the end of June 1995, 24 Air Mobile Brigade landed at Ploce, Croatia, as part of a larger deployment of French and UK forces to reinforce and support UNPROFOR. The Brigade's air mobility was provided by six Pumas and six Chinooks. Although both the Puma and Chinook Forces were both involved in operational

A BAe Harrier GR7 returns to Gioia del Colle after a mission over the Balkans in the late 1990s. Equipped with forward looking infra-red (FLIR) sensors and a cockpit compatible with night vision goggles (NVG), this version of the aircraft introduced a night combat capability to the RAF Harrier force. (Crown Copyright)

Jaguars of 6, 54 and 41 Squadrons of the Coltishall Wing. The aircraft in the foreground is a GR1B carrying a Ferranti TIALD pod. During operations over Bosnia in the autumn of 1995, TIALD-equipped Jaguars designated targets for Harrier GR7s to attack with LGBs. (Crown Copyright)

detachments in Northern Ireland, the overall burden for the Pumas had at least been eased by the disbandment, in July, of 1563 Flight in Belize.

After further violations of the UN safe areas, NATO launched a brief but intensive air campaign against the Bosnian Serb air-defence system. The first attacks were flown on 30 August 1995. The Harrier detachment at Gioia flew two waves on the first day, each comprising two TIALD-equipped Jaguars designating targets for a pair of Harriers dropping LGBs. Over the next 14 days, the Harriers flew 144 daylight combat missions and dropped 48 LGBs against 19 targets. A further 30 free-fall bombs were dropped on eight more targets. After the campaign, air operations over Bosnia returned to the routine of reconnaissance and armed over watch. In February 1997, the Harriers of 3 Squadron handed responsibility for the Balkan detachment back to the Jaguars of 41 Squadron.

IRAQ & RWANDA

Two armoured divisions of the Iraqi Republican Guard were reported to be moving towards the Kuwaiti border in early October 1994, triggering Operation *Driver*, a reinforcement of UK forces in the Gulf region. Six more Tornados were sent to Dhahran from Brüggen on 11 October to supplement the six aircraft already there and a further VC10 tanker was sent to Bahrain. The extra Tornado GR1 aircraft enabled an increased number of patrols in the southern NFZ from 13 October. Operation *Driver* also involved the deployment of 45 Commando RM from its base at Arbroath to Kuwait. The move was undertaken over 19 to 22 October by a relay of Hercules and TriStar transport aircraft. By the end of the deployment there had been 126 RAF transport flights into Kuwait International airport.

On 25 June 1996, a terrorist truck bomb destroyed part of the accommodation area in Dhahran used by Coalition personnel, so the whole operation was moved to Prince Sultan Air Base (PSAB) at Al Kharj, some 80 miles south of Riyadh. The transfer was made without losing any of the operational task. While the flying operation

remained virtually unchanged, the morale of Brüggen's Tornado GR1 crews was not improved by the prospect of living in tents next to the runway in temperatures approaching 50°C and the lack of an opportunity to escape to Bahrain. After Iraqi military activity in the north of the country and cruise missile strikes by US forces, the southern NFZ was expanded to cover the airspace up to the 33rd Parallel in September 1996.

When civil war erupted in Rwanda in 1994, much of the population sought refuge from the genocide that was being committed by fleeing into the jungle of Eastern Zaire. Two years later, efforts were still being made by the UN to track down all of these refugees and there was concern that a multi-national force might be required to protect them. A Canberra PR9 of 39 Squadron flew to Entebbe, Uganda, on 20 November 1996 to carry out a four-week survey of the jungle areas.

A Tornado F3 over the Balkans during an Operation *Deny Flight* sortie in the mid-1990s. The aircraft, flying from Gioia del Colle, is operated by a crew from 43 Squadron: note the unit markings of the 'rival' 11 Squadron have been crudely over-painted. (43 Squadron Archive)

The English Electric Canberra PR9 photographic reconnaissance aircraft first entered RAF service with 58 Squadron in 1960 and the type remained a front-line aircraft until 2006. This aircraft was operated by 39 Squadron, the last unit to operate the type. (BAe Heritage)

The survey indicated that the problem was not as severe as had been feared, so a further armed UN force was not required.

Back in Iraq, a team of inspectors established by the UN Special Commission (UNSCOM) had been monitoring Iraq's compliance with UN directives on biological and chemical warfare since the end of the Gulf War. However, when the Iraqis declared in early November 1997 that they would no longer co-operate with UNSCOM, the US-led Coalition reacted by increasing its military presence in the area. Since the Saudis were unwilling to allow

the RAF Tornados at PSAB to carry out offensive operations from their territory, HMS *Invincible* was diverted to the Persian Gulf, carrying FAA Sea Harriers and eight Harriers of 1 Squadron. The ship initially remained in the Mediterranean Sea as diplomatic moves and counter moves over Iraq ran their course in the UN over the winter months. During this time, the Harriers flew missions over the Balkans in early December and again in early January 1998. As the crisis deepened, HMS *Invincible* arrived in the Persian Gulf in late January and its aircraft started to fly patrols over southern Iraq as part of Operation *Jural* from 29 January. Each mission comprised four Harrier GR7 bombers escorted by four Sea Harriers.

In the meantime, the Kuwaitis had expressed a willingness to host combat aircraft and after 48 hours' notice, nine Tornados from 14 Squadron left Brüggen for Kuwait on 9 February 1998. A further four aircraft deployed directly from the UK. The Tornados deployed to Ali Al Salem (AAS) Air Base, which lay some 25 miles to the west of Kuwait City and was still in the semi-destroyed state in which it had been left after the Gulf War. The Tornado detachment established itself amongst the ruined HAS sites over the next two days; weapons were delivered to AAS and the TIALD pods that were being used by 17 Squadron for Operation *Jural* were flown in from Al Kharj so that the detachment was ready for offensive operations on 11 January.

However, neither the Tornados nor the Harriers were required to carry out attack operations: diplomatic initiatives had quickly defused the crisis and a new agreement between Iraq and UNSCOM was signed on 17 February. However, both aircraft types flew sorties in the Southern NFZ for the next three months. The Harriers of 1 Squadron were replaced by those of 3 Squadron when HMS *Illustrious* replaced HMS *Invincible* during the first week of March. HMS *Illustrious* left the Gulf in mid-April, leaving an RAF presence of 12 Tornado GR1 aircraft at AAS and a further six aircraft at PSAB.

Relations between Iraq and UNSCOM deteriorated again in late 1998 and Iraq was issued with a deadline to comply with UN directives or to face the consequences. The RAF contingent in the Gulf region was further enhanced by the presence of a Nimrod R1 from 51 Squadron, which deployed to Kuwait International airport; the two VC10 tankers from 101 Squadron remained on standby at Bahrain. When the deadline for Iraqi compliance passed on 16 December the Coalition mounted airstrikes, which the US military named Operation *Desert Fox*. LGB-armed Tornado GR1

bombers flew three operational waves early that evening. The first four-ship was tasked against the SAM-3 site and a radio relay site near Basra; the second wave attacked an ammunition store and a hangar on Tallil airfield, as well as a radio relay station just to the north at An Nasiriyah. At Tallil, it transpired that the target hangar had contained the Aero L29 drone aircraft which were being modified to carry biological weapons. The third four-ship attacked a Republican Guard barracks at Al Kut.

The following day six more Tornados from 617 deployed to AAS to support the operations. But they were not required for action. On 18 December, two formations of Tornados were launched against the SAM-3 site at Tallil and the Republican Guard Barracks at Al Kut, once again. A third wave also carried out further attacks against targets in the Al Kut area.

On the third night of operations the targets for the first formation were once again in the vicinity of Al Kut. This time the Tornados were armed with the new 2,000lb Paveway III LGB, which was designed for use against hardened targets such as bunkers. The first four-ship delivered its weapons successfully, but a second wave which had been tasked against targets near Basra was cancelled before it crossed the border into Iraq; the aircraft returned to AAS with their weapons.

A NEW DIRECTION

After 30 years of Cold War preparations for a conflict in central Europe, the period from 1990 to 1998 had seen a fundamental shift in focus towards Iraq and the Balkans. The RAF fast-jet force, which had trained for so long to carry out relatively short-range missions at low level now found itself prosecuting long-range operations from medium-level with laser-guided weapons. And as operational involvement moved towards more direct support of troops on the ground, so the importance of the support helicopter increased.

CHAPTER 9

OPERATIONS CONTINUE

1999-2008

Despite eight years of continuous operations by RAF aircraft acting as part of a larger Coalition over Iraq and seven years over the Balkans, both regions remained highly volatile at the end of the 1990s, much like smouldering embers waiting to burst into flame once more. At least other areas of British responsibility across the globe seemed to have stabilized during the decade. The Falklands remained unchallenged and Belize was now secure enough not to need the presence of Harriers and Pumas. In Northern Ireland, the Good Friday Agreement promised an end to the Troubles and to Operation *Banner*.

At the beginning of 1999, all operations over Iraq had been amalgamated into Operation *Resinate*: *Resinate North* covered the operations out of Incirlik into the northern NFZ and *Resinate South* covered operations from AAS and PSAB into the southern NFZ. Early in the year 12 Squadron handed over the commitment for the 12 Tornado GR1 aircraft at AAS in Kuwait to 2 Squadron. Across at PSAB in Saudi Arabia, six Tornado F3 fighters had taken over from the Tornado GR1 bombers in order to police the southern NFZ. However, after the 'Desert Fox' operations of December 1998 the Iraqi government had stated that it would no longer recognize the legality of the NFZs, and Coalition aircraft operating over southern Iraq were subsequently often fired upon by Iraqi anti-aircraft guns. In the north of the country, six Jaguar GR3 aircraft based at Incirlik made up the UK contribution to 'Northern

Operations in Iraq and Afghanistan in the early 2000s were characterized by the capabilities of the support helicopter. The Boeing Vertol CH-47D Chinook HC2, which equipped 7, 18 and 27 Squadrons, could carry up to 55 troops or 10 tons of cargo. (Crown Copyright)

The Intelligence Surveillance Target Acquisition and Reconnaissance (ISTAR) force operating over the Balkans included Nimrod R1 Elint aircraft of 51 Squadron, flying from Practica di Mare, near Rome, and Boeing E-3D Sentry Airborne Warning and Control System (AWACS) aircraft of 8 and 23 Squadrons, operating from Aviano, Italy. (Crown Copyright)

Watch.' Previously relatively quiet in comparison to its southern counterpart, the northern NFZ was also now disputed by the Iraqis and aircraft, here, too were regularly fired upon by anti-aircraft guns. Although no weapons were dropped by RAF aircraft over the northern NFZ, airstrikes by Tornado GR1 (and later Tornado GR4) aircraft against Iraqi anti-aircraft positions and air defence units became a regular feature of operations in the southern NFZ from 1999. The Tornado F3 crews also became accustomed to Iraqi MiG-25 Foxbat and Mirage F1 aircraft attempting to dash into the NFZ to take a shot at the AWACS and Rivet Joint

aircraft; however, the Iraqi aircraft invariably ran out of the NFZ when they were locked up by the Tornado F3 Foxhunter radar.

KOSOVO

In late 1998, another war erupted in the Balkans, this time in Kosovo. After attempts to resolve the conflict through diplomacy had failed, NATO commenced air operations against Serbia in March 1999. The RAF aircraft already in theatre as part of the larger NATO/UN operations in the Former

Republic of Yugoslavia comprised eight Harriers of 1 Squadron, based at Gioia del Colle, supported by two TriStar tankers from 216 Squadron operating from Ancona. Three Sentrys from 8 and 23 Squadrons were also based at Aviano as part of the NATO Airborne Early Warning component. Additionally, a Nimrod R1 of 51 Squadron was based at Practica di Mare. The Harriers flew the first offensive sorties of Operation *Engadine* over Kosovo on 24 March 1999. That night, four Harriers armed with Paveway II (PWII) LGBs accompanied by two more TIALD-equipped Harriers were tasked against an ammunition storage facility. However, the pilots had to abort their mission when they found their targets obscured by explosions and smoke caused by other nearby attacks. A second mission by six Harriers the following night was successful against a military complex at Keskovac, but the eight Harriers which launched on 26 March were recalled because heavy clouds over Kosovo obscured the target area. The weather also prevented Harrier operations the next night.

This experience was typical of the Kosovo campaign: poor weather conditions over the Balkans made LGB attacks challenging and the problems were exacerbated by unfamiliarity amongst both Harrier and Tornado crews with the nuances of laser-guided operations. This, in turn, was the result of inadequate training thanks to a chronic shortage of equipment in the preceding years. On 27 March, four more Harriers arrived at Gioia del Colle, bringing the detachment's total to 12 aircraft, and a further two TriStars and three VC10s deployed to Ancona to bolster the AAR detachment. Throughout the campaign, the TriStars and VC10 tankers at Ancona flew AAR missions for other NATO forces as well as RAF aircraft, refuelling aircraft from the US Navy, Canada, France, Italy and Spain. Three VC10 tankers from 101 Squadron also deployed to Brüggen to support long-range bombing missions from there by the Tornado GR1 aircraft of 9, 14 and 31 Squadrons.

Harriers carried out successful self-designated LGB attacks on a munitions depot in Pristina on the night of 28 March. Numerous sorties were cancelled over the next week because of the weather and a daylight armed reconnaissance sortie, hunting for Serbian tanks and artillery on 4 April, produced no results. However, that evening six Tornados from 9 and 14 Squadrons carried out their first mission of the campaign. From Brüggen the aircraft flew in two three-ships, each accompanied by a VC10, over eastern France to the Mediterranean coast, then routed via Corsica east across Italy. The transit also included AAR brackets, which were carried out in challenging conditions. In the southern Adriatic, the aircraft rendezvoused with a pre-strike pair of TriStar tankers, before crossing the border into Serbia, where they were greeted with heavy anti-aircraft fire. The first two attacked the highway bridge at Jezgrovice (along the shores of Lake Gazivoda 40 miles northwest of Pristina) with 1,000lb PWII LGBs, while the second two delivered 2,000lb PW IIIs onto the rail tunnel near Mure (some 50 miles north of Pristina) on the boundary between Kosovo and Serbia. All NATO aircraft shared the same planned weapon impact time that night with the objective of achieving a simultaneous cut of road and rail links into Kosovo. After completing their attacks, the aircraft returned home via the same route, having first refuelled again from the TriStar tankers. The Tornados landed back at Brüggen in daylight after a seven-and-a-half-hour flight. This was the first time since World War II that RAF bomber crews had flown offensive operations from their home base.

Six Brüggen-based Tornados from 9 and 31 Squadrons, attacked hardened storage bunkers at Pristina airfield the following evening and on 6 April ten Harriers carried out daylight attacks against four groups of Serbian ground forces in Kosovo, using RBL755 Cluster Bombs Units (CBUs). That night another wave of Harriers bombed an ammunition facility in Kosovo and six Tornados attacked Pristina Barracks. Then, once again the weather intervened and there were no offensive sorties by RAF aircraft over the region for the next two days.

Harrier operations resumed on 8 April with ten sorties mounted against military vehicles in two

A Boeing E-3D Sentry AEW1 of 23 Squadron, one of seven aircraft procured by the RAF in 1990 to replace the Avro Shackleton AEW3 in the airborne early warning role. During operations over the Balkans, RAF Sentrys were integrated into the NATO early warning force. (Crown Copyright)

locations, one in the south and one in the west of Kosovo. Two days later, six Harriers attacked a military storage area and a radio relay station in daylight; however, eight night sorties tasked against military vehicles were recalled because the targets had moved location.

Brüggen-based Tornados carried out their fourth mission on 12 April, when six aircraft attacked the ammunition storage facility at Čačak and targets on the nearby airfield at Ladeveci, near Obvra, some 70 miles south of Belgrade. The following day ten Harriers attacked an oil storage depot, a military radio relay and a military radar in Kosovo. Because of poor weather once again, the aircraft dropped their weapons, a mixture of 1,000lb bombs and RBL755 CBUs, through cloud.

The next two Tornado missions, against Nis airfield on 14 April and a military communications site near Ivanjila three days later, were not entirely successful because of weather and equipment problems. Meanwhile the Harriers of 1 Squadron had carried out a number of successful CBU attacks on Serbian forces in Kosovo, including command posts and armoured vehicles, between 16 and 20 April. Then the weather closed in and for the next week a number of Tornado and Harrier missions were cancelled, either pre-launch or shortly after take-off.

On 27 April, 15 Harrier sorties were launched from Gioia del Colle to bomb an ammunition storage site at Besinje. The aircraft had to drop their CBUs through cloud, but the following day the weather had improved sufficiently for a further 11 Harrier sorties some of which were armed with LGBs. That night the Tornados returned to launch an attack on the airfield at Podgorica in Montenegro, just a short distance inland from the Adriatic coast. Over the next two nights, the Tornados carried successful attacks against the ammunition storage site at Valjevo, about 40 miles southwest of Belgrade, and the oil storage at Vitanovac, a few miles southeast of Obvra. The improvement in the weather also brought increased tasking to the Harriers: 18 sorties on 30 April included an LGB attack on the bridge at

Kokin Brod in western Kosovo, 12 aircraft attacked an army barracks and rail bridge at Djakovica in Serbia on 1 May and more than 30 sorties were flown against Serbian army and police units in Kosovo over the next three days.

A more direct route from Brüggen to Serbia, through the Czech Republic, Slovakia, Hungary and Croatia, was authorized at the end of April. This routing, which reduced sortie times to around five hours and required just one pre- and one post-strike AAR bracket, was used for the first time on 2 May for an attack by six Tornados of 9 and 14 Squadrons on the airfield at Ladeveci airbase, near Obvra. Defence suppression for the mission was provided by four F-16CJ Wild Weasels and two EA-6B Prowlers. In the target area, the Tornados met with heavy anti-aircraft fire, and eight SAM-3s were also fired at the formation. However, all aircraft dropped their LGBs successfully and all returned safely to Brüggen.

The weather caused another break in Tornado operations until 10 May, but Harrier missions continued on 7 May with an attack on Sjenica airfield (with 1,000lb bombs dropped through cloud) and over the next week up to 20 sorties per day were flown against Serbian forces in Kosovo. The targets, which included fuel storage, artillery units, armoured vehicles and communications sites, were attacked with a mix of CBUs and 1,000lb bombs.

Tornado missions resumed on 10 May with an attack on the storage at the barracks at Leskovac, some 45 miles northeast of Pristina. The following night the Barë Road Bridge at Mitrovica was attacked and on 14 May the longer southerly route to Serbia was used in order to attack the oil storage facility at Sjenica airfield. This mission was not entirely successful, as low cloud interrupted the guidance of some weapons during the last few seconds of the attack.

On 19 May, a formation of Tornados from 9 and 31 Squadrons was tasked against a special police depot approximately ten miles west of Belgrade, which was very heavily defended by anti-aircraft guns as well as SAM-3s. Both units were then temporarily

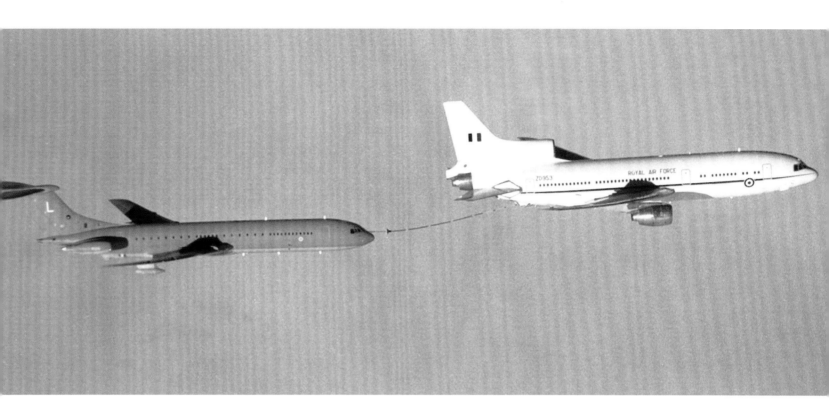

stood down from operations while they deployed to Solenzara, in eastern Corsica. After a brief break, Harrier operations continued on 21 May, but they were severely hampered by the weather. Most of the 18 Harrier sorties on 22 May could not release their weapons because of the weather conditions and on 24 May only eight sorties were flown out of a planned total of 20 sorties. However, that night the weather cleared sufficiently for six Tornados from 9 and 14 Squadrons to attack the fuel storage at Batajnica airbase, outside Belgrade.

The Tornados also attacked the ammunition storage at Ralja, 30 miles southeast of Belgrade on 26 May. During this attack, three SAM-6s were launched against the Tornados, which were able to evade the missiles. On this day 29 sorties were flown over Kosovo by the Harriers of 1 Squadron.

On 27 May, the Tornados bombed a SAM support facility near Belgrade and the following day the ammunition storage sites at Boljevac 100 miles southeast of Belgrade and Sremska Kamenica, near Novi Sad, were also bombed. These missions marked the end of long-range direct operations from Brüggen: the Solenzara detachment was fully operational with

12 Tornados from 9 and 31 Squadrons and the remaining Tornado GR1 operations over Serbia were mounted from there. Two additional VC10 tankers had also been sent to Ancona to support the aircraft at Solenzara.

Over 29 and 30 May, ten Harriers attacked vehicles, mortar positions, artillery and armour in Kosovo with RBL755 CBUs and eight Harriers attacked Serbian troops in dug-in positions with a mix of CBUs and 1,000lb bombs. For the next week, around 20 Harrier sorties were launched each day from Gioia del Colle, targeting Serbian forces, concentrating particularly on artillery and mortar positions. The first missions flown by Tornados from Solenzara on 4 and 5 June were thwarted by the weather and neither was able to carry out their attacks. However, on 7 June six Tornado GR1 aircraft from 31 Squadron flew the first daylight sortie to be carried out by RAF Tornados. Four aircraft fired ALARM missiles at a SAM-6 battery near Sjenica, while four aircraft carried out a successful LGB attack on the airfield. On the same day, the Harriers of 1 Squadron carried out 20 sorties against artillery and mortar

A VC10 K4 of 101 Squadron refuels from a TriStar of 216 Squadron over the Adriatic. The VC10 was the more flexible tanker for refuelling tactical aircraft, because its two underwing-mounted Hose Drum Units (HDUs) enabled two aircraft to refuel simultaneously; the TriStar had only a single HDU mounted in the rear fuselage. (Crown Copyright)

Supported by VC10 tankers from 101 Squadron, the Tornado GR1s of IX, 14 and 31 Squadrons flew long-range night interdiction sorties over Kosovo and Serbia in 1999 from their base at Brüggen. The aircraft were armed with Paveway II and III Laser-Guided Bombs (LGB). (Froome)

positions in Kosovo. These were the last sorties of the campaign: a ceasefire was declared on 10 June 1999 and a multi-national ground force, KFOR, moved into Kosovo.

The British contribution to KFOR was 5 Airborne Brigade which was supported by eight Chinook HC2 helicopters from 27 Squadron and six Pumas from 33 Squadron. Most of the troops were flown into Skopje by a mixed force of TriStar, VC10 and Hercules aircraft in early June. Most of the RAF aircraft in theatre were withdrawn over the summer, leaving six Harriers at Gioia del Colle, two TriStars at Ancona and two Sentrys at Aviano. The support helicopter force was also reduced.

AFRICA

In response to catastrophic flooding by the Limpopo and Save Rivers in southern Mozambique, four Pumas of 33 Squadron were transported to Maputo in chartered Antonov An-124s. From there, they flew relief operations from 5 March until 19 March, after they were relieved by five Sea King helicopters of 820

Squadron FAA which arrived aboard the RFA *Fort George* on 11 March. The Pumas delivered over 425 tons of supplies to areas affected by severe flooding and rescued 563 people.

After the breakdown of law and order in Sierra Leone, British forces were dispatched in May 2000 to secure the capital Freetown and to evacuate British and other entitled personnel from the country. Troops from the UK Rapid Reaction Force were flown into Dakar in neighbouring Senegal by RAF transport aircraft. Meanwhile, four Chinooks also deployed to Dakar via long-range ferry flights from the UK, staging via Gibraltar, the Canary Islands, Mauritania and Senegal. The aircraft were crewed by personnel from all three Chinook units, 7, 18 and 27 Squadrons. The helicopters were used to evacuate 500 civilians from Freetown to Dakar, from where they were flown to the UK by Hercules. Eight Hercules aircraft were retained at Dakar to support the ground forces in Sierra Leone and a daily resupply flight was mounted from the UK.

HMS *Illustrious* arrived in theatre on 11 May, bringing with it a mixed force of FAA Sea Harriers and five Harriers of 3 Squadron. Over the next months, the Harriers flew reconnaissance missions and also mounted flypasts over various locations as a 'show of force'. HMS *Ocean* brought with it another two Chinooks in June. Two Chinooks operated with Indian Special Forces during an operation on 10 July to relieve Indian Army Gurkha troops and a British liaison officer, who were pinned down by rebels of the Revolutionary United Front (RUF). In another operation on 10 September, three Chinooks provided airlift for a force of 1Para and SAS troops to rescue troops of the Royal Irish Regiment who had been captured by another rebel gang known as the 'West Side Boys.' During this successful operation, named Operation *Barras*, the Chinooks used aircraft-mounted the General Electric M-134 Minigun to provide covering fire for the troops.

AFGHANISTAN

On 11 September 2001 terrorists from the Al-Qaeda organization flew hijacked airliners into the World Trade Center in New York and the Pentagon in Washington DC. As a result, the US commenced operations in Afghanistan to remove the threat posed by Al-Qaeda and the Islamist Taliban government in the country.

US aircraft started offensive operations over Afghanistan on 9 October 2001. The UK participation was the provision of AAR support to the US Navy in the form of two TriStar tankers from 216 Squadron and four VC10 tankers from 10 and 101 Squadrons based in Oman. These aircraft flew daily sorties from October 2001 and throughout the following year. Additionally, two Sentrys with crews from 8 and 23 Squadrons deployed to Thumrait to join USAF E-3C Sentrys operating over Afghanistan. Sentry crews flew missions up to 14-hour long controlling and co-ordinating airstrikes. Nimrod MR2 aircraft also carried out maritime patrols in the Indian Ocean, in support of the US Navy, while Canberra PR9 reconnaissance aircraft of 39 Squadron and Nimrod R1 Elint aircraft of 51 Squadron provided photo-reconnaissance and electronic surveillance respectively.

An agreement was reached in December 2001 to set up an International Security Assistance Force (ISAF) in Afghanistan. The UK contribution to

Boeing C-17A Globemaster IIIs of 99 Squadron in the early morning mist. The type entered service in 2001, giving the RAF a strategic airlift capability for the first time since the mid-1970s when the Short Belfast was withdrawn. (Knight)

ISAF (Operation *Fingal*) amounting to three battalions, started to deploy by Hercules C4/5 to Bagram, Afghanistan on 30 December 2001. The operation by UK forces to destroy the Al-Qaeda infrastructure in southeastern Afghanistan (Operation *Jacana*) was reinforced three months later: on 27 March 2002, 45 Commando (Cdo) RM deployed to Kabul in the TriStars of 216 Squadron. Air mobility within Afghanistan was provided by three Chinooks from 27 Squadron. Based at Bagram and the Forward Operating Base (FOB) at Khowst, the helicopters flew over 1,000 sorties in support of 45 Cdo.

A TIALD/LGB-armed Tornado GR4 of 14 Squadron based at Ali Al Salem Air Base, Kuwait, flies a holding pattern near the Iraqi border awaiting authorization to carry out an airstrike against Iraqi air-defence systems. (David Hales)

IRAQ

Initial preparations for large-scale military intervention in Iraq started in late 2002. In four consecutive days of offensive missions starting on 18 November, the Tornado GR4 detachment at AAS, crewed by crews from 14 Squadron, attacked Iraqi air defence installations at Tallil, Al Kut, Shaibah and Al Uzayr. The weapons used included the new Enhanced Paveway (EPW) LGB which was equipped with a Global Positioning System (GPS), allowing it to be dropped accurately onto target co-ordinates if the weather prevented laser designation. Formations of six Tornados, which were supported by USAF McDonnell-Douglas KC-10 Extender tankers, comprised four bombers armed with LGBs and two aircraft equipped with the new Raptor reconnaissance pod to record battle-damage assessment. In three more days of offensive action between 14 and 16 December, the Tornados bombed radars, and communications sites at Abu Zawbah (between Basra and Al Kut), Al Kut and An Nasiriyah.

The force deployment for Operation *Telic*, the invasion of Iraq, was carried out in half the time it had taken for Operation *Granby*. The four new Boeing C-17A Globemaster III transport aircraft of 99 Squadron joined the Hercules C1/3 aircraft of 47 and 70 Squadrons, the Hercules C4/5 aircraft of 24 and 30 Squadrons, the VC10s of 10 and 101 Squadrons and the TriStars of 216 Squadrons all of which participated in the airlift of personnel and equipment into Kuwait and Saudi Arabia. Meanwhile, a tactical air force was being assembled in theatre. The 12 Tornado GR4 aircraft of 31 Squadron at AAS were boosted by the arrival of a further six aircraft, with additional crews from 2, 9, 13 and 617 Squadrons and another 12 Tornado GR4 aircraft (with crews from 2, 12, 14 and 617 Squadrons) deployed to Al Udeid airbase in Qatar. Twelve Harrier GR7 aircraft of 1 and 4 Squadrons arrived at Al Jaber airfield in Kuwait on 23 February 2003 to form 'Harrier Force South'; another nine aircraft from 1 and 3 Squadrons were based at Azraq,

Jordan, to form 'Harrier Force West.' Also in Jordan were two Canberra PR9 reconnaissance aircraft of 39 Squadron, four Hercules and eight Chinooks.

At PSAB, too, there was a major deployment: here the RAF force included 14 Tornado F3 fighters from 43 and 111 Squadrons, four Sentrys from 8 and 23 Squadrons, four Nimrod MR2 MPAs from 120, 201 and 206 Squadrons, a Nimrod R1 from 51 Squadron and seven VC10 tankers from 101 Squadron. Four TriStar tankers were based at Bahrain and two further Nimrod MR2 MPAs at Seeb, Oman.

The balance of support helicopters was based at AAS under the auspices of the Joint Helicopter Force (JHF). Six Chinooks from 18 Squadron and seven Pumas from 33 Squadron joined 12 Lynx AH7/9s and ten Gazelle AH1s of the AAC. Working closely with FAA helicopters from ships in the Gulf these helicopters provided airlift during the initial amphibious assault on the night of 20 March 2003 by 40 and 42 Cdo on the Al Faw peninsular. Harrier Force South provided CAS throughout the night armed with Hughes AGM-65 Maverick Air-to-Ground Missiles (AGMs) and the new Enhanced Paveway (EPW) II LGBs, which could also be dropped accurately onto Global Positioning System (GPS) co-ordinates if laser guidance was not possible. Meanwhile Tornado GR4 aircraft attacked artillery positions as well as other military installations, as far north as Al Kut, with LGBs.

On the following night, four Tornados operating from AAS launched the first MBDA Storm Shadow stand-off missiles against Iraqi air-defence bunkers at Taji and Tikrit; in all a total of 27 of these missiles would be fired during the campaign. Tornados operating from Al Udeid bombed targets including the Republican Guard barracks at Saribadi, some 30 miles to the southwest of Baghdad. All of these missions were met with spirited resistance from the Iraqi defences including SAM-2 and SAM-3. Unfortunately, a Tornado GR4 of 9 Squadron was shot down while returning from a mission by a US Raytheon MIM-104 Patriot missile, killing the crew.

In the west of the region, the Harriers flying from Azraq were part of a force committed to hunting for SCUD missile launchers in the western desert. They were joined by Tornado GR4s equipped with the Raptor pod and Tornado GR4As with their specialist low-level reconnaissance capability. Additionally, the Canberras at Azraq flew three three-hour sorties each day in search of missile launchers. Unusually for maritime patrol aircraft, the Nimrods at PSAB were also involved in these operations, where their radio and surveillance equipment proved to be very useful. Sentrys, Hercules and Chinooks also made up a force of some 30 RAF aircraft which were permanently allocated to anti-SCUD operations.

During the 2003 Iraq war the BAe Nimrod MR2 was increasingly diverted from the maritime patrol role and used overland in support of ground troops. The sensor and communications suites fitted in the aircraft proved very useful to ground forces searching for Iraqi troops in the open desert. (BAe Heritage)

After the first few days of the war, the tasking for both Harrier and Tornado GR4 was for Kill-box Interdiction CAS (KICAS), a US Marine corps concept whereby Iraq was divided into discrete 'kill-boxes,' each measuring 30 miles by 30 miles. If aircraft were tasked into an 'open' kill-box they could attack any targets, such as military vehicles, which they found in the area; if it was a 'closed' kill-box, the crew would be controlled by a Forward Air Controller (FAC) onto specific targets. In the case of Harrier Force South, tasking one night included locating a vehicle-mounted SSM near Tallil, which was engaged by two aircraft using Maverick and Paveway II. With AAR available, KICAS sorties might last up to six hours. Although VC10 and TriStar tankers were on hand to refuel the RAF aircraft, nearly half of the tasking for the RAF tankers was in support of the US Navy and US Marine Corps aircraft.

By the end of the second week of operations, US forces were on the outskirts of Baghdad, and Tornado offensive missions as well as Raptor reconnaissance sorties reached into the northern areas beyond the city. On 11 April, a pair of Tornado GR4 bombers destroyed a SAM-2 system near Tikrit. Defensive

CAPs mounted by the Tornado F3 fighters also moved north, reaching the Baghdad area. The ground war was largely over by early April and British forces settled into the role of an occupying force with responsibility for the Basra region.

NATO IN AFGHANISTAN

At the end of 2003, NATO took responsibility for the ISAF in Afghanistan and the British military presence in the country was increased accordingly. Six Harriers from 3 Squadron deployed to Kandahar on 24 September 2004, for what was intended to be a nine-month detachment, to provide CAS to ISAF troops. Each of the constituent units of the Joint Force Harriers (JFH), comprising 1, 3, 4 and 800 (FAA) Squadrons, took turns for a two-to-four-month tour of duty in Afghanistan; 1 Squadron followed 3 Squadron and 4 Squadron then took over in April 2005 by which time the Harrier detachment had become a permanent part of Operation *Herrick* and the strength had been increased to eight aircraft. Harriers flew in pairs, usually by day, armed with CRV-7 rockets and EPW II LGBs and equipped with TIALD pods. The Harriers were Coalition, rather than exclusively UK, air assets and the area of operations stretched as far as the borders with Pakistan, Iran, Turkmenistan and Uzbekistan. Pre-planned sorties might involve over-watch of convoys or army units, as well as reconnaissance sorties using the DJRP; however, pilots had to be ready to be diverted from any task to respond to a Troops In Contact (TIC) incident where close air support was needed. In most cases a high speed low-level flypast, a Show of Force (SoF), was sufficient to persuade the enemy forces to disengage, but there were also occasions when weapons would have to be expended. Two aircraft also maintained Ground CAS (GCAS) readiness to respond any TIC if no Coalition aircraft already in the air were available. In a GCAS scramble the aircraft would expect to be airborne within a few minutes and the pilots would contact the Joint Tactical Air Controller (JTAC) for target information.

The deployment of the new Augusta Westland Merlin HC3 helicopters to Iraq in March 2005 to form 1419 Flight freed the Chinooks to be re-allocated to Afghanistan. By mid-2006 there were eight Chinooks of 1310 Flight operating in Afghanistan. The prime tasks of the support helicopters included airlifting personnel and supplies to Forward Operating Bases (FOBs) and Patrol Bases as well as inserting or extracting Coalition ground troops during 'deliberate operations.' On operational sorties into high threat areas, the Chinooks might also be escorted by AAC Augusta-Westland Apache AH1s. Additionally, two Chinooks remained on immediate standby at Camp Bastion as part of the Immediate Readiness Team (IRT) to carry the Medical Emergency Response Team (MERT) to casualties whenever they were needed and to evacuate the casualties either back to Camp Bastion or to Kandahar. From 2004, three Hercules were also based in Afghanistan to provide in-theatre air transport but this was increased to four aircraft during 70 Squadron's tenure as lead squadron in 2006. Medical teams were also on hand with the

A BAe Harrier GR7A over the mountains of Afghanistan. After seeing action during the Iraq war in the previous year, the GR7s of 1, 3 and 4 Squadrons (RAF) and 800 Naval Air Squadron (NAS) were deployed to Kandahar in 2004 to provide close air support to the ground forces of the NATO-led International Security Assistance Force (ISAF). (Crown Copyright)

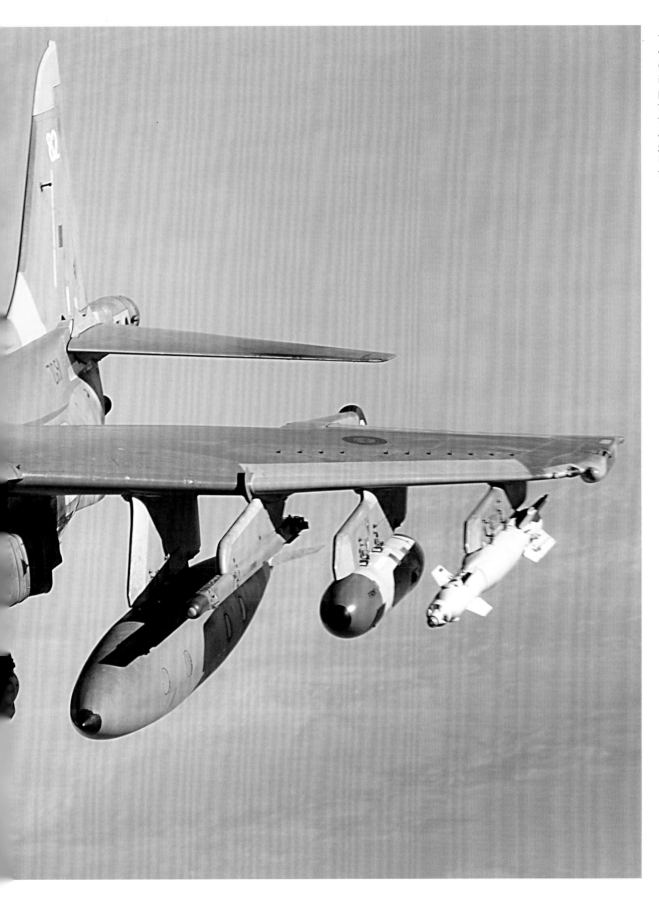

The BAe Harrier GR9, which superseded the GR7A in 2007, had many improvements over its predecessor including the capability to use the Hughes/Raytheon AGM-65 Maverick air-to-ground missile and the Lockheed Martin Sniper targetting pod. (USMC)

Hercules to transport casualties within theatre. Further medical specialists in the Critical Care Air Support Team (CCAST) accompanied casualties back to the UK on either a TriStar of 216 Squadron or a Globemaster of 99 Squadron, so that critically injured personnel could be repatriated for specialist care within 24 hours of being wounded.

AAR support for operations over Afghanistan was provided by TriStar tankers based in Oman. Also in Oman were Nimrods of 120 and 201 Squadrons; as previously in Iraq, these aircraft were used for overland surveillance and to support the army directly by providing radio relay for troops but the newly-fitted Wescam MX-15 Electro-optic/Infra-red sensor also gave them the capability to provide over-watch to army patrols in the field. Unfortunately, Nimrod operations over Afghanistan were cut short when an aircraft exploded in mid-air after it suffered a fuel leak while supporting operations in Helmand in September 2006.

The tasking for Chinooks and Harriers increased dramatically in spring 2006 when the UK took over responsibility for the security of Helmand Province, and the British task changed, as an Army report later put it, from a military operation into a war. Reflecting the increased need for CAS at night, the Harrier detachment started to operate two pairs by day and a pair at night. The Harrier tasking rose from approximately 3,000 hours per year involving less than 50 weapon releases in 2005 to around 4,500 hours per year and over 320 weapon releases, including about 80 LGBs. In the same year, 34 Squadron RAF Regiment was the first RAF Regt unit to deploy to Afghanistan to take up base protection duties at Kandahar.

BALTIC AIR DEFENCE

In March 2004, NATO established a Quick Reaction Alert force of four NATO fighters at Šiauliai in Lithuania, to provide air defence cover for the Baltic States against incursions by Russian aircraft. Each member of the Alliance took its turn to provide aircraft for a four-month period. Four Tornado F3 aircraft, from 11 and 25 Squadrons, carried out the task from 14 October 2004 until January 2005.

LEBANON

An outbreak of violence between Israel and Hezbollah forces in Lebanon during July 2006 led to the evacuation of British subjects from Beirut. This was carried out by ships of the RN, but two Chinooks of 27 Squadron were deployed to Beirut to ferry evacuees to HMS *Illustrious* from 21 July.

IRAQ - POSTWAR

After the war in Iraq a significant British Army presence remained in the south of the country. Initially, the Army's tactical airlift requirements were met by five Chinooks of 1310 Flight and six Pumas of 1563 Flight based at Basra International Airport, but the Chinooks were replaced by Merlins in 2005. Basra was also used as a hub for the Hercules of 24, 30 and 70 Squadrons for air transport movements in and out of the Middle East and within theatre. Although there were nominally only three aircraft based in Basra, the number of aircraft passing through fluctuated and sometimes there were more Hercules at Basra than at Lyneham. Based at Baghdad in support of Special Forces operations were four Chinooks from 7 Squadron (later replaced by Pumas) and a Hercules C1 from 47 Squadron.

A detachment of between six and eight Tornado GR4 aircraft provided CAS for ground troops. The Tornados were initially based at AAS, but moved to Al Udeid in September 2003. Like previous such detachments, it was manned by elements of each of the Tornado GR4 squadrons in turn. Dedicated AAR for the Tornados was from two VC10s based at Bahrain. With long transits

Opposite: A General Atomics MQ-9A Reaper Remotely Piloted Air System (RPAS) of 39 Squadron on the final approach to Kandahar. It is armed with two GBU-12 500lb LGBs and four Lockheed Martin AGM-114 Hellfire missiles. During a mission the aircraft would be 'flown' remotely by a crew at Creech Air Force Base, Nevada, but the take-off and landing would be performed by a crew at Kandahar. (Stradling)

between Qatar and the operating area over Iraq, Tornado sorties often lasted for seven or eight hours. The aircraft were equipped with TIALD pods and armed with EPW II LGBs and most tasking involved over-watch of convoys or troop patrols. Sometimes the aircraft would be called in for a SoF, which was often enough to persuade dissidents to refrain from attacking British or Iraqi army troops, but occasionally a bomb drop would be needed. Military activity in Iraq peaked during the insurgency of 2004–2007, but the flying task remained relatively mundane in that time. In 2007, the Northrop/Rafael Litening III targeting pod replaced the TIALD pod on Tornado GR4: the newer pod provided much better resolution that its predecessor – a capability which was badly needed in the urban environment where much of the insurgent activity was occurring. However, by 2008 it was clear that the Iraqi government had gained the upper hand and that the British forces would not be needed for much longer.

AFGHANISTAN CONTINUES

The more capable Harrier GR9 was introduced into the Afghan theatre in June 2007. The aircraft was fitted with the AN/AAQ-33 Sniper Advanced Targeting Pod which also offered a much-improved capability over the TIALD pod. Furthermore, the new 500lb PW IV LGBs, which had a much-reduced capacity for 'collateral damage,' added to the flexibility of the new aircraft variant. Another new aircraft type introduced to the Afghanistan theatre in 2007 was the General Atomics Aeronautical Systems MQ-9A Reaper Remotely Piloted Air System (RPAS) or 'drone'. The first of five Reapers of 39 Squadron started flying from Kandahar in October 2007. Although a two-man crew would take off and land the aircraft using a control console in Kandahar, the operational crews, each comprising a pilot, a sensor operator and a mission intelligence coordinator (MIC), were based at Creech AFB

(formerly Indian Springs) to the northwest of Las Vegas. Capable of 18-hour missions, the Reapers were ideal platforms for extended surveillance or for over-watch of convoys or patrols: the infra-red sensors could show where earth had been disturbed by the laying of Improvised Explosive Devices (IEDs) ahead of convoys. Reapers were also armed with GBU-12 LGBs and AGM-114 Hellfire missiles so they could engage targets if necessary and indeed over the course of the Afghanistan campaign, the Reapers would release more weapons in a seven-year period than the total weapons delivered by the combined Tornado and Harrier detachments over ten years.

Although the operational tempo in Afghanistan peaked in 2006, it nevertheless remained at a high pitch throughout the next two years. The Chinooks of 1310 Flight were heavily committed to army operations in Helmand, carrying out a number of air assaults on Taliban strongholds. In August and September 2008 over 2,000 troops were involved in Operation *Eagle's Summit* to ensure the safe delivery of a 200-ton turbine from Kandahar airfield to the hydro-electric power station at the Kajaki dam in northern Helmand Province. The Chinooks played a critical role in moving troops between positions to clear and secure the route to ensure the safe passage of the turbine.

BREATHING SPACE?

With operations over Iraq apparently coming to an end and relative peace in the Balkans, it seemed in late 2009 that the RAF could concentrate solely on Afghanistan. The period of continuous, and sometimes simultaneous, operations since 1991 had also coincided with almost continuous reductions in the size of the RAF: the new decade brought with it an opportunity for the service to consolidate its strength and to start being proactive rather than reactive in preparing for the new challenges of the 21st century.

CHAPTER 10

A CENTURY OF OPERATIONS

2009-2018

After a period of nearly 20 years in which Iraq had dominated the operational life of the RAF, the UK operations in the country wound down in early 2009. The last Tornado GR4 mission over Iraq was flown by a 13 Squadron crew in May 2009. A small contingent of Puma HC1 helicopters of 1563 Flight was retained in Baghdad to support Foreign and Commonwealth Office personnel and in addition, small detachments of Merlin helicopters remained in Kuwait and Hercules at Basra to provide transport in and out of Iraq. However, all of these elements had left the country by July 2009. By then the operational focus had switched decisively to Afghanistan. In 2009, the larger part of the RAF's support helicopter force, ISTAR assets and the Joint Force Harrier were all committed to Operation *Herrick* in Afghanistan.

Meanwhile, the Falkland Islands, which had themselves been the operational focus nearly three decades previously, received a major upgrade in defensive capability. Four Typhoon FGR4 aircraft from 11 Squadron flew from RAF Coningsby to Mount Pleasant airfield via Ascension Island, arriving on 18 September 2009, to re-equip 1435 Flight. Also based in the Falklands were 1312 Flight, operating a Hercules and a VC10 K4 tanker and 1564 Flight, equipped with Chinook HC2s for air mobility and a Sea King HAR3 for search and rescue.

The Lockheed Martin F-35B Lightning II fifth generation multi-role fighter will provide the RAF with a deep interdiction capability when the Tornado GR4 is withdrawn from service. (Crown Copyright)

An infra-red decoy flare is ejected from the BOZ-107 pod on a Tornado GR4 over Afghanistan. The aircraft is also armed with 500lb Paveway IV Laser-Guided Bombs (LGB) and MBDA Brimstone Dual-Mode Seeker (DMS) missiles. (Stradling)

AFGHANISTAN

The early summer of 2009 in Afghanistan saw the launch of Operation *Panchai Palang*, a Coalition land offensive to drive out the Taliban from areas of Helmand Province. In the hours before dawn of 19 June, ten Chinooks of 1310 Flight inserted 350 troops of 3rd Battalion Royal Scots into positions behind the Taliban defensive lines at Babaji, to the northwest of Lashkar Gar. The assault was supported by over-watch by Reapers from 39 Squadron and Harriers flown by pilots from 4 Squadron.

The release of Tornado GR4s and Merlins from Iraq meant that these aircraft could then be deployed to Afghanistan. Eight Tornados from 12 Squadron had arrived at Kandahar on 16 June 2009 and they formally took over from the Harrier detachment on 24 June. Like the Harrier detachment, the Tornado detachment was manned in turn by personnel from the UK squadrons on temporary four-month tours: 31 Squadron took over the detachment in October 2009, handing over sequentially to 9 then 2, 13 and 14 Squadrons during the course of the next year. Missions over Afghanistan were flown in pairs, by aircraft equipped with the Litening III targeting pod and armed with the new 500lb Paveway IV laser-guided bomb (PW IV LGB) and the MBDA-built Brimstone dual-mode seeker (DMS) missile. With their smaller

warheads and their consequent lower footprint of collateral damage, both of these weapons were better suited to counter-insurgency operations than the previous generation of weapons used over Iraq. Many Tornado sorties were flown in direct support of ground forces, frequently providing armed over-watch for convoys in transit or troops on foot patrol; reconnaissance sorties were also flown routinely, using the Raptor reconnaissance pod. Most sorties were supported by AAR, giving typical sortie lengths of between three and five hours. Two VC10 tankers from 101 Squadron relieved the TriStar tankers of 216 Squadron at Seeb, Muscat, in 2009 to support operations over Afghanistan. However, Tornado crews could

also expect to use USAF KC-10 and KC-135 Stratotanker tankers. Indeed, the VC10s often refuelled USN and French Air Force aircraft.

The tasking for the Tornado Force remained at similar levels to the Harrier Force, around 6,000 hours a year. Like the Harriers, Tornados were kept at 30min readiness for GCAS, although if scrambled they would expect to be airborne in half that time. Tornados were also often re-tasked from other sorties to respond to calls for support from Troops in Contact (TIC) incidents or to cover ISAF convoys which had been involved in roadside IED incidents. If Coalition ground forces were engaged by Taliban groups, often a Show of Presence flypast would deter the enemy, but if necessary this tactic

A Harrier GR9 over the mountainous terrain of Afghanistan. The Harrier force handed responsibility for the operational commitment over Afghanistan to the Tornado force in 2009. (Crown Copyright)

could be escalated into the more intimidating Show of Force (SoF). Capable of supersonic speeds and generating a vast amount of noise in reheat, a Tornado SoF could be particularly effective, especially at night using the aircraft's unique TFR capability to get to low level when other types could not do so. As a last resort, weapons could also be used and each detachment might expect to see one or two 'kinetic' events each month. Although the number of precision-guided weapons expended by the RAF over Afghanistan remained almost constant at about ten per month from 2007 to 2013, the Tornados dropped considerably less munitions than the Harriers. The difference was made up by the Reapers of 39 Squadron, which accounted for over three-quarters of the weapons expended.

The number of hours flown by Reapers over Afghanistan doubled over the period 2009 to 2010 to over 10,000hr per year, as more aircraft were deployed into the theatre. By September 2010 there were enough aircraft at Kandahar to fly multiple sorties simultaneously over Afghanistan. Along with Raptor reconnaissance data, the Reapers were a vitally important part of the RAF's Intelligence, Surveillance, Target Acquisition and

Reconnaissance (ISTAR) capability in the region. Crucial ISTAR assets were the Nimrod R1 of 51 Squadron and the Raytheon Sentinel R1 of 5 Squadron operating from Seeb. The Sentinel used its Synthetic Aperture Radar and Moving Target Indicator systems to monitor ground movement in large areas of Afghanistan. One of the main objects of the surveillance operations was to establish a picture of normal activity in the country, so that abnormal activity could then be detected. Another ISTAR platform that made its debut in Afghanistan in 2009 was the Raytheon Shadow R1, which was operated by a flight from 5 Squadron based at Kandahar. Shadow carried much of the surveillance equipment which had previously been used by the Nimrod MR2 over Afghanistan.

The first Merlin helicopters were transported to Afghanistan by Globemaster transports of 99 Squadron in mid-November 2009. At Camp Bastion, six Merlins of 1419 Flight crewed by personnel from 28 and 78 Squadrons on temporary four-month tours of duty joined the Joint Helicopter Force Afghanistan which also included eight Chinooks of 1310 Flight (crewed by 7, 18 and 27 Squadrons), as well as RN Westland Sea King HC4s,

Opposite: A Tornado GR4 is accompanied by a Northrop Grumman EA-6B Prowler electronic warfare aircraft over Afghanistan on that country's election day, 20 August 2009.

Below: A Raytheon (Beechcraft) Shadow R1 of 14 Squadron at Kandahar. Equipped with a Hughes Wescam MX-15 electro-optical/ infra-red sensor and an electronic surveillance suite, the Shadow provided ISTAR for army units.

The workhorse of the RAF tactical transport fleet, a Lockheed C-130J Hercules C4 takes off from Camp Bastion in Afghanistan. Amongst the improvements made to this model over the C-130K were more powerful Rolls-Royce (Allison) AE 2100-D3 turbo-prop engines and a two-pilot 'all glass' flight deck. (Crown Copyright)

AAC Apaches and Westland Lynx AH7s (and later AH9As). The prime tasks of the support helicopters remained those of re-supplying the forward deployed troops at FOBs and Patrol Bases and of providing air mobility for Coalition ground troops during 'deliberate operations.' At Camp Bastion, two Chinooks continued to be held at immediate readiness to respond to casualty incidents as part of the Incident Response Team (IRT). On operational troop movements or IRT scrambles, the Chinooks and Merlins might also be escorted by Apaches. By late 2010, the Chinooks in theatre had all been modified to the Chinook HC3 standard. Chinooks were armed with two M134 Miniguns, one in each front side window, and an M60D machine gun on the ramp.

Further support to the air efforts over Afghanistan were the Sentrys of 8 Squadron, based at Seeb, and the Hercules C4/5 detachments (manned by personnel from 24 and 30 Squadrons) at Kandahar and Camp Bastion. The Hercules were used to transport freight and personnel within theatre. Although the Globemasters, which accounted for around 40 return flights between the UK and Afghanistan each month, were authorized to land at Camp Bastion, there were still around 24 TriStar flights per month which landed at Kandahar.

Much of the freight and many of the passengers from these flights would then have to be transported the 100 miles to Camp Bastion. In order to relieve the task of the Chinooks, the Hercules C4/5s were also used for low-level supply drops, carried out at night, to resupply FOBs and Patrol Bases which were inaccessible by heavy vehicles because of Taliban activity.

With 24-hour operations by five different helicopter types as well as Hercules and Globemaster movements and refuelling stops by Shadows, the airfield at Camp Bastion was extremely busy. The airfield had originally been intended to accommodate around 12 aircraft movements a week, but by mid-2010 the actual figure was already running at over 3,000 movements a week. At 3,000ft above sea level, with ambient temperatures around 40°C, it was also close to the operating limits of many aircraft types. Conditions were also very difficult at helicopter landing sites in Helmand, which might vary from purpose-built sites with tarmac or matting surfaces to open areas of desert which created dust clouds obscuring all visual references, to confined spaces surrounded by tall trees. Added to this, the helicopters might be landing in the midst of a firefight. In the summer of 2010, Chinook pilot Flt Lt I.A. Fortune of 27 Squadron won the DFC after he continued to fly his damaged aircraft after being wounded in the head during a MERT extraction.

In August two more Tornados were added to the detachment in Kandahar, bringing the total to ten aircraft, in readiness for increased tasking during the Afghan national elections. When 2 Squadron returned to RAF Marham at the end of July, they had flown approximately 500 operational sorties, of which around 100 were GCAS scrambles.

A Battle Group operation by Coalition forces started on 13 February 2010. The aim of Operation *Moshtarak* was to wrest control of the town of Marja, southwest of Lashkar Gar in Helmand Province, from the Taliban. The initial troop insertion was carried out by four Chinooks from 1310 Flight, which delivered over 600 soldiers into Taliban-held territory in just over two hours.

Over the next few days, Tornados carried out over-watch of the operation, using their Litening pods to assist troops on the ground to locate groups of insurgents. Using the Litening pod, Tornados were also able to track and follow suspicious persons or vehicles, often for prolonged periods of time, and to guide friendly forces to intercept them, or to engage them using PW IV LGB or Brimstone missiles. The operation continued for the next few months. Another large-scale ground operation, this time led by the Afghan National Army (ANA) to reassert government control over western Kandahar Province commenced in April 2010. Much of the work of the Tornado detachment in the summer of 2010 was in support of this Operation *Hamkari* and the number of 'kinetic' events increased towards the end of the year.

Six Agusta-Westland Merlin HC3 helicopters were deployed to Afghanistan to complement the Chinook force in 2009. The type could carry up to 24 fully-equipped troops. (Crown Copyright)

Troops of 40 Commando RM prepare to board a Chinook HC3 during operations in Afghanistan in 2012. The type was the workhorse of the RAF tactical helicopter force in Afghanistan and ground operations were heavily dependent on the type for air mobility. (Crown Copyright)

Typical of smaller-scale ground operations carried out over the autumn and winter months was Operation *Zamary Kargha*, which commenced at dawn on 15 November when two Chinooks inserted troops from 5th Battalion Royal Scots and Afghan National Police (ANP) close to the village of Hoorzai in Helmand Province. With the elements of surprise and mobility, the combined army and ANP force were quickly able to drive the Taliban out of the area. At the end of November 2010, 1419 Flight celebrated its first anniversary of their deployment in Afghanistan, in which time the Merlins had carried nearly 40,000 troops and over

750 tons of freight including artillery pieces, land rovers and light strike vehicles.

The airfields at both Kandahar and Camp Bastion were protected by elements of the RAF Regiment as well as other Coalition force protection units. Early 2011 saw 34 Squadron RAF Regt responsible for the security of Camp Bastion and 15 Squadron RAF Regt for Kandahar. Later in the year, 58 and 51 Squadrons RAF Regt would also serve in Afghanistan.

The district of Nahri Saraj, to the west of the Musa Qala river and almost halfway between Kandahar and Camp Bastion, had the reputation as the most violent corner of Afghanistan. On 26 May 2011, a force of 22 aircraft, including RAF Chinooks and Merlins as well as US Marine Corps aircraft, delivered a large force of ANA and Coalition troops into the village of Loy Mandeh at the opening of Operation *Omid Haft*, to take back the region from the Taliban. The operation was supported by over-watch from Reapers of 39 Squadron as well as the Tornados from 617 Squadron, which had carried out much of the preparatory reconnaissance work using the Raptor pods. Ground operations in the region continued into the summer, and in late July two Chinooks inserted 3 Commando Brigade Reconnaissance Force (BRF) into Nahri Saraj to destroy a Taliban bomb-making factory. The helicopters landed under small arms fire to deliver the troops, who were able to destroy the factory successfully.

LIBYA

The start of a revolution in Libya triggered an operation to evacuate British and other foreign citizens from the country in February 2011. Three Hercules C4/5 transports from 47 Squadron deployed to Valetta, Malta on 22 February, from where they were tasked with the rescue of personnel from remote desert airstrips amongst the oilfields in central Libya. Over the next few days two Sentrys from 8 Squadron and a Nimrod R1 from 51 Squadron arrived at Akrotiri to support the operation. These were followed by Sentinels of 5 Squadron. The Hercules collected some 429 people during sorties on 26 and 27 February and evacuated them to Malta. The airlift was not without incident: one aircraft was damaged by small arms fire shortly after take-off from a desert strip.

In early March operations over Libya were expanded after a UN Resolution authorized the enforcement of a No-Fly Zone over Libya, ostensibly to protect civilians from attack by the Gaddafi regime. Control over this operation was granted to NATO and UK involvement, which included both naval and air forces, was nicknamed Operation *Ellamy*. The RAF contribution to the air contingent which established the NFZ on 19 March 2011 was ten Typhoon FGR4 aircraft from RAF Coningsby. The aircraft and personnel, drawn mainly from 11 Squadron but augmented by both 3 and 29 Squadrons, deployed

A Eurofighter Typhoon FGR4 armed with LGBs at dusk during an operational sortie over Libya in 2011. Operation *Ellamy* was the first occasion that Typhoons were used in the air-to-ground role dropping LGBs. (Beevers)

at short notice to Gioia del Colle on 20 March; a pair of Typhoons were flying operational Combat Air Patrols (CAPs) within the NFZ the next day. Four Tornado GR4 aircraft from 9 Squadron also deployed to Gioia to carry out reconnaissance and attack missions. Offensive operations over Libya had started on 19 March when Coalition forces, including four Tornados from 9 Squadron armed with Storm Shadow long-range missiles, attacked the Libyan air defence installations. The Tornados operated from their home base at RAF Marham and completed a 3,000-mile round trip, supported by VC10 and TriStar AAR tankers of 101 and 216 Squadrons, during the mission. A second Storm Shadow mission by four Tornados from 13 Squadron was aborted shortly before weapon release for fear of hitting civilians in the target area.

Four more Tornados launched from Marham on 22 March and after flying an armed reconnaissance mission over Libya, they recovered to Gioia del Colle to join the Tornado detachment there. Meanwhile, an extensive airlift by RAF Hercules and Globemasters was under way between the UK and various Mediterranean bases to position personnel and stores for both air and naval operations.

While the Typhoons flew CAPs to enforce the NFZ, the Tornados flew armed reconnaissance sorties; both aircraft types worked closely with the ISTAR aircraft in theatre. As the operation progressed the Sentrys and VC10 tankers moved from RAF Akrotiri to Trapani in Sicily to reduce their transit flying time and maximize their time on station; the Sentinels moved to join the fast jet aircraft at Gioia del Colle. During operational missions, overall command and control was provided by the Sentry, which directly controlled the air defence aircraft. For offensive missions, the Sentinel played a central role in directing the attack aircraft. The Sentinel would check in with the Sentry for details of the day's areas of interest and would then examine those areas with its Synthetic Aperture Radar and identify any potential targets, such as armoured vehicles or SAM systems. The positions of these were passed back to the Sentry, which in turn transmitted target details

to the Tornados as they transited to the operational area. The Tornados could then use their own Litening pod sensors to locate and identify targets and then engage them using PW IV LGB or Brimstone Dual Mode Seeker (DMS) missiles. Using this mode of operation, Tornados used Brimstone missiles to destroy three armoured vehicles near Misrata and two more further to the east in Ajdabiya on 25 March. Tornados accounted for a further 22 tanks, armoured vehicles and artillery pieces in the same locations over the next two days. Another long-range mission was launched from Marham on the morning of 28 March, to destroy ammunition bunkers in the Sabha area in the southern Libyan Desert. The aircraft, armed with Storm Shadow missiles, were refuelled by TriStar tankers during the mission.

Over the next few days the Tornados targeted armoured vehicles, including main battle tanks, as well as SAM systems. In this phase of the operation, the Sentinel's Moving Target Indicator system proved to be a particularly valuable asset: it enabled the Sentinel to identify vehicle movement and to data-link the information to Typhoons on CAP, who in turn could pass the information to Tornados in the operating area. The focus of operations shifted to Sirte on 2 April and tanks and a number of armoured vehicles in the vicinity were destroyed by Tornados over the next few days, using PW IV LGBs and Brimstone DMS. The number of Tornados at Gioia del Colle was increased to 12 on 6 April, but the most notable increase in ground-attack capability was the switch to offensive operations by the Typhoons. The first operational mission by a mixed formation of Tornados and Typhoons was flown on 7 April.

Armed reconnaissance missions continued over both Misrata and Ajdabiya during the first half of April; on 8 April five tanks were destroyed. During the week, a further four Tornados were deployed to Gioia del Colle bringing the RAF contingent there to a combined strength of 22 Tornados and Typhoons. Mixed-type patrols continued and on 18 April a Tornado and a Typhoon attacked a rocket launcher and an artillery piece near Misrata. At the beginning of May personnel from 2 Squadron took

over the Tornado GR4 detachment from 9 Squadron. A similar changeover of the Typhoon detachment from 11 Squadron to 3 Squadron took place a month later. On 6 May two Tornados attacked a concentration of FROG-7 and SCUD ballistic missile systems near Sirte, destroying about 20 FROG launchers and damaging a number of SCUD launchers. On the same day, Tornados also accounted for one tank, two armoured vehicles and a rocket launcher. The first Typhoon self-designated laser attack took place on 12 May when a Typhoon dropped an Enhanced Paveway (EPW) II LGB on self-propelled guns near Sirte. Further attacks took place over the following days, including bombing a command bunker near Tarhuna by Tornados and Typhoons on 17 May.

The Libyan naval base at Al Khums, near Misrata was attacked two days later. Tornados hit two corvettes in the harbour and also bombed a facility in the dockyards used for constructing inflatable fast attack craft. In a further series of airstrikes on 24 and 25 May Tornados and Typhoons attacked a coastal radar station at Brega, near Ajdibiya, and four heavy armoured vehicles near Zlitan, near Misrata.

A Tornado and a Typhoon between them dropped five Paveway IVs and four EPW IIs respectively on point targets within a vehicle depot a Tiji, to the southwest of Tripoli.

At the beginning of June, the Nimrod R1 Elint aircraft of 51 Squadron were withdrawn from service. These aircraft, which had flown almost 350 hours in support of operations over Libya, were replaced in the RAF inventory three years later by the Boeing RC-135W Airseeker (also known by the US designation 'Rivet Joint'). Although the pace of operations slowed somewhat from early June, they did not cease completely. On 10 August six Tornados carried out another long-range Storm Shadow strike from Marham, to attack Libyan command and control bunkers. Eight days later, Tornados operating from Gioia del Colle sunk a patrol craft transporting troops from the Az Zuwar oil refinery to the west of Tripoli. The following day the responsibility for manning the Tornado detachment at Gioia del Colle passed once more to 9 Squadron.

On the morning of 25 August, Tornados located and destroyed a long-range SAM system near Al Watiya

The RAF replaced the ageing BAe Nimrod R1 Elint aircraft with the Boeing RC-135W Airseeker (also known as 'Rivet Joint') in 2011. Despite its antiquated airframe, the RC-125W is equipped with state-of-the-art electronic intelligence gathering equipment. (Crown Copyright)

on the Tunisian border and that afternoon a joint force of Tornados and Typhoons attacked a command and control facility near Tripoli airport. That night a formation of Tornados flew from Marham to fire Storm Shadow missiles at a large headquarters bunker in Sirte; once again they were supported by AAR on this long-range mission. Another Storm Shadow mission was flown from Marham on 14 September by Tornados supported by TriStar tankers. This time the targets were vehicle depots and buildings near Sabha in the southern desert, which were being used by pro-Gaddafi mercenaries. The Storm Shadow strike was co-ordinated with another attack by Gioia-based Tornados which fired some two dozen Brimstone DMS missiles at a formation of tanks and armoured vehicles near Sabha. Just over a week later, on the morning of 23 September, Tornados dropped 16 Paveway IV LGBs on point targets within a barracks and ammunition storage facility. The following day a formation of Tornados destroyed a radar installation and control bunkers in Sirte with LGBs.

As Operation *Ellamy* wound down, the Typhoons returned to RAF Coningsby on 26 September,

A Boeing C-17 Globemaster of 99 Squadron at Évreux airbase, France during UK support for French operations in Mali. (Knight)

leaving a force of 16 Tornados at Gioia del Colle. The NATO operation itself ended on 31 October 2011, by which time RAF aircraft had flown over 3,000 sorties over Libya, of which two-thirds were strike sorties. The Tornados returned to Marham on 1 November.

RE-EQUIPMENT AND DEPLOYMENTS

The fallout from the Strategic Defence and Security Review (SDSR) carried out by the government in 2010 included the withdrawal of the Harrier Force later in that year and the disbandment of two Tornado GR4 units, 13 and 14 Squadrons. With the disbandment in March 2011 of 111 Squadron, the last Tornado F3 unit, responsibility for the UK air defence rested solely with the Typhoon FGR4 units 3, 6 and 11 Squadrons. As part of the security arrangements for the Olympic Games in London in 2012, four Typhoons from 11 Squadron were redeployed to RAF Northolt on 9 July to mount QRA for the duration of the Games.

Additionally, a Sentry from 8 Squadron provided command and control for air defence contingency operations during the Games. The Typhoons returned to Coningsby in mid-August.

In January 2013, French forces started a campaign against Islamist insurgents in northern Mali, many of whom had moved into the country after the civil war in Libya. A number of NATO countries offered assistance to the French, including the UK. Two Globemasters from 99 Squadron deployed to Évreux, from where they provided a heavy airlift capability, carrying large armoured vehicles to the Mali capital, Bamoko. The Globemasters continued to fly into Bamoko until 21 April, when they returned to Brize Norton. Meanwhile a Sentinel from 5 Squadron and had deployed to Dakar in Senegal on 25 January. Over the next six months, the Sentinel flew 66 sorties in support of French operations.

Islamist terrorists were also active in Syria, which, like many of the Mediterranean dictatorships at that time, was engulfed in a civil war. Because of the proximity of Syria to Cyprus, Operation *Luminous*, comprising measures to defend the Sovereign Base Areas, was initiated in August 2013. Six Typhoons from 11 Squadron and a Sentry from 8 Squadron deployed to Akrotiri on 29 August. After a ten-week detachment during which the Typhoons flew over 220 sorties, including working with HMS *Dragon*, a Type 45 destroyer, the aircraft returned to the UK in mid-November. In August, 1312 Flight in the Falklands had been re-equipped with a TriStar tanker, which in turn was replaced by an Airbus Voyager K3 in February 2014.

AFGHANISTAN WIND DOWN

Air activity over Afghanistan over the period 2012 to 2014 had fallen into something of a routine. During the period, UK operations started to wind down slowly as more of the security functions were passed to the ANSF. The tasking for the various RAF

A Typhoon of 6 Squadron intercepts a Tupolev Tu-95MS Bear-H bomber aircraft of the Russian Federation Air Force in September 2014. After a long absence following the end of the Cold War, Russian long-range aircraft began to probe the UKADR again. (Crown Copyright)

contingents was in support of the various ground operations, many of which were led by the Afghan National Security Forces (ANSF). For the Tornado Force, this meant generally Raptor reconnaissance missions with occasional SoFs or providing over-watch to search for IEDs ahead of convoys. Although Tornado GCAS sorties were launched, many of them achieved their aims by an SoF rather than having to deliver weapons. For the Support Helicopter Force, this meant 'deliberate operations,' of which there might be about 20 per month as well as IRT sorties, often under fire, and supply and movement sorties. The ISTAR aircraft continued their surveillance to identify any unusual activities and to monitor developments among the insurgents. The RAF Regiment was also closely involved in operations and

in February 2012, 2 Squadron RAF Regt successfully carried out a joint assault with the US Marines against a Taliban bomb-making factory and heroin facility. The Reapers of 39 Squadron continued their surveillance missions and carried out an increasing proportion of the air task. In 2014 Reapers were flying 15,000hr a year as opposed to just 5,000 hours by Tornados. Although Reapers carried out a number of strikes with Hellfire missiles, the rate of weapon expenditure had dropped considerably by 2014. There was a small victory in the campaign against the Taliban's drugs trade on 12 August 2012 when a Reaper tracked a suspicious vehicle until it could be intercepted by USMC and ANSF. A large quantity of heroin and opium was discovered hidden in the vehicle. Two more heroin-transporting vehicles were also intercepted in the same mission.

A General Atomics MQ-9A Reaper Remotely Piloted Air System (RPAS) of 39 Squadron. These 'drones' played an increasingly important role during operations over Afghanistan, and in the last years of the campaign, the majority of 'kinetic events' were carried out by unmanned, rather than manned aircraft. (Crown Copyright)

As a result of the decrease in the number of UK ground forces in Afghanistan, the tasking for the Joint Helicopter Force had reduced by about a third in the three years since 2013. The Merlins of 1419 Flight were withdrawn from Afghanistan in June 2013 and on their return to the UK both 28 and 78 Squadrons were disbanded and the helicopters were transferred to the FAA for use by the Commando Helicopter Force. The last Tornados, flown by crews from 31 Squadron departed from Kandahar on 10 November 2014. The Chinooks of 1319 Flight had also been reduced to just three airframes and on 1 April 2015 they, too, were withdrawn and were replaced in theatre by the Puma HC2 helicopters of 33 Squadron. In subsequent operations over Afghanistan, nicknamed Operation *Toral*, the Pumas were used to transport personnel and troops around the country. The tasking peaked between April and May 2016 because of a major changeover of personnel deployed to Afghanistan. In that short period, the Pumas moved nearly 2,000 passengers and four tons of freight.

POLICING BALTIC AIRSPACE

After a ten-year break, RAF aircraft were once again assigned to NATO's Baltic Air Policing operation. In March 2014, an RAF Sentry joined the NATO AWACS force operating in Polish and Romanian airspace to provide reassurance to the easternmost countries of the Alliance. Two months later, four Typhoons of 3 Squadron deployed for a four-month tour of duty to Šiauliai in Lithuania where they joined a Polish MiG-29A unit. The NATO force also included Danish F-16 Fighting Falcons based at Ämari in Estonia and French Mirage 2000s at Malbork, Poland. During an operational scramble in mid-June, the Typhoons intercepted a formation of Tupolev Tu-22 Backfire bombers and Sukhoi

While more spectacular operations took place overseas, the RAF Search and Rescue (SAR) force was always ready, 24 hours a day and 365 days a year, to aid those in distress at sea or in remote areas. The Westland Sea King HAR3 equipped 22 and 202 Squadrons until the SAR role was contracted out to civilian operators in 2015. (Crown Copyright)

A Russian Air Force Sukhoi Su-27 Flanker with a Typhoon FGR4 of 3 Squadron over the Baltic Sea in June 2014. Typhoons had been launched to intercept a large group of Russian aircraft which included a Tupolev Tu-22 Backfire bomber, four Su-27 fighters, one Beriev A-50 Mainstay early warning aircraft and an Antonov An-26 Curl transport. (Crown Copyright)

Su-27 Flanker escorts. Later, two more Typhoons escorted a large formation of Su-27 Flanker and Sukhoi Su-34 Fullback aircraft over the Baltic.

The following summer the pattern was repeated by four Typhoons of 6 Squadron, which deployed on 1 May 2015, this time to Ämari. The detachment was kept busy by Russian aircraft which operated without any communication with Air Traffic Control centres and without displaying any identifying transponder codes. The squadron's fourth QRA launch was on 8 June, when an Ilyushin Il-20M Coot surveillance aircraft was

intercepted and shadowed, before the Typhoons were re-tasked to intercept a further contact which proved to be an Antonov An-26 Curl transport aircraft. During their four months in Estonia, the 6 Squadron Typhoons were scrambled on 17 occasions to intercept over 40 Russian aircraft.

In the third consecutive summer deployment, four Tornado FGR4s of 2 Squadron detached to Ämari on 28 April 2016. On this occasion, they shared responsibility for the operation with four F-16AM Fighting Falcons of the Portuguese Air Force based at Šiauliai. The first operational

scramble was on 11 May, when An-26 Curl, Antonov An-12 Cub and Ilyushin Il-76 Candid aircraft were intercepted and shadowed. The next launch, five days later, intercepted two Su-27 Flanker fighters escorting an Il-20 Coot-A reconnaissance aircraft, which were flying to the north of Estonia; during this sortie, two more Su-27s were detected and the Typhoons also intercepted them. By the end of August 2016, the Typhoons had been involved in 21 QRA launches, which had resulted in the interception of 42 Russian aircraft. Four German Air Force Typhoons took over from the RAF detachment on 31 August.

NIGERIA

After the Islamist terror group Boko Haram kidnapped 200 girls from a school at Chibok in Nigeria in April 2014 the UK government decided to assist Nigeria in its fight against the terrorists.

A Sentinel from 5 Squadron was despatched to Accra in Ghana, along with a Shadow R1 from 14 Squadron. Over the following two months the Sentinel carried out surveillance of areas of Nigeria, feeding its information into a UK-manned Intelligence Fusion Cell in the Nigerian capital Abuja. Following the departure of the Sentinel, three Tornados from 2 Squadron deployed to the French military airfield at N'Djamena, Chad in late August 2014. From here the aircraft spent two months flying further reconnaissance sorties over Nigeria.

IRAQ & SYRIA

By early 2014 a terrorist organization known as Islamic State in the Levant (ISIL) had driven Iraqi government forces out of a number of cities in western Iraq. The group had already taken advantage of the chaos of the Syrian civil war to assume control of much of the northeastern region of that country.

A Raytheon Sentinel R1 Airborne Stand-Off Radar (ASTOR) aircraft of 5 Squadron departs from RAF Waddington to participate in operations over West Africa in 2014. (Crown Copyright)

A Tornado GR4 based at RAF Akrotiri, Cyprus, on an operational sortie over Iraq. The aircraft flew in support of ground forces, including the Iraqi Army, Syrian Democratic Forces (SDF) and Kurdish Peshmerga, fighting the ISIL terrorist organization. (Crown Copyright)

Many of the inhabitants of Iraqi towns and cities were displaced by the brutal ISIL regime, in particular, the Yazidi population in the Sinjar area. On 9 August, two Hercules dropped humanitarian aid to Yazidi refugees on Mount Sinjar. Six Tornados of 2 Squadron were then deployed to Akrotiri to assist with further drops. The Tornados were to use their Litening targeting pods to direct the Hercules to safe drop zones on the mountain. The Tornados were, in turn, supported by an Airbus Voyager tanker. Four Chinooks were also deployed to the theatre in case evacuation of refugees was necessary. Two more aid drops were carried out by Hercules on Mount Sinjar on 13 and 14 August, after which the Tornados were tasked for reconnaissance missions over northeastern Iraq, using the Raptor pod. Ten such missions were flown to gather intelligence about ISIL forces between 13 and 16 August. Meanwhile further ISTAR assets had deployed into the theatre, including Sentrys from 8 Squadron, Airseekers from 51 Squadron, Sentinels from 5 Squadron and Shadows from 14 Squadron.

The Hercules flew two more sorties to deliver relief supplies over Amerli (to the west of Kirkuk) on 30 and 31 August. From mid-September, the Tornados started to fly regular reconnaissance sorties over Iraq. Operating from Akrotiri and equipped with the Raptor pod, the aircraft, supported by the Voyager, flew in pairs, routing into western Iraq via Israel and Jordan. The British government authorized the use of weapons over Iraq in late September and the RAF's offensive force at Akrotiri was augmented by two more Tornados. The aircraft were armed initially with Paveway IV LGBs and later with MBDA Brimstone DMS missiles; the first weapons were dropped by Tornados on 30 September. Throughout the next six months the Tornados operated in support of the Iraqi army in the area of Ramadi and also Kurdish Peshmerga forces fighting in northern Iraq. Two Reaper UAVs were also deployed into theatre for surveillance and close air support tasks: the first live weapons drop from a Reaper was on

10 November when a Hellfire missile was fired to prevent an ISIL group from laying IEDs. Along with offensive operations over Iraq, surveillance sorties were also flown by both Tornados and Reapers over Syria. As with previous operations over Iraq and Afghanistan, each Tornado GR4 squadron took its turn to provide personnel for a four to six-week detachment at Akrotiri.

Typical targets attacked by Tornados and Reapers in Iraq included ISIL APCs, vehicles, artillery and mortar teams. The aircraft also disabled earthmoving equipment where it was being used to build improvised fortifications in ISIL-held areas. Both aircraft types typically expended live weapons on about ten sorties per month. In early April 2015, intensive sorties were flown against ISIL forces preparing to attack Kurdish positions to the southwest of Mosul. The aircraft also flew over-watch missions ahead of advancing Kurdish troops to clear the area of IEDs and ambushes. Over the summer months the focus of Iraqi army operations in Anbar Province progressed from Bayji to Tal Afar and Fallujah. These ground offensives relied heavily on Coalition air support including RAF Tornados and Reapers. A good illustration of the diversity

A Typhoon FGR4 on an operational sortie over Iraq. Operating with Tornado GR4s and Reaper drones, the Typhoons were heavily involved in the battle for Mosul between 2015 and 2017. (Beevers)

An Airbus A330 Multi-Role Tanker Transport (MRTT) Voyager KC2 tanker refuels two Tornado GR4s during an operational sortie over Iraq in March 2015. The RAF fleet comprises nine aircraft in the 'core fleet' in daily use by 10 and 101 Squadrons and another five aircraft operated by the Air Tanker Consortium in the 'surge fleet' which can be called into service if there is a surge in tasking. (USAF)

of tasks carried out by RAF aircraft over Iraq was on 23 July 2015. On that day, two Tornados on a CAS mission in support of Peshmerga forces near Sinjar used a Paveway IV LGB to destroy a building close to the frontline, from which a sniper was engaging Kurdish forces. The aircraft were then called on to neutralize a mortar position, which they did using another Paveway IV. Further south, a Reaper destroyed an ISIL supply vehicle using a Hellfire missile, before providing surveillance for Coalition aircraft conducting an airstrike on ISIL positions. Meanwhile another Reaper operating over western Iraq identified a building

from which ISIL forces were firing on Iraqi army troops; another Coalition aircraft was tasked to destroy the building. The Reaper then neutralized a nearby heavy machine-gun position using a Hellfire missile.

Surveillance and CAS missions by Tornados and Reapers continued over northern and western Iraq through the summer and a large number of weapons were expended. On 15 September, a Reaper identified a cache of ISIL weapons stockpiles on the banks of the Euphrates and destroyed one stockpile, coincidentally destroying in the same blast a small boat which was being

used to transport the weapons. The Reaper then remained on station and directed other Coalition aircraft onto the remaining targets. Exactly two months later, a Reaper supported an attack by French aircraft against a terrorist facility near Raqqa in Syria. A typical day's work over Iraq in the autumn of 2015 is illustrated by operations on 25 November: in the morning, a pair of Tornados carried out attacks against three groups of ISIL fighters near Mosul using Paveway IV LGBs; they also destroyed an ISIL vehicle with a Brimstone, before moving westwards to neutralize a heavy machine-gun post near Sinjar with a further Paveway IV. That night, a second pair of Tornados then continued to support Kurdish forces in the Sinjar area, including destroying another heavy machine-gun position. Meanwhile a Reaper carried out an attack on a building within a terrorist-held compound near Mosul, destroying it with a GBU-12 LGB.

By late 2015, RAF surveillance platforms, including Airseeker, Reaper and Sentinel, were responsible for approximately 33 percent of the intelligence by the Coalition in Syria, while the Tornado/Raptor combination was responsible for approximately 66 percent of the intelligence gathered by the Coalition in Iraq. RAF Sentry aircraft were integrated into the control structure of the Coalition and on a typical sortie they might also expect to control simultaneously around 40 Coalition aircraft operating over Syria and Iraq. The British government authorized offensive operations over Syria on 1 December 2015 and the first of these was carried out the following day. Tornados attacked six wellheads in the Omar oilfield with Paveway IVs in order to disrupt the ability of ISIL to fund its activities through oil revenue. The following day the RAF's offensive forces at Akrotiri was further expanded by the deployment of two additional Tornados (bringing the total in theatre to ten) and six Typhoon FGR4s. The number of Reapers in theatre had also been increased previously. A mixed force of Tornados and Typhoons revisited

the Omar oilfield on 4 December. On the same day, Tornados and Typhoons flew CAS missions for Iraqi and Kurdish forces and a Reaper also provided CAS for Kurdish forces.

For much of December 2015 and January 2016 the Tornados and Typhoons provided CAS for Iraqi army operations near Ramadi as well as Kurdish Peshmerga fighting near Mosul. On 23 December, a Typhoon patrol dropped eight Paveway IV LGBs on targets in the Mosul area, destroying four buildings and a tunnel, which between them contained ammunition stores, several heavy machine guns and a sniper position. Meanwhile two pairs of Tornados supporting Iraqi troops in action near the centre of Ramadi carried out six attacks on targets in close proximity to friendly forces. Using Paveway IV LGBs, they neutralized three Rocket Propelled Grenade (RPG) teams, a sniper and two groups in close combat with Iraqi troops. That evening a further pair of Tornados destroyed two buildings occupied by ISIL personnel near Mosul.

On 10 January 2016, Tornados were operating in pairs near the self-proclaimed ISIL capital at Raqqa. One section attacked an ISIL command and control centre near Raqqa, while another section attacked a tunnel complex. A third patrol, working in co-ordination with a Reaper, used Brimstone missiles to disable cranes and other heavy engineering equipment being used by ISIL to repair damage to the wellheads in the Omar oilfield. The following day marked the 1,000th sortie flown by Reapers against ISIL since October 2014. In early March a Reaper was amongst Coalition aircraft supporting an offensive by the Syrian Democratic Forces (SDF) to the southwest of Al Shaddadi, in eastern Syria. Intensive air operations continued throughout early 2016, in the areas around Ramadi, Mosul and in north-eastern Syria. Between January and March, Typhoons carried out 104 airstrikes over Iraq and two over Syria, dropping some 252 Paveway IV LGBs while the Tornados mounted 52 airstrikes over Iraq and 15 over Syria, using 147 Paveway

A Puma HC2 of 33 Squadron over Afghanistan. This version of the helicopter has more powerful engines and an improved flight management system. In Afghanistan, the Puma HC2s were based in Kabul supporting Operation *Toral*, the training of Afghan Army troops by NATO forces. (Crown Copyright)

IVs and 42 Brimstones. The Reapers were also busy in that period, firing 47 Lockheed Martin AGM-114 Hellfire missiles over both theatres, and dropping five GBU-12 LGBs.

From April, the region between Qayyarah and Hit provided a new focus for the Iraqi army and therefore for RAF CAS operations. As part of a larger Coalition operation on 21 April Tornados dropped 2,000lb Enhanced Paveway (EPW) III LGBs on a tunnel and bunker complex on terraced hills above the River Euphrates. Tornados also used 1,000lb Enhanced Paveway II LGBs to destroy ISIL command centre near Raqqa on 20 May and an Improvised Explosive Device (IED) factory in northern Syria ten days later. The following day was a busy one in which a pair of Tornados destroyed two heavy machine-gun positions that were engaging Iraqi troops advancing near Fallujah; at

the same time a Typhoon patrol destroyed an ISIL headquarters building near Mosul, and a Reaper provided targeting information for Coalition aircraft attacking an engineering vehicle which was constructing defences near Qayyarah. The Reaper then engaged two mortar teams with Hellfire missiles. The Typhoons and Reaper then joined the operations over Fallujah and the Typhoons destroyed another heavy machine-gun position. The Reaper monitored ISIL personnel as they loaded weapons into a truck, before destroying the vehicle with a Hellfire missile. Meanwhile, another Reaper supporting Iraqi forces near Hit destroyed an ISIL machine-gun team and a vehicle-mounted anti-tank gun with Hellfire missiles.

Storm Shadow long-range missiles were first employed against ISIL targets on 26 June 2016 when two Tornados fired four missiles against a former Iraqi military bunker in western Iraq that ISIL was using as a weapons facility. The following day Typhoons and a Reaper worked once again with Syrian Democratic Forces (SDF) in eastern Syria. Tornados also dropped EPW IIIs on 31 July while operating as part of a larger Coalition force attacking a Saddam Hussein-era palace complex on the banks of the River Tigris near Mosul which was being used as a major training facility by ISIL. Meanwhile Tornados, Typhoons and Reapers had been engaged in intensive operations over Manbij supporting the SDF in northern Syria as well as Sharqat and Qayyarah in western Iraq and Mosul in northern Iraq. Operations also continued over the Omar oilfield: on 31 August two Tornados attacked tanker vehicles attempting to transport oil from the area. Four Paveway IV LGBs and four Brimstone missiles were fired at the convoy, resulting in the destruction of a number of ISL vehicles.

Most of the air-support effort flown by the RAF during October 2016 was based around Mosul, where Iraqi forces were attempting to isolate the city from the southeast in conjunction with Kurdish forces operating to the north. Tornados, Typhoons and Reapers were all busy on a daily basis working closely with ground forces. In addition, on 31 October two Tornados once again launched Storm Shadow long-range missiles, while participating in a Coalition airstrike against bunkers at a former Iraqi military facility near Haditha. Meanwhile the battle around Mosul continued into the following months. On 11 November Tornados and Reapers worked over Mosul, while Typhoons operated with the SDF north of Raqqa. Typhoons also provided CAS to Iraqi forces as they liberated the ancient Assyrian capital of Nimrud on 14 November. Despite poor weather in December, Tornados were still able to provide precise air support to Iraqi ground forces as they fought their way into Mosul. The aircraft were able to drop Paveway II and IV LGBs through cloud with sufficient accuracy to destroy targets in very close proximity to friendly forces. Eastern Mosul was captured by Iraqi forces on 24 January 2017, but the battle to clear the western half of the city raged through the next few months. RAF aircraft continued to support SDF forces fighting around Raqqa, but the main focus through February and March was the Iraqi army operation in and around Mosul. Tornados, Typhoons and Reapers cut lines of communication to prevent ISIL reinforcements from reaching the battle and also cut roads within the city to stop ISIL from deploying truck bombs. Mortars and snipers were also neutralized both within the city and in outlying areas. Although the major part of the RAF missions in March were in support of operations in Mosul, reconnaissance sorties continued to be flown over Syria and on 18 March an ISIL headquarters building was identified some five miles to the east of Raqqa; this was destroyed by a Tornado which dropped a Paveway IV onto the target.

SOUTHERN AIR POLICING

Four Typhoons from 3 Squadron deployed to Mihail Kogălniceanu Air Base near Constanţa on the Black Sea coast of Romania on 24 April 2017. These aircraft were part of the NATO Southern Policing Mission, an analogous operation to the Baltic Air Policing Mission, and remained in Romania from May to August. The first operational scramble occurred during July, when two Russian Tupolev Tu-22M3 aircraft approached the Romanian border; however, the Russian aircraft remained in international airspace and the Typhoons did not close to visual range.

TYPHOONS, TORNADOS & HURRICANES

In Iraq, the battle for western Mosul continued until early July, with Typhoons, Tornados and Reaper drones providing CAS for the Iraqi army by targetting enemy snipers and mortar teams. The Iraqi army had retaken Mosul by 24 July, but combat operations continued around Tall Afar, Sharqat and Qayyarah through the autumn. Typical targets attacked by Typhoons included a truck carrying armed insurgents across the desert to the northwest of Tikrit on 19 August: despite being driven at high speed, the truck was neutralized by a PW IV.

Meanwhile regular patrols by Typhoons had started over Raqqa in April 2017 and targets in the eastern outskirts of the city were attacked on 21 May in support of SDF ground forces. Over the next six months, RAF aircraft continued to provide daily close air support for the SDF often flying in 'mixed pairs' comprising a Tornado and a Typhoon: the aircraft targeted snipers and mortar teams which were engaging friendly forces during house-to-house fighting, as well as buildings being used by terrorists. By 10 August, ISIL had been cut off from the River Euphrates and as the SDF closed in on the city, ISIL elements started to move eastwards along the River Euphrates towards Deir Ez-Zur. RAF aircraft carried out six attacks over Raqqa on 2 September and a week later Reapers were active over Deir Ez-Zur, where teams of terrorists on motorcycles were neutralized using Hellfire missiles.

Throughout the rest of September, Typhoons, Tornados and Reapers operated over Raqqa, as well as northern Iraq. One particularly busy day was 23 September when two pairs of Typhoons and a further two pairs of Tornados each carried out a number of attacks around Hawijah in Iraq: the targets included command posts, weapons stockpiles and also a number of truck bombs which had been placed to block the approach roads into the city. In early October, the focus of operations returned to Raqqa, where the battle for the city was reaching its conclusion: in the final days, the role of RAF aircraft was pivotal, as it had been throughout the long campaign to liberate the city. The SDF announced that they had completely taken the city on 17 October, after a year-long campaign during which time RAF aircraft had engaged 213 targets in and around the city. However, the fighting in Syria continued around Deir Ez-Zur, and Typhoons, Tornados and Reapers continued to be called upon to neutralize ISIL mortar teams, snipers and strongpoints.

In the late summer of 2017, the Caribbean was hit by two devastating Hurricanes, known as *Irma* and *Maria*. Hurricane *Irma* struck the Leeward Islands on 6 September, where it wrought major damage on the British Virgin Islands, Turks and Caicos Islands and Anguilla. Two days later a Globemaster, a Voyager and an Atlas were dispatched from RAF Brize Norton carrying 200 troops from 40 Commando RM, as well as engineers, medical specialists and essential supplies. The aircraft flew to Barbados, which was the nearest suitable runway. Over the next few days, further Globemasters transported three Puma HC2 helicopters to the region. The second hurricane, *Maria*, struck the Windward Islands on 18 September and once again extensive damage was caused, particularly in Dominica. When HMS *Ocean* arrived in the area four days later it brought two RAF Chinooks as well as its own complement of helicopters. Meanwhile a shuttle service comprising a Hercules and an Atlas had been set up to distribute supplies such as food, bottled water and shelters from Barbados to the storm-damaged islands. In addition, a Globemaster assisted the French government to transport heavy equipment to Guadeloupe.

THE FUTURE

After an extended period of cutbacks in the military services, the 2016 Defence White Paper announced a modest expansion of the RAF in the following few years. Arguably the most important facet was the reintroduction of the maritime patrol and anti-submarine role, one of the core roles of the RAF in World War I, World War II and throughout the Cold War. Boeing Poseidon aircraft will take on this role and a cadre of aircrew who have been flying maritime patrol aircraft with the US, Canadian and Australian forces will ensure that the RAF's maritime capability will continue seamlessly from where it left off. The Tornado, the RAF's

longest serving bomber aircraft, will be replaced by the Lockheed Martin F-35 Lightning II, but much of the surveillance and attack work is likely to be taken on by a growing UAV force, including the General Atomics Protector. The introduction of the Airbus A-400M Atlas aircraft will also give the RAF an enhanced air-transport capability.

In numbers of operational squadrons, the RAF entering its second century is almost the same size as the service that emerged immediately after World War I. Its deployments are similar, too: in 1919 RAF aircraft operated in the Baltic and Black Sea areas to deter Russian aggression and in 1920 they operated in the Middle East to maintain law and order. Indeed, the operational experiences of the last 20 years in Iraq and Afghanistan would have been very familiar to the RAF personnel who served in those regions in the 1920s and 1930s. But there are also many differences: today's aircraft, whether they be tactical transports, air-to-air refuelling tankers, support helicopters or all-weather fighters, are all immensely more capable than those of a century ago and those who fly, service or support them all benefit from a 100 years of corporate expertise. As it celebrates its centenary, the RAF continues to strive for *Per Ardua Ad Astra*.

The Airbus A-400M Atlas which will replace the Lockheed C-130 Hercules in RAF service. The aircraft can carry a larger load than a Hercules, and is also capable of operating into a smaller airstrip than the Boeing C-17 Globemaster. (Crown Copyright)

INDEX

ACKNOWLEDGEMENTS

Writing this book would not have been possible without considerable help from a number of people. I am very grateful to Vic Flintham and Graham Pitchfork who were very supportive at the outset of the project and allowed me access to their photograph collections. I would also like to record my thanks to the incredibly helpful staff at the RAF Museum, in particular the Curator of Photographs Andy Renwick, and Ian Alder, the manager of the RAFM Reserve Collection, both of whose support was invaluable. At the Air Historical Branch, Lee Barton was most helpful and Mick Davis at *Cross & Cockade International* was generous to a fault. I am also very grateful to Phil Jarrett for providing a number of excellent images for the early chapters and to Richard Cooke for allowing me to use his fantastic shots from the late 1970s.

Many thanks indeed to the following individuals who very kindly allowed me to use their private photographs, which I believe give a unique perspective on more recent operations: Paul Beevers, David Bellamy, Paul Froome, Andy Glover, David Hales, Tim Kerss, Chris Knight, Paul Lashmar, David Lewis, Mike Lumb, Nigel Nickles, Peter Rolfe, Mark Sheppard, Chris Stradling, Andy Thomas and Derek Tuthill.

Where there was meagre detail in published sources, I sought help from a number of eye-witness experts to help me to understand some aspects of recent operations. I'm very grateful to the following for their advice and expertise: Tim Kerss (Jaguar operations over the Balkans), Malcolm Rainier DFC (Jaguar operations during the Gulf War), Pete Birch (Jaguar Mid Life Update and TIALD integration), Andy Tagg and Sean Bell (Harrier GR7 operations), Gareth Jones and John Platt (Nimrod operations). I'm also grateful to Philip Weyers, grandson of Jan Smuts, for enlightening me on aspects of the 'Oubaas.'

I am extremely grateful to Air Chief Marshal Sir Stuart Peach for writing a foreword to this book. Sir Stuart and I were contemporaries on 31 Squadron flying Tornado GR1s from Brüggen in the late 1980s, where he earned my utmost respect for his professional expertise and his encyclopaedic grasp of 'the big picture.'

Finally, many thanks to Marcus Cowper at Osprey Publishing for his support and to my indefatigable editor, Jasper Spencer-Smith, a man once described as a cross between a ram and an armadillo, whose imagination first envisaged this book and whose patience I have tested to the limits during the production process.